I'd Just as Soon Kiss a Wookiee

The William and Bettye Nowlin Series in Art, History, and Culture of the Western Hemisphere

I'd Just as Soon Kiss a Wookiee

Uncovering Racialized Desire in the Star Wars Galaxy

GREG CARTER

University of Texas Press *Austin*

Copyright © 2025 by the University of Texas Press
All rights reserved
Printed in the United States of America
First edition, 2025

Requests for permission to reproduce material from this work should be sent to permissions@utpress.utexas.edu.

♾ The paper used in this book meets the minimum requirements of ANSI/NISO z39.48-1992 (R1997) (Permanence of Paper).

Library of Congress Cataloging-in-Publication Data

Names: Carter, Greg, 1970– author.
Title: I'd just as soon kiss a Wookiee : uncovering racialized desire in the Star Wars galaxy / Greg Carter.
Description: First edition. | Austin : University of Texas Press, 2025. | Series: The William and Bettye Nowlin series in art, history, and culture of the Western Hemisphere | Includes index.
Identifiers: LCCN 2024047408 (print) LCCN 2024047409 (ebook)
    ISBN 978-1-4773-3158-3 (hardcover)
    ISBN 978-1-4773-3159-0 (paperback)
    ISBN 978-1-4773-3160-6 (pdf)
    ISBN 978-1-4773-3161-3 (epub)
Subjects: LCSH: Star Wars films—History and criticism. | Race in motion pictures. | Motion pictures—Social aspects—United States.
Classification: LCC PN1995.9.S695 C36 2025 (print) | LCC PN1995.9.S695 (ebook)
LC record available at https://lccn.loc.gov/2024047408
LC ebook record available at https://lccn.loc.gov/2024047409

doi:10.7560/331583

Contents

List of Illustrations **vii**
Preface **ix**

Introduction **1**

1. The History of On-Screen Science Fiction Interracial Intimacy (1902–1987) **29**

2. What Are You, Darth Vader? (1977–1980) **55**

3. Early Fanship, the Invisible Jetpack, and Black Fans (1977–1982) **73**

4. Princess Leia, Lando Calrissian, and Fan Imaginations (1977–1983) **91**

5. Don't Ask the Prequels Where Babies Come From (1999–2005) **115**

6. Four Ships Sailed. Which Would Land? (2012–2016) **141**

7. Social Media, Fans, and Interracial Relationships (2015–2020) **169**

Conclusion **193**
Notes **205**
Index **245**

Illustrations

0.1. Blueprint showing organic and cybernetic parts making up Darth Vader's body. **21**

0.2. *Bricklandia Comic*, no. 1, making light of Princess Leia's distaste for kissing Chewbacca. **27**

1.1. Gus, played by a white actor in blackface, accosts Flora Cameron in D. W. Griffith's *The Birth of a Nation* (1915). **32**

1.2. Leonard Nimoy's 1968 letter to a fan, encouraging her to persevere with her racial mixture. **47**

1.3. Glynn Turman as Preach in Michael Schultz's *Cooley High* (1975). **50**

2.1. Lee Shelton shoots Billy Lyons in Timothy Lane's 2007 comic chapbook telling the story of the song "Stagger Lee." **64**

2.2. James Earl Jones as the Jack Johnson stand-in Jack Jefferson in the play *The Great White Hope* (1968). **66**

2.3. Mort Drucker's cover illustration for *Mad* magazine suggesting that Darth Vader was Mr. T's character in *Rocky III* (1982), Clubber Lang. **71**

3.1. *National Lampoon*'s 1974 poster warning against showing the telltale signs of nerddom. **79**

3.2. Scene from Richard Pryor's 1977 skit bringing his Black sensibilities to the *Star Wars* cantina. **83**

3.3. Amiyrah Martin and her husband offer their friendship to Black *Star Wars* fans on YouTube. **90**

4.1. Lando Calrissian (Billy Dee Williams) flirts with Princess Leia (Carrie Fisher) in *The Empire Strikes Back* (1980). **98**

4.2. Hannah Foxx, here with another licensed sex worker at Carson City's Moonlite Bunny Ranch, attests to the popularity of the "slave Leia" fetish. **111**

5.1. Tim Bisley (Simon Pegg) berates a child fan of Jar Jar Binks in a 2001 episode of *Spaced* (1999–2001). **119**

5.2. Image from Ahmed Best's 2018 tweet sharing his suicidal depression following the racist backlash against him. **129**

5.3. Mellody Hobson and George Lucas attend Backstage at the Geffen on March 22, 2015, in Los Angeles. **138**

6.1. "Only in the Darkness Can You See the Stars," fan art by Heidi Hastings depicting Kylo Ren's abduction of Rey as a bridal carry. **144**

6.2. Anti-Semitic image from 2014 asserting that the pairing of Daisy Ridley and John Boyega was part of a Jewish conspiracy. **150**

6.3. One of the photos from Victor Sine and Julianne Payne's cosplay photo shoot that went viral in March 2016. **165**

7.1. Christina Cato, a Black woman fan, discusses her experience as a droid builder with *Our Star Wars Stories* host Jordan Hembrough. **179**

7.2. December 31, 2019, tweet by John Boyega, including a collage critiquing Lucasfilm's depiction of romance in the sequel trilogy. **188**

Preface

"A long time ago, in a galaxy far, far away . . ." The first imagery in *Star Wars* (1977) consisted of these words, in blue letters, superimposed over empty space.[1] Even before the score marched in, the title card cast the viewer into the realm of legend, hinting that this would be a creation myth, answering the question "Where did we come from?" But once the small spaceship entered the screen, pursued by the big spaceship, we saw that this was a futuristic world with technology far beyond our own. Tatooine, the desert planet where we spent half of the movie, looked run-down like a frontier town, but it also featured advanced elements like levitating vehicles. The Death Star was sanitary but required trash compactors to manage rubbish. Characters hinted at a distant past that, most likely, was far more futuristic than our present. This shuffling of narrative perspective thoroughly confused me at age seven.

But in 1977, as now, I regard the framing as the opening of a fairy tale, a mere flourish. *Star Wars* would not provide a suitable origin myth, but I already had plenty of those. First, raised in a religious household, I knew key biblical stories by then. But how useful was the allegory of Adam and Eve when kids were mean, teachers could not bother to learn my name, and cross burnings were still a thing in Maryland that year? Besides, I became an atheist at age twenty-one. Second, the original *Roots* (1977) aired the previous January. For eight nights, I watched the dramatization of Alex Haley's genealogical work as if it were my own. Kunta Kinte's descendants survived enslavement, rape, and intimidation. Since the Ku Klux Klan was active two exits down I-83, *Roots* guided me to be careful in the present.[2] Third, I was racially mixed and knew that global, historical forces brought my parents together. *Roots* informed my racial identity as a child, but that shifted around age twenty-one, and again ten years later, and again after the deaths of Trayvon Martin and Michael Brown. My attitude toward temporality persisted well into the writing of this book. By its end, I will share my new insights with you.

I am amazed that *Star Wars* has been more consistent in my life than the major affiliations I was raised with; that nearly a dozen movies and three award-winning television shows are readily available at my fingertips; and that journalists, professors, and students come to hear my thoughts on *Star Wars* and race. By plying methods, rigor, and contextualization I have developed as a scholar, I have mined a subject I have delighted in since age seven, producing a work that will earn me my "acafan" merit badge! Combining *academic* and *fan*, this portmanteau describes scholars who research fans for humanistic reasons, who have personal affection for the pop culture object of their interest, and who feel allegiance to both academia and fan communities.[3]

Being an acafan becomes more complicated the further one is from the white, male, straight, US context so prevalent when discussing these topics. Henry Jenkins's call "to expand the borders of fandom studies to reflect shifting conditions of reception, production and circulation, to engage with a more diverse sets [sic] of fan communities and to address new areas of concern" is also an admission that the field has privileged white and heteronormative perspectives since its inception.[4] As andré m. carrington intimated about the value of other perspectives, "Fandom is, in a way, a scholarly attention to material that other people consume and let go. It's a scholarly attention to things that people look at and think critically about, but maybe you know that criticism is more skeptical, is more negative, and they reject it. For me, fandom sometimes means you stick with it and see where it takes you and that's a really constructive way to be a scholar, in my view."[5] The racial analysis of pop culture is what most audiences, fans, and scholars seldom regard. They do not understand that, for many underrepresented groups (especially African Americans), critical consumption is a survival skill, a defense mechanism, and a commitment to catalyzing what the mass media gives them. Even though racial talk seems to inundate us, racial analysis remains devalued in fandom studies, in fan communities, and in society. *I'd Just as Soon Kiss a Wookiee* interjects *Star Wars*, a topic both personal and universal, into a conversation about racism, a theme most do not want to engage.

Choosing to write about a "fun" topic does not liberate one from the market forces that regulate how to be a scholar and a fan, who may choose to follow this path, and what rewards await. I had to get a doctoral degree, secure a tenure-track job, and place a previous monograph with a university press. Erin A. Cech writes, "When we praise passion, we reward privilege," in reference to an NPR report that stated, "Employers can take advantage of workers who work for passion."[6] As she explains in *The Atlantic*, "Put frankly, the white-collar labor force was not designed to help workers nurture self-realization projects. It was designed to advance the interests of an organization's stockholders."[7] Perhaps, if I had a different disposition, I could have become an influencer on social media, but that would have taken just as much diligence to a path predetermined by corporate gatekeepers.

Lastly, I did not write a book about *Star Wars* because I was following Joseph Campbell's advice to "follow your bliss."[8] I wrote this because it was the most bearable thing I could come up with, posttenure, following my first book. It was the best thing I could come up with as the state where I am employed attacked collective bargaining, defunded education on all levels, and interrogated the value of the humanities. It was the best thing I could come up with as Donald Trump and his allies pushed our tenuous democracy closer to dictatorship. It was the best thing I could come up with as, daily, the coronavirus killed as many Americans as the September 11 attacks, and I could not leave the house. So, I created this timely, rigorous, and imaginative work for you, *hypocrite lecteur,—mon semblable,—mon frère*, who embraces the myth of the acafan; for my outer persona, who resides in academia in the United States in the twenty-first century; and for my private self, who has been pondering the role of race in *Star Wars* since 1977.

I did not do it alone. I would like to thank the following. The Critical Mixed Race Studies Association, of which I was president from 2017 to 2019, has been my intellectual home. My colleagues in the Department of History at the University of Wisconsin–Milwaukee set a model many would envy. The Honors College and students of my seminar, History 399: Seeing Race in Modern America, gave me a forum to hone ideas that would appear in this book. The Office of Undergraduate Research supported the work of my undergraduate research assistants: Lauren Robertson outlined the perspectives of minority fans in 2018. Lauren Clausing helped disentangle the voices responding to *The Rise of Skywalker* in 2020. And in 2023–2024, Scott Emanuel White Jr. gathered sources that laid the foundation for the exploration of race, gender, and sexuality in chapter 4.

Beyond UWM, Jasmine Mitchell, author of *Imagining the Mulatta: Blackness in U.S. and Brazilian Media*, offered feedback on early versions of the chapters that appear here. Jordan Gonzales, my copy editor, helped transform those chapters into a coherent whole, then sent sixteen thousand words to the recycle bin. Billy Korinko and the Cassandra Voss Center at St. Norbert's College invited me to give a talk that led to the crystallization of the ideas in chapter 5. David K. Seitz, author of *A Different Trek: Radical Geographies of "Deep Space Nine,"* provided good cheer that got me through the final revisions.

At the University of Texas Press, I thank Jim Burr, Mia Uribe Kozlovsky, and other staff members for their enthusiasm in making this book a reality.

Additional conversations with these minority fans outside academia revealed a spectrum of encounters with the galaxy far, far away: Keith Chow, Rana Emerson, Brandon Jackson, Derrick Johns, Amiyrah Martin, Leon Julian Powell, Holly Quinn, David Richeson, Jason Sperber, Shawn Taylor, and the departed John Thomas. Some white friends helped too, namely Daniel Casasanto, David Papas, Laura Staum, and Salem Vouras.

If this book displays persistence, candor, and verve, credit my mother, Clarice Carter, who taught me those traits, and much more.

Again, Natasha Borges Sugiyama is my partner in all things. I cannot imagine having completed this without her.

Our daughter, Nina Sugiyama Carter, has grown in beauty, intelligence, and perceptiveness. The Force will be with you, always.

Lastly, our son, Anton Sugiyama Carter, has a reading off the charts . . . over twenty thousand! We will watch your career with great interest.

I'd Just as Soon Kiss a Wookiee

Introduction

The Galaxy Not So Far Away

Science fiction can be set in the past, present, or future and told from a narrative perspective that is independent of those moments. It can tell stories *from* any temporal point of view, and those stories can be *about* any temporal point of view, offering answers to the following questions: What mistakes did we make? How can we improve the present? How have we already shaped the future? In other words, science fiction has a lot in common with the aims of the discipline of history, so it is no surprise that *I'd Just as Soon Kiss a Wookiee: Uncovering Racialized Desire in the Star Wars Galaxy* brings together two phenomena prominent since the 1970s: the science fiction movie franchise *Star Wars* and the increased acceptance of interracial intimacy. In both realms, prohibiting interracial (or interspecies) intimacy has maintained the belief in racial difference and, in turn, racial inequality. My objective is to uncover the link between George Lucas's creation and our real world. It becomes apparent in how audiences respond to the saga. Finding what mainstream (i.e., predominantly white) fans think of *Star Wars* is super easy.

In addition to selling goods and purveying pornography, discussing *Star Wars* seems to be the main reason the internet was developed. Additionally, forums, clubs, and conventions offer clearinghouses of mainstream perspectives. Pointing out the "unbearable whiteness of fandom and fan studies," Mel Stanfill highlights the neglected matters of race: "[The two] engage in structural whiteness through participation in mainstream American culture's default to whiteness and through engagement with default-white media. As a result, there is a need for fan studies to name whiteness as it functions in fandom and interrogate its workings as well as attend to the experiences of fans of color in predominantly white fandoms and the particular cultures and practices of fandoms of color."[1]

The racial whiteness of fans and the cultural whiteness of fanship is taken for granted without even examining said whiteness. Meanwhile, the closer a fan's perspective is to US, het, cis, middle-class norms, the less likely they are to take an interest in uncovering those assumptions. But these fans are not adept at discussing race, so many of the low-hanging fruits they express are superfluous. Relying solely on these will lead to the same narrow understanding that already prevails. On the other hand, interpretations by minority fans are essential, but they are hard to find. No one method can capture them, especially when considering a time span of nearly five decades. As part of the negligence toward racial identity and racism in fanship, fan studies scholars have overlooked both Black critical thought and Black fan activities. Scholars like John Fiske have given mealy apologies for the shortage, while others have ignored whole realms of fanship to maintain the narrative of science fiction fanship as colorblind, progressive, and inclusive.[2]

My goal is not only to write history, but to offer perspectives beyond the linear, sequential master narrative that the saga itself favors. Taking seriously the fantasies of underrepresented groups can help us rethink the present, past, and future. Toward this end, this book provides a collection of pro-interracial thinkers, artists, producers, and fans who have reimagined "a long time ago" into a utopia. In this, I am inspired by Alexis Lothian's "archive of feminists, queers, and people of color who insist that the future can and must deviate from dominant narratives of global annihilation or highly restrictive hopes for redemption."[3] Likewise, this book follows José Esteban Muñoz: "Queer fantasy is linked to utopian longing, and together the two can become contributing conditions of possibility for political transformation. Utopia's rejection of pragmatism is often associated with failure. And, indeed, most profoundly, utopianism represents a failure to be normal."[4] Both of these call for a galactic battle against what Lothian calls the "relentless onslaught of future generations" and Muñoz calls the "force of political pessimism."[5]

Key Concepts

Before I delve into three main commonalities between a galaxy far, far away and the United States, I want to introduce three other concepts that have guided me in undertaking this project. First, Stuart Hall's theory of encoding and decoding messages in media reminds me that media producers use verbal and nonverbal elements to encode messages into popular culture. Writing in 1973, Hall concentrated on the dominant–hegemonic encoding position, presuming that messages came from the ruling class and served their interests, which generally protect the social order as it is. From advertising to news outlets, from popular music to motion pictures, media producers use verbal and nonverbal elements to send messages that protect capitalism, sexism, and white privilege. Because many audiences have biases, agendas, and experiences like the producers' own, they also decode from the dominant–hegemonic positions. In these cases, there is negligible slippage between the two, and the system continues to operate in favor of the ruling class.

But audiences may or may not decode those messages in the ways the producers intended. They may take a negotiated position, accepting some of the premises and jettisoning others. Or they may take an oppositional position, rejecting the messages outright, resulting in reactions the producers did not expect, sometimes disrupting the intended cycle of production, circulation, use, and reproduction. However, even if their reactions frustrate the ruling class, they have not engaged with the text incorrectly; their perspectives have led them to interpretations congruent with their experiences. In the United States, racial minorities, the poor, women, and other marginal groups are more likely to take positions oppositional to elite producers. This will be apparent from initial reactions to Darth Vader in the first *Star Wars* movie through hopes for a romance between Rey and Finn coming to fruition in the last.[6]

The next concept follows Hall's third route in name and spirit. The oppositional gaze, as coined by bell hooks, originates from the perspective of Black women viewers, who have had to engage in the "pleasure of deconstruction" when viewing films with no representations of people like themselves. When most Black people in the United States first had the opportunity to look at film and television, they did so fully aware that mass media was a system of knowledge and power reproducing and maintaining white supremacy. To stare at television or mainstream movies, to engage their images, was to engage their negation of Black representation. It was the oppositional Black gaze that responded to these looking relations by developing independent Black cinema. Black viewers of mainstream cinema and television could chart the progress of political movements for racial equality via the construction of images. Hooks writes, "Identifying with neither the phallocentric gaze nor the construction of white-womanhood as lack, critical black female spectators construct a theory of looking relations where cinematic visual delight is the pleasure of interrogation."[7] We are now accustomed to satiric routines produced by *Saturday Night Live*, *Mystery Science Theater 3000*, and *Honest Trailers*. But the oppositional gaze has offered a space for critique, interpretive innovations, and creative possibilities for as long as American mass media has existed, because that is how long some have known that mass media is not for them.

Third, Toni Morrison analyzed in her essay collection *Playing in the Dark: Whiteness and the Literary Imagination* the treatment of Blackness by white authors, showing that, even when they pushed Black characters to the margins, writers like Edgar Allan Poe, Nathaniel Hawthorne, and Ernest Hemingway relied on them to define their own whiteness: "Through significant and underscored omissions, startling contradictions, heavily nuanced conflicts, through the way writers peopled their work with the signs and bodies of this presence—one can see that a real or fabricated Africanist presence was crucial to their sense of Americanness."[8] The admirable individualism of the white American characters, as well as their terrible brutality, are products of having to deal with the presence of African Americans. Calling this influence "American Africanism," Morrison's intervention is equally applicable to American films like *Star Wars* because of the characterization of nonwhites and nonhumans. But this project also provides a corollary to the white racial frame, white narcissism, and white solipsism. Even though the most privileged in society see everything through a lens that benefits themselves, historically, their sense of themselves has been formed by a sense of others, even in absence. Though interracial intimacy and mixed race identity seem minimal in *Star Wars*, their appearances are worthy of analysis because they help us understand the rest.

This book contextualizes the five-decade *Star Wars* phenomenon historically because, as products of their times, they mirror our society's beliefs, provide allegories for difficult topics, and showcase how we treat one another. I use the metaphor of "mirroring" to describe science fiction because it occurs in real time. As an analogy, I offer racial categories on the US Census, which reflect the nation's thinking on race, our global role, and the place of newcomers in our society. Yet, changing the categories affects the way we think about race, one another, and our society. Often these changes trickle down to us through news makers communicating the results of the decennial. In turn, we talk about one another with the same categories. Since the census works in ten-year cycles, the reflection occurs much more slowly than it does for popular culture.

I also employ the metaphor of mirroring because of the primacy of visual representations in these materials. I am using the interactions between groups perceived to be biologically different in *Star Wars* to illuminate the story of race in the United States. As Matthew Pratt Guterl writes, discrimination "is also the story of the everyday assessment, or scan, of the body as text, and the culturally informed interpretation of the signs and symbols seen in the profile, the posture, and the comportment of a person's carriage."[9] This often makes all the difference between privilege and oppression, inclusion and exclusion, and even life and death.

This book draws out the interactions among humans, aliens, and droids to show how they mirror the real world. Creating a tally sheet and trying to recall every interspecies relationship in the movies, I saw that the most common was servitude, where one holds another as a laborer, lesser partner, debtor, or henchman. Cooperation, my label for relationships where both are equals working for a common goal, was a close second. In the movies, these relationships existed between people on the same team. Often, they were already ideologically aligned, like the Rebel Alliance pilots of different species blowing up the second Death Star. But I also included activities as mundane as sharing libations at the Mos Eisley cantina. *Star Wars* is, as the name suggests, a violent world, but interactions where individuals attacked someone from a different group were the third-most numerous. I expected intimacy, the central theme of this book, to be the rarest, but it finished ahead of violence and friendship.

Third, this book compares representations and tropes in *Star Wars* with those of other popular science fiction franchises, whether motion pictures or television. I do not argue for consistent, linear progress, suggesting that demeaning stereotypes have vanished, opportunities on both sides of the camera have equalized, and narratives approach universal inclusion. On the contrary, things have transformed in fits, stops, and clusters. By "clusters," I mean periods of time when trends coalesce in observable ways. For example, in the early 1990s, morphing technology appeared in Michael Jackson's chart-topping "Black or White" music video, James Cameron's blockbuster film *Terminator 2: Judgment Day* (1991), and several television commercials, transforming the human body. These instances of morphing did not mean that representations would always emphasize its malleability, just that there was a notable pattern at the time. For example, as I discuss in chapter 2, a cluster of symbolic interracial intimacy appeared between 1977 and 1987, and another formed between 1997 and 2008.

Last, this book examines the perceptions, attitudes, and activities of *Star Wars* fans. Just as many assume the movies are free of racial issues, some have claimed that the United States has reached a "postracial" state where racial difference is irrelevant. The increased visibility of racially mixed figures and interracial relationships contributed some to this misconception.[10] But developments post-2008 showed that the United States was far from postracial. In the first year of Barack Obama's administration, the United States Secret Service reported racist threats to the president. News outlets like Fox News called for a race war. The Tea Party movement rallied for candidates at the other end of the spectrum from the racially mixed president. The early exit polls from the 2016 election showed that a wide variety of white voters—not just working-class and male—voted for Trump, a candidate who made racism, sexism, and ignorance fundamental to his campaign (and later, his administration). The United States had continued to be hyperracial, and long-standing patterns in interracial marriage remained. Anti-intermarriage laws historically have kept apart white and Black people. To this day, these two groups are the least likely to marry anyone of a different race.[11]

If 17 percent of Americans believe there is something "morally wrong" about interracial marriage; if 43 percent of the country opposes the Black Lives Matter movement; and if 47 percent of voters chose Donald Trump in 2020, then those same proportions of *Star Wars* fans would do the same.[12] The genre of science fiction has enjoyed a reputation of being progressive, and the study of fans has also promoted the idea of its fans being progressive. But this is not necessarily true. During recent years, the proof is apparent both in the conformity fandom demands and, in the case of *Star Wars*, in the retrograde reactions to John Boyega, Kelly Marie Tran, and Kathleen Kennedy.

This book bears methodological kinship with Daniel Bernardi's *"Star Trek" and History*, which also balances an analysis of the text with an examination of the logics of *Star Trek* and an evaluation of the creators' production decisions. Works like Adilifu Nama's *Black Space* and andré m. carrington's *Speculative Blackness* share this work's attention to the presence and absence of people of color in science fiction. *I'd Just as Soon Kiss a Wookiee* follows Rukmini Pande's vindication of minority fans in the face of hostile fan environments, negligent fanship scholars, and indifferent media producers. I apply historical analysis, critical race theory, and media reception theory to declarations by producers, statements in the public record, and activities by fans of all backgrounds. I switch rapidly between these methods, and often the sources prove that they belong in more than one category.[13]

In this examination of the *Star Wars* phenomenon, I have gathered a wide variety of sources often overlooked, putting them shoulder to shoulder with readily accepted ones. The opening chapters draw on the history of science fiction film, along with racial science and postcolonial theory. The lives of George Lucas and Gene Roddenberry shed light on franchise creators' willingness (or hesitancy) to portray interracial relationships on-screen. Accounts of the production teams of the original trilogy movies address race indirectly in discussing the visual language of costumes, lighting, and special effects. Independent fanzines and publications licensed by Lucasfilm contained the wealth of knowledge early fans would crave. Consistently excluded from the mainstream conceptions of what fans enjoy, the activities of Black and other underrepresented fans can be found in first-person recollections, the minority press, and even hip-hop lyrics. Announced in 1997, the prequel trilogy proliferated just as the internet became a medium for community building, so message boards, reviews, and fan sites recorded the voices of that era. Social media continued to provide the fora for discussion of the sequel trilogy, so mining YouTube, Twitter, Tumblr, and other blogs produced many of the sources for the later chapters of this book. Some are rare because of mere demographics, some are obscure because media outlets exclude them, and some are hard to find because their speakers have sequestered themselves to more private realms. But, by utilizing a wide variety of sources in this history of *Star Wars* and interracialism, I want to expand notions of what counts as a valid perspective to consider.

The audience for this book consists of students and scholars in American studies, media studies, ethnic studies, and critical mixed race studies. Courses in race and media, fan studies, and Black studies will be likely homes for its lessons in representations, reception, and resistance. For undergraduates, various selections will illuminate their way toward developing critical skills. Graduates will find intersections between this and other seminal texts, as well encouragement in developing their own arguments. Scholars will likewise benefit from this book's unconventional take on popular culture since 1977. In addition, a trade audience of *Star Wars* fans looking for a perspective different from the mainstream will also enjoy *I'd Just as Soon Kiss a*

Wookiee's unique approach. Followers of blogs like *The Nerds of Color* and *Black Girl Nerds* and Tumblrs like *MCU Fandom Hates People of Color* will celebrate this book's coverage of the *Star Wars* phenomenon.

On the other hand, more conservative *Star Wars* fans will be frustrated. This book does not partake in fan service, conjuring beloved moments of the saga to delight the devotees. It does not present fan theories about events in the galaxy far, far away. It is not an exhibit of mastery of *Star Wars* trivia. It is not an indictment of George Lucas, Lucasfilm, or, since its 2012 purchase of his company, Disney. It does not rank *Star Wars* among other science fiction franchises in terms of progressiveness. That simplification would miss the point; in addition to being mirrors of their times, science fiction works undertake a wide variety of messages. *Star Wars* has addressed themes like bravery, loyalty, and inner peace that place it among classics in the Western tradition. Indeed, handlers of the franchise have stopped short in matters of interracial intimacy, but the saga's warnings against the militarism, technophilia, and despotism offer lessons for our times.

Three Commonalities in Terms of Race

I believe that George Lucas's racial influences were US-specific, not Asian, European, or Latin American. Led by these US ways of thinking, even only semiconsciously, George Lucas created the saga with the United States in mind. For this reason, I present here three main commonalities between the United States and the galaxy far, far away in terms of race. Since this is a work focusing on interracial intimacy, this list begins with the regulation of mixture. After all, you cannot tell the story of bondage without the story of mixture, because that was present at the beginning, complicating the guidelines of who was free and who was enslaved. Nor can you tell the story of white supremacy without the story of mixture, because that relies on the notion of racial purity. Questions around freedom, inheritance, and identity that arose with the slave system have had mixture at their cores. The disruptive potential of racial mixing in the United States has been a nuisance for scientists, intellectuals, and politicians, beginning with the same colonial period as the beginnings of white supremacy. Cases from the seventeenth century would challenge the rules of categorization and lead to more rigid standards. Following Bacon's Rebellion—a 1676 uprising of bonded servants, both Black and white—Virginia's House of Burgesses defused the rebels by establishing privileges that came with white male status and cementing the association between African descent and inheritable enslavement. Efforts to stabilize racial identity had been instrumental in securing property, defending slavery, and qualifying as a litigant in court before the first anti-intermarriage laws of the 1690s.

Later, as the stakes increased leading up to the Civil War, associations between mixture and degeneracy grew. Antimixing discourses flourished in popular culture, notably with blackface minstrelsy; in literature and drama, with the tragic mulatto stereotype; in the law, with anti-intermarriage statutes; and in the natural sciences, which promoted the notion of polygenesis. Proslavery scientists argued that humans spawned on different continents around the world. This schema placed whites at top and claimed that other races were distinct species, casting mixture between the types repugnant. They claimed that mulattoes would pass away, unable to produce viable offspring (like mules). *Types of Mankind*, by George Gliddon and Josiah Nott, the culmination of their work to bolster slavery with scientific authority, echoes in common thinking about race to this day: that pure races exist, centered around the continents; that specific groups have specific talents; and that mixed people are halfway between their parent groups, confused, and aspiring to join the superior whites. Slavery ended, but states criminalized interracial relationships, making their undesirability common sense across the nation.[14]

In the early twentieth century, progressive social scientists striving for racial equality cast mixed minorities as the last hope for their inferior parent groups. Meanwhile, the nation at large fixated on racial passing in situations like the Rhinelander case and movies like *Imitation of Life* (1934). Racial thinking had changed from proslavery to social Darwinism to eugenics, but the project remained the same: white supremacy. In other words, they ensure that whiteness occupied the center above all. Preferences for monoracial conceptions of America have limited the analysis of a society where mixture has always been present. For more than four hundred years now, we have developed a resistance to discussing mixture, considering the mixed, or admitting our unease with ambiguity.[15]

But what happens if we put intimate exchanges between racial groups at the center of the examination of race and history in the United States? That is, how would discussions of those themes expand by utilizing the ambiguities arising from interracial intimacy? Is it possible to end the mass denial? I argue that this approach brings together more themes than monoracial thinking does, and perhaps puts us on a path away from the separate-but-equal thinking that Pande has observed.

Indeed, the terms have shifted and changed across time and place. At different moments, the meaning of *race* has relied on kinship, biology, and culture. The set of "races" prevalent in the United States has fluctuated between three and five or more, depending on who has done the classification. Similarly, the meaning of *mixture* has applied to marriages between European nationalities; types of humankind considered different species; and the fusion of culinary, musical, and linguistic idioms. I argue that interracial intimacy (the sexual relations between people considered members of disparate origins) is a site where multiple historical themes intersect. Thus, thoughtful conversations about mixed race can produce narratives that keep more themes in view.

I call this "mixed race analysis," and it is a tool that scholars of racial mixing have been using since the 1990s. Some of the earlier works, like Maria P. P. Root's "A Bill of Rights for Racially Mixed People" and G. Reginald Daniel's "Beyond Black and White: The New Multiracial Consciousness," seemed to focus on validation; but examined more carefully, they were also calling for a reform in the ways we think about race.[16] Influenced by Black studies, the field has moved to a more critical stance. In tracing the "critical turn" in the interdisciplinary study of mixed race, Daniel and coauthors Laura Kina, Wei Ming Dariotis, and Camilla Fojas, describe the field as follows: "[It] encompasses these areas of analysis with an emphasis on all things related to 'mixed' race. This includes renderings and studies of racial mixing, interraciality, multiraciality, transracial adoption, and interethnic alliances, among others. Ethnic studies and critical race studies are key components of critical mixed race studies and continue to advance similar inquiries and scholarly discourses about race, culture, and society."[17]

Much of the work in this field appreciates two or more perspectives. One or two of these may draw from the experience of a minority group in the United States. It brings together disparate sources to reconstruct unheard voices. Having to eke out tools to consider the intersections of margins, it often draws from more than one discipline. It takes as a starting point that meanings are in flux, especially the borders between them. It maintains that concepts taken for granted are highly constructed.

Rather than consider mixed race analysis a new approach that corrects the ills of existing focuses in African American, Latino/Chicano, Asian American, and American studies, I emphasize that the study of mixed race is integral to each of them. Rather than the successor to implicitly obsolete approaches, it can be a thread that runs through any or all of them, just as the analytic lenses of gender and class are. This is especially true when anti-racist ends motivate the scholarship on race in the United States. I argue that mixed race analysis is most effective as one aspect of an array of reforms, rather than a good in and of itself. Scholars need not identify as a specialist in this field to contribute in these ways. However, as Minelle Mahtani points out, the following are not identical: first, "studies that broadly consider mixed race identity; second, the newly emerging field that is called critical mixed race studies or critical mixed race theory; and finally, critical race theory." She argues "that a critical mixed race studies is possible only through a prolonged exchange both with critical race theory and with anticolonialism and anti-imperialism debates, which do, of course, inform critical race theory as well."[18] One way to distinguish works that fit the critical label from works that merely examine mixed race is to ask whether they put whiteness at the center, as polygenesist science, early twentieth-century "mulatto studies," and laments by white mothers have done. Second, do they serve mixed people only, celebrating their comeliness, reappropriating other minority achievements to a multiracial umbrella, or casting racially mixed people as the heroes of American race relations? Last, are they rooted in collective, historical experiences, or utopian wish making?

Critical mixed race studies scholars using this sort of analysis have addressed topics relevant to racial mixing globally: identity formation, marriage, government enumeration, transnationalism, and empire. The fact of mixture is readily apparent in these, but often subjects, places, and relationships do not lend themselves to conversations about mixed race. *I'd Just as Soon Kiss a Wookiee* offers an example of how to do mixed race analysis when the subject at hand is parsimonious toward this line of questioning. My hope is that this book will serve as a model for others who see interracial intimacy (close encounters between people of different racial groups), interracialism (the less intimate varieties of interaction), or mixed race (racial mixing as a by-product of contact) beneath the surface. Upon completion of this book, readers will find in their toolboxes equipment to consider familiar things from a rare, yet emergent perspective.

Altogether, mixture is a useful analytic lens, producing innovative perspectives and insights into the mainstream, including race and sex in *Star Wars*, a nexus obscured by our society's historical denial of racial mixture, as well as its contradictory treatment of intimacy in general. Movies rely on vague tropes to present intimacy, romance, and kinship, even though the Motion Picture Association film rating system loosened its standards in 1968. Depictions of violence can be seen in movies of any rating, but nudity may only appear in PG or higher. More than brief nudity requires a PG-13 rating, and nudity in a sexual context requires an R rating. Even before examining the saga for interracial intimacy, we must ask whether there is sex in *Star Wars*. From the early days of the movie's popularity, the common answer was no. As *Time* magazine wrote in its review of *Star Wars* in 1977, "The result is a remarkable confection: a subliminal history of the movies, wrapped in a riveting tale of suspense and adventure, ornamented with some of the most ingenious special effects ever contrived for film."[19] In naming it movie of the year, the author argued, "It has no message, no sex and only the merest dollop of blood shed here and there. It's aimed at kids—the kid in everybody."[20] This became the conventional wisdom about *Star Wars*: that it was fine entertainment for all ages, and that it provided wholesome escapism from real-world issues. But it was rated PG, not G, so *Time*'s author must have given the movie a pass for severed arms, incinerated bodies, and people shot dead in bars. The reality is that *Star Wars* was violent, cast aspersions on the military–industrial complex, and depicted the servitude of nonhumans. As the story of a boy becoming a man through adventure, it is full of Freudian symbols. Guns, lightsabers, and mechanical probes proliferate nearly every scene. Dialogue becomes comically sexual once we learn the idioms of intercourse ("Luke, at that speed, do you think you'll be able to pull out in time?"). Explanations of relationships become unbelievable when we evaluate them against what we already know (for example, that Luke and Leia are siblings).

The centrality of servitude is the next commonality between the galaxy far, far away and the United States. Bondage, slavery, and cheap labor have shaped life around the Atlantic since European colonists began classifying laborers along racial lines. Africans kidnapped by the Portuguese and stolen by English privateers arrived in 1619 in Virginia, the earliest of the British colonies on the East Coast, and were immediately sold into bondage. Since the slave system was still developing, some were indentured servants like the poor whites before them, rather than slaves. Soon began the process of lining up racial classification and social status described above, which was completed in the latter part of the seventeenth century, when (pure) whiteness became free, equal, and protected by the law, while the presence of nonwhite ancestry became servile, unequal, and vulnerable to the law.[21]

Star Wars introduced us to a universe replete with advanced infrastructure, miraculous technology, and architectural wonders without explaining how they were built, or when humans had colonized these planets. George Lucas's movies are not exposition-rich like *Lord of the Rings* or *Game of Thrones*. Glimpses of labor show a scheme like many in Orlando Patterson's work on slavery and social death, including the United States. His book *Slavery and Social Death* laid out a comparison of slave systems globally across history, ultimately defining slavery as "the permanent, violent domination of natally alienated and generally dishonored persons." Because Patterson was developing a unified theory that would include antiquity, he deemphasized African descent and opened the conversation to elite slaves, not just menial workers. Across many contexts, people become slaves through a process of defeat, dehumanization, and alienation. The social status of slaves, as well as their social relations, all came from their relationships with their masters. Slaves were considered subhuman, with no agency of their own. However, slave societies depended on the labor of these "socially dead" people. They did all the work, including duties dangerous or taboo to others. Ultimately, slavery is a parasitic relationship in which masters hold people and extract labor from them, and their society would crumble without them.[22]

Let's take C-3PO as our guide in discerning parallels with Patterson's framework in the first *Star Wars* film. After Luke's Uncle Owen has purchased him and R2-D2, he mentions that their former master was a Captain Antilles. Like many slaves, the two have changed masters. C-3PO expresses the belief that Uncle Owen and Luke are their new masters, scolding R2-D2 for continuing his quest to find Obi-Wan Kenobi. Both Threepio and Artoo are outfitted with restraining bolts that, activated by remote control, are even more effective than shackles; they control their movements and mark them as unfree beings. Additionally, Threepio addresses Luke as "Master." He speaks when he's spoken to. He offers his talents in protocol and translation to his master. He is dependent on Luke, following his commands, seeking his protection, and feeling great shame in the young man's apparent demise in the trash compactor ("Curse my metal body!"). Threepio's signature outlook is panicky, dependent, and pessimistic; in his words, he and Artoo are doomed, sure to be melted down, or smashed into who knows what. When they land on Tatooine, Threepio laments, "How did I get into this mess? I really don't know how. We seem to be made to suffer. It's our lot in life." On the one hand, this echoes the Buddhist noble truth that life is suffering. But Threepio is also commenting on their station in society as manufactured beings, made to suffer as a slave is born to suffer.

The film drops us in medias res in the galaxy far, far away, making it seem natural that humans do heroic work like prepping for battle, administering a city, or soldiering. (I would call soldiers with masks socially dead, while those with faces are more likely to be viable members of society.) With no prequels, sequels, or licensed texts to provide the backstory behind the proliferation of humans, *Star Wars* invites us to fill this in with our preconceived notions and familiar imagery. Most of the first half of the movie takes place on Tatooine, the desert planet resembling the settings of Western movies like *The Searchers* (1956), *The Good, the Bad and the Ugly* (1966), and *Once Upon a Time in the West* (1968) that influenced Lucas. Those also presented the story of westward expansion as a given, illustrated by the landscapes and demonstrated by the relationships other peoples had to brave white men, whether vulnerable white women, lecherous American Indians, or shifty Mexicans. On Luke Skywalker's home planet, women fix breakfast; droids do menial work like tuning water vaporators, loading freighters, or monitoring the halls; Indigenous people scavenge, pilfer, and pirate; and foreigners conspire in the alcoves of bars. Most likely, nonhumans were the ones doing the hard labor of building the galaxy. The preconceived notions, the familiar imagery, and the number of on-screen relationships in which nonhumans serve humans suggest this. Throughout all nine movies, the origin story of human diaspora remains a mystery, but relationships resembling those in United States history remain.

The last major commonality between the galaxy far, far away and the United States is the predominance of white racial status—especially white masculinity—which laws began codifying in the seventeenth century, as mentioned above. These privileges have produced ways of thinking relevant to this exploration of race in the *Star Wars* saga. The most prominent is the white racial frame, as defined by Joe Feagin. The product of four hundred years of conditioning, the white racial frame is a "comprehensive and complex" way of thinking applicable to almost every aspect of American life. Generally, the white racial frame views whites as superior and people of color as less essential in the United

States. Going deeper, whites see their domination and their enrichment as unremarkable. Going deeper still, abstractions, stereotypes, and associations of "inferior racial others" are constructed and accepted. This framing is taken for granted and rarely challenged by whites. In fact, society has rewarded acting within the white racial frame, so there are benefits to complying to it. It reflects the hegemony ("the dominance of one group over other groups, with or without the threat of force, to the extent that, for instance, the dominant party can dictate the terms of trade to its advantage") of whiteness over others.[23] One must actively adopt a counterframe to oppose it, and whites are highly unlikely to do so: "In summary, the dominant white racial frame is more than a way of interpreting the world; it typically becomes central to a white person's way of life, to their character. Whites shape their lives and actions from within it."[24]

The white racial frame theory goes deeper than just the appearance of stereotypes, which are products of just part of the process: "Considered more comprehensively, the white racial frame includes a broad and persisting set of racial stereotypes, prejudices, conceptual ideologies, interlinked interpretations and narratives, and visual images. It also includes racialized emotions and racialized reactions to language accents and imbeds inclinations to discriminate."[25] The white racial frame shapes responses and, since it is often used unchecked, actions. So, the white racial frame precedes racial formation theory, which focuses on actions (frequently by leaders). As opposed to the implicit bias model, which argues that we may be unaware or mistaken about thoughts and feelings, Feagin and his colleagues who work with the white racial frame theory have shown that "truly unconscious racist framing of discriminatory behavior" is rare. Often, subjects show "differing levels of personal awareness of racial framing."[26]

Responses to *Star Wars* also come from the white racial frame, whether in the ways Feagin describes or in various forms of white solipsism that I offer here to better discern ways white audiences think about matters related to race and racism, in both the real world and the galaxy far, far away. I draw attention to Adrienne Rich's definition of white solipsism as the tendency "to think, imagine, and speak as if whiteness described the world."[27] If the white person were to explicitly express their feelings, they would sound something like "I can only see topics from my point of view. I can only recognize a problem in the ways that it affects me." During the revolutionary period, colonists described their relationship to King George III as slavery when they did not experience slavery themselves. In fact, this made them detest the enslaved, and only a few followed their revolutionary fervor with abolitionism. During the same period, many Americans needed the mixed, tragic mulatto character to feel sympathy for abolition. Often portrayed as a light-skinned woman who turned out to be the daughter of a landowner and one of his slaves, the tragic mulatto believed she was white until the truth came out, sometimes (as in William Wells Brown's *Clotel* and Dion Boucicault's *The Octoroon*) when her father died. Her chaste heart, excellent upbringing, and physical beauty would attest to this whiteness, but the Black parentage would deem them invalid. Quickly, her white fiancé would desert her, she would be sold to settle the estate, and she would suffer at the hands of violent white men, until she died. Her embodiment of whiteness—and then her inevitable fall from whiteness—gained white audiences' sympathy in the antebellum period.[28]

Star Wars is a product of the white racial frame, and Feagin's theory is so useful for examining interracial intimacy and *Star Wars* precisely because it is easy to deny the connection. But the servitude, white predominance, and disciplining of mixture appear in a galaxy far, far away because of their power in the real world, not because of an in-galaxy event. Never in the original trilogy do they say something like, "The Empire forbids consorting between different species"; rather, it is just taken for granted that you do not do that. So, even though the galaxy far, far away is a place of fantasy, many of its mores comply with those of our world.

Star Wars movies are reflections of not only George Lucas and the other creators, but all of us more broadly, in a particular historical moment. It is squarely a product of the post–civil rights era, and this book uses *Star Wars* to tell a history of that time through popular culture. In terms of diversity, gender, and inclusion, the movies can disappoint. Some argue it is not science fiction at all. But like its creator, *Star Wars* is quintessentially American, showing a pastiche of influences. So many elements echoed previous films that it seemed familiar.[29] Like many Americans, *Star Wars* is liberal, but not anti-racist, expressing good intentions, yet weak convictions. Near the end of his life, Martin Luther King Jr. described these people and their resistance to change: "Whites, it must frankly be said, are not putting in a similar mass effort to reeducate themselves out of their racial ignorance. It is an aspect of their sense of superiority that the white people of America believe they have so little to learn. . . . Loose and easy language about equality, resonant resolutions about brotherhood fall pleasantly on the ear, but for the Negro there is a credibility gap he cannot overlook."[30] King described how each step toward equality led to "an ever-present tendency to backlash." The same has been true in the decades since then. Eduardo Bonilla-Silva describes the times since the landmark civil rights gains: "In contrast to race relations in the Jim Crow period, however, racial practices that reproduce racial inequality in contemporary America are (1) increasingly covert, (2) embedded in normal operations of institutions, (3) void of direct racial terminology, and (4) invisible to most whites."[31]

But as the post–civil rights era extends from 1965, it transitions into new sub-eras. I resist the urge to delineate these with specific years. But I will point out that the three trilogies of movies came out in remarkably different times. The first *Star Wars* film redefined the blockbuster in an era when we went to theaters to see movies, ventured to stores to buy collectibles, and kept our eyes peeled for any tidbit of the franchise we could catch on one of three television networks. The prequel trilogy began twenty-two years later, with the internet just beginning to bring together fans, big-box stores deluging us with merchandise, and every media outlet stoking expectations of *The Phantom Menace* (1999). The sequel trilogy commenced sixteen years after that, with every pop culture product you'd ever want available all the time, social media and the internet amplifying the most marginal of positions, and viewers following routes to encounter the saga beyond the movies. So historical contextualization is essential in discerning the shifts from era to era. Still, the history of the *Star Wars* phenomenon and race runs parallel with the history of race relations in the post–civil rights era for the creators, the story lines, and the fans. This is why this book's analysis focuses mainly on the United States, rather than taking a comparative, global approach.

Frequently Asked Questions

What is *interracial intimacy*? This term encompasses interracial marriage, sex across racial lines, and creation of mixed offspring. Its seemingly neutral tone makes it applicable to consensual and forced relations. It encompasses a variety of relationships, including those outside of marriage and those not producing children. Rising in popularity since the 1990s, *interracial intimacy* supplants terms bearing racist undertones:

Amalgamation had been used in a positive sense in the late eighteenth and early nineteenth centuries, until antiabolitionists hijacked it. Specific to the Southwest and American Indians, *mongrelization* always meant degradation, as the root word indicates. The invention of anti-Lincoln journalists during the 1864 election, *miscegenation* was designed to sound scientific but was always used in the negative sense. *Race mixing* became popular in scientific writing of the twentieth century. Taken at face value, it sounds like a matter-of-fact description of the phenomenon, but its employment by eugenicists and social Darwinists gives *race mixing* a negative connotation. *Social equality* raised its head before the Civil War, during Reconstruction, and through the Jim Crow era. In the hands of abolitionists and other activists for racial justice, it referred mostly to equality and citizenship. Protectors of slavery, separation, and white racial purity often used it as a euphemism for consensual interracial relations. But their opponents immediately connected it to an upending of sexual norms. So, from the antebellum period, through the civil rights movement of the 1950s and '60s, they rejected social equality as forced interracial sex.

Because it complicates monoracial conceptions of family, I include interracial and transnational adoption as forms of interracial intimacy. The mixing of this fundamental unit of society by including a child of a different race or nationality is intimate business. In the 1950s, proponents often stated this in a patronizing way, with white Americans introducing poor kids to democracy. Along with international adoption, interracial adoption also has placed a high number of racially mixed kids with monoracially identifying parents. Women who became pregnant with someone of a different race were likely to put their babies up for adoption. Through 1994, when the Multiethnic Placement Act stated that race matching was not a prerequisite, transracial adoption was the norm domestically, and mixed children were placed with monoracial, minority homes. Mixed Black kids were placed with Black families to preserve their Black identities. Meanwhile, international adoption commonly placed Asian, Latin American, and African children with white families.

How much *Star Wars* are we covering here? The *Star Wars* universe has included novels, comics, video games, merchandise, and television shows in addition to the movies. Prior to its 2012 purchase by Disney, Lucasfilm maintained a storytelling hierarchy system that placed George Lucas's films at the pinnacle. Comics that told stories of an alternate reality and video games that followed paths depending on the players' actions ranked furthest from the canon. After Disney acquired the franchise, it jettisoned all the previous novels, comics, and video games from the canon, keeping only the movies and the recent television shows. Around the same time, it established the Lucasfilm Story Group, a committee of company veterans who make available to writers and directors their knowledge of *Star Wars* storytelling logic. I greatly respect those creators and the fans who consume those media (now called "Legends," rather than "canon"), but I will be mostly sticking to the motion pictures in the Skywalker saga. First, most people familiar with *Star Wars* are casual fans who stop with the movies, so I will too. Second, the movies have had the longest lifespan (nearly fifty years), so they offer some constancy when discussing a cultural phenomenon that has been in flux.

I use the term *operate as* to encourage a different kind of knowledge that considers that what a character looks like and how they are considered in their fictional world may resemble something different in our real society. It describes what racialized characters might recall beyond their physical appearance. For example, the house elves in the *Harry Potter* series don't even appear as humans, but they echo representations of enslaved Black people in the United States. Discerning that they operate this way highlights their position in society, as well as the prickly aspects of the Wizarding World. Saying that these magical creatures operate as slaves also alerts us to stereotypes in J. K. Rowling's creations. Last, when discussing racial mixture, seeing how characters "operate as" reminds us that physical appearance is unreliable.

What do aliens, droids, and cyborgs operate as racially? The distinctiveness of humans, aliens, and droids recalls racial science from the antebellum period, mentioned above. These ideas influenced science fiction writers, often through tropes of hybridity. Notably, Lucas also limited hybridity to a minimum. But the ways humans, aliens, and droids interact echo Gliddon and Nott. Humans are one race, each species of alien is a race, and each kind of droid is a race. I consider aliens (sentient, biochemical beings, often humanoid) to be equal in capacity as humans. Yet, as stated above, those in servitude are "socially dead." Biologically, aliens are separate species (not just types) from humans, and different species do not produce shared offspring in *Star Wars*. They seem to find each other repellent.

Droids (sentient, mechanical, in many shapes, analogous to what we call robots) may have skills superior to humans, but those skills exist to serve humans. Droids are property. The standard for constructing robotic personalities is Isaac Asimov's "Three Laws of Robotics," which first appeared in his 1942 short story "Runaround." These guided his own work, later science fiction, and adaptations:

1. A robot may not injure a human being or, through inaction, allow a human being to come to harm.
2. A robot must obey the orders given it by human beings, except where such orders would conflict with the First Law.
3. A robot must protect its own existence if such protection does not conflict with the First or Second Laws.[32]

Robots are honest, conscientious, and subservient to humans. These laws set the foundation for their decision-making. Of course, complications arise when available options violate one law or another, or when a robot realizes it has free will. The adventures of R2-D2 demonstrate that droids in the galaxy far, far away can prioritize orders from one human over others. They can conceal and even lie. They can harm humans, aliens, and droids if the victims are enemies of their master. They develop personalities based on experiences and have emotions like those of humans. The three laws of *Star Wars* may look something like this: First, a droid must fulfill its primary purpose as designed by the maker. Second, a droid must obey commands given by its master. It must assist in defeating its master's enemies. Third, a droid's existence (and well-being?) depends on its master. A droid may come into great harm assisting its master. Above all else, *Star Wars* droids comply with their purpose. So, a droid built for battle can harm humans. Each kind of droid is its own species. They are asexual. They can build relationships with other sentient beings, but always platonic. They cannot reproduce.

A cyborg, as defined by Donna Haraway, is "a cybernetic organism, a hybrid of machine and organism, a creature of social reality as well as a creature of fiction."[33] In her "Cyborg Manifesto," she argues that the science fiction trope is instrumental to expanding our understanding of women's lived experiences in our current times. As "creatures simultaneously animal and machine," cyborgs challenge many presumptions of Western thought. Haraway uses the science fiction characters to promote feminism, socialism, and phenomenology. Cyborgs are the closest thing to mixed characters in *Star Wars*, but their mixed bodies are symbols of servitude rather than liberation. *Star Wars* follows other science fiction works in subordinating cyborgs to humans. Lando Calrissian's assistant, Lobot, wears a computerized implant fused to the back of his head, making him available to the administrator's beck and call. General Grievous, whose mostly mechanical body presages Darth Vader's, is the military commander of Count Dooku's Separatist movement. And Darth Vader's mechanical breathing announces his dependence on the mechanical components of his body, as well as his position as the Emperor's principal henchman.

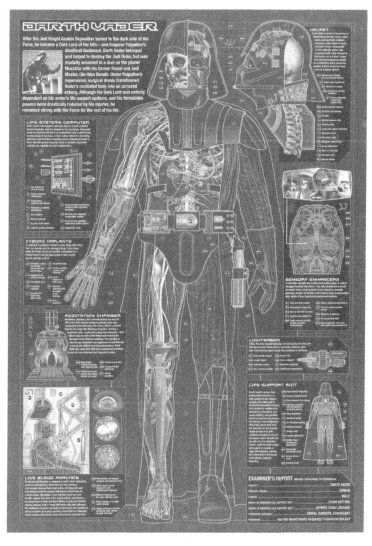

Figure 0.1. Blueprint showing organic and cybernetic parts making up Darth Vader's body. Credit: Chris Trevas and Chris Reiff.

Chapters

Chapter 1, "The History of On-Screen Science Fiction Interracial Intimacy (1902–1987)," compares interracial intimacy in science fiction movies and shows of the twentieth century. This chapter traces the uses of symbolic interracial intimacy, ambiguous bodies, explicit interracial intimacy, and mixed offspring. Focusing on the central villain of the original trilogy, chapter 2, "What Are You, Darth Vader? (1977–1980)," takes seriously the position that Darth Vader is not simply a white man in a black suit. Following the admonitions of Manthia Diawara and bell hooks concerning oppositional reading practiced by Black viewers, I argue that considering Darth Vader African American when *Star Wars* debuted in 1977 was not so far-fetched. Chapter 3, "Early Fanship, the Invisible Jetpack, and Black Fans (1977–1982)," situates the activities of African American *Star Wars* fans up to the 1983 release of *Return of the Jedi*, showing how the privileging of whiteness grew in fanship, a supposedly colorblind arena. Reconfiguring the "invisible knapsack," Peggy McIntosh's list of hidden benefits of white privilege in everyday life, I suggest that white fans are equipped with a sort of invisible jetpack that increases their mobility and lifts them above the concerns of others, making it easier to enjoy their diversions in a carefree way. Chapter 4, "Princess Leia, Lando Calrissian, and Fan Imaginations (1977–1983)," critiques the conventional wisdom saying that Darth Vader represented authority, militarism, and brutality, while Princess Leia represented the institutional dimensions of freedom. I argue that *The Empire Strikes Back* (1980) tells the story of her sexual exploration as much as it builds the father–son conflict. The fifth chapter, "Don't Ask the Prequels Where Babies Come From (1999–2005)," argues that the backlash against the prequel trilogy (1999–2005) had, in part, a racial basis. Fans who had never questioned the primacy of white characters now had to accept more minority ones than ever. The betrayal these fans felt mirrored their distaste for multiculturalism, affirmative action, and demographic shifts of the outside world. Chapter 6, "Four Ships Sailed. Which Would Land? (2012–2016)," relies on a variety of minority geek voices to reveal their underappreciated perspectives, especially regarding the intraracial "ship" between two white characters (Rey and Kylo Ren) or an interracial one between two characters (Finn and Rey). The seventh and final chapter, "Social Media, Fans, and Interracial Relationships (2015–2020)," brings us to a highly anticipated moment: the conclusion of the Skywalker saga in *The Rise of Skywalker*, released in December 2019.

"If She's Leia, You Can't Be Luke!"

I end this introduction with a vignette about the early days of shipping, canonical authority, and cosplay that demonstrates the boundaries of inclusion, the influence of pop culture, and the reason I titled this book *I'd Just as Soon Kiss a Wookiee*. In May 1978, a year after *Star Wars* and eighteen months after *Roots*, second grade ended, and I was free to play *Star Wars* all day long with two other kids who lived on my block. *Star Wars* had stuff that was supposedly for boys, like laser guns, but it also had stuff that was supposedly for girls, like kissing. But playing *Star Wars* with Michael and Jennifer showed that both sexes had mastery of both realms. Fairy tales, advertising, and adult television had already introduced us to society's rules about both shooting and kissing, best summarized by the maxim "Boy meets girl, boy loses girl, boy gets girl." If a story had more than one boy, only one of them could get the girl, as in *Some Like It Hot* (1959). If a story had more than one boy and more than one girl, pairings followed tiers based on their desirability, as in *Sabrina* (1954). If the boys were of different races, then the white one got the girl; after all, since heroism meant white masculinity, minority men were disqualified. Later, when interracial buddies appeared onscreen, storytelling rules went out the window in favor of protecting white purity. Even the oldest story conventions of Western storytelling were subordinate to Hays Code prohibitions, which enforced society's racial prejudices.

Michael was also eight years old that year. He lived two doors away, had an older brother, and went to the neighborhood public school. Print was his thing. He read every *Star Wars* comic and novel he could get his hands on, as soon as they appeared at Waldenbooks. Jennifer lived down the block and across the street. She was a grade ahead of us but went to the same school as Michael, and she was the youngest of three. She could recite every line of the movie, scene by scene; her siblings had taken a tape recorder into the theater. (Remember, this was before home video or the internet.) The previous Halloween, she emerged from her house in a full Princess Leia costume, not the plastic deal Michael and I got. I was the one with the action figures. I had the full, original series of twelve 3.75-inch figures, the Death Star play set, the landspeeder, the radio-controlled R2-D2, the X-wing fighter, the TIE fighter, and the carry case. *And I shared.*

I was their mixed but Black-identifying friend. They were my Jewish neighborhood, white friends. We knew we were different from most people, but in ways different from each other. Michael and Jennifer respected my odd identity, and I respected theirs. My private boys' school, white friends lived in more stately neighborhoods. Returning in the fall, those boys would slip "the club," "our boat," and "our cabin" into descriptions of where they played *Star Wars*. Together, Jennifer, Michael, and I crisscrossed in the backyards connecting the homes on my side of the street. Trees were planets, and the line at the bottom of the hill was the end of the galaxy. Straight sticks were lightsabers, and bent ones were blasters. Each time we played, one rule held firm: once you picked who you would be you had to commit, and the other two friends had to respect that.

On the first day of summer, the three of us had decided to pick up the action right after the medals were given out. We were agreeing that Luke and Leia should be together—Luke is the hero, and they've kissed. Han is not trustworthy. Jennifer then reenacted the "A princess and a guy like me" scene. "Han should be able to tell Luke already likes her. And then Luke blew up the Death Star, which makes him a greater hero." As an amendment, Jennifer offered that "they've kissed twice. For luck." She gasped and then added, "I only wish Ben were here."

"Wouldn't it be cool if Darth Vader showed up?" Michael supposed. "I'm Darth Vader."

I claimed Luke, and Jennifer claimed Han Solo.

"You can't be Han Solo," Michael proclaimed. I agreed.

"Why not?"

"He's male."

"Then I'll be R2-D2," Jennifer teased, "the true hero of *Star Wars*."

"He's male too. They call him *him*."

"But he's a robot, he's not starting a family. I've been R2-D2 and C-3PO lots of times."

"You can be Chewbacca," Michael offered.

"Being Chewbacca is hard," Jennifer protested, "all that gargling."

"You can be Princess Leia," I offered.

"Yes, that's what I'm known for. Fine, I'm Leia, Michael is Darth Vader, and Greg is Luke."

It was set, as if "Action!" had been called on set. Jennifer and I got into positions. Michael yelled abruptly, "No!" and we looked back immediately. "If she's Leia, you can't be Luke!"

"Why not?" I asked.

"Because you two do not belong together." I had a sense he was talking about Jennifer and me, not Leia and Luke.

"But we're playing, pretending," Jennifer offered. "We've played these roles before."

"But Greg can't be Luke."

"I have been before."

"And I've been Leia before."

Having read all those comics and novels endowed him with authority, and our disagreeing with him hurt his feelings. Couldn't we see what would unfold? "You two have never been Luke and Leia after the awards ceremony. You'll probably kiss!"

Jennifer began singing, "Luke and Leia sitting in a tree, K-I-S-S-I-N-G! First comes love, then comes marriage, then comes a baby in a baby carriage!" She puckered up and began to chase me. She looked nothing like Princess Leia. Although just nine, she looked like a big aunt with too much lipstick hoping for a kiss at a family gathering. I yelled, "Noooo!" because the jumbling of Princess Leia, an aunt, and a neighborhood girl confused me. Michael yelled, "Noooo!" because he saw our play a different way: in stripes of white and nonwhite that should not dissolve into each other. Running from Jennifer, I went straight toward Michael. Perhaps he would rescue me from this auntie/neighbor/princess who wanted to slobber one on me. Instead, he put out his hand and pinched his fingers together like he was rubbing Elmer's glue off them. By the time I noticed the rage in his face, I was already on him. He was trying to crush my throat, à la Darth Vader. I ran into him, and his telekinetic strangling hand snapped right into his face. As soon as we were both on the ground, his nose was bleeding, and his rage face drooped in agony. "Oww! Oww! Oww! Oww!" he screamed as he raced toward his house. I sat in the grass and watched Jennifer follow him. Her tall socks had blue stripes near the top, just like the Baltimore Colts.

I was not the "real" Luke Skywalker, who was a fictional character in a fictional world. Did they know this? Maybe their grasp on the fiction was weaker than my own. Did I want a kiss from Jennifer? It had not crossed my mind, but sure. Did I want to run off with Princess Leia? Sure. Did I think Michael was wrong and hateful? Yes. I hoped he would not sell me out, saying I was the cause of the bloody nose. He could still want me punished because I was poised to blur the color lines. The prospect of my sexual opportunities surpassed the novelty of my racial mixture. Michael now saw me as a new kind of threat, just as Black men became a new kind of threat after the Civil War. My parents had taught me over the dinner table, Alex Haley had taught me in *Roots*, and the evening news had taught me through images of marching Klansmen to beware this kind of resentment.

Early in *The Empire Strikes Back*, which was set some point after the destruction of the first Death Star, Princess Leia and Han Solo are bickering in the corridors of the rebel hideout, providing us a scene that illustrates these points and provides the title of this book. He argues that she does not want him to leave the base without giving her a goodbye kiss. She protests, "I'd just as soon kiss a Wookiee!" referring to the species of Han's copilot, Chewbacca. Han Solo responds that he could arrange such a kiss and storms off, leaving her fuming. She has insulted Chewbacca before, calling him a "walking carpet." Chewbacca is sentient but not worthy of intimacy. Although intelligent, strong, and brave, the Wookiee follows Han's orders. That kiss would be less meaningful than one from her principal, white, human male suitor. This exchange is just one of many one-liners between characters in the *Star Wars* movies, perhaps forgettable to those who do not ponder these relationships. It takes for granted Chewbacca's subservience to Han Solo, Wookiees' minority status, and the superiority of humans in all their relations with nonhumans. It works on a comic level because the values of a galaxy far, far away must be like those of the United States; it is preposterous to imagine a human female and Wookiee male kissing. The common sense of the galaxy far, far away, like that of our society, discourages people from fraternizing with others deemed too biologically different.

In the summer of 1978, Michael thought of me differently than he thought of Black people, but he also did not think of me as white. He thought of Chewbacca differently than he thought of cantina aliens, but he also did not think the Wookiee was worthy of a kiss. He was mad because a situation arose where I would have license to practice interracial intimacy. Michael thought of himself and Jennifer as white—perhaps not WASPs, but white, nonetheless.

Jennifer likely also thought of herself as white. During the original trilogy years, Princess Leia was the white chick to be. There was no cool, universally accepted Jewish girl in *Star Wars*. Jennifer's ability to become

Figure 0.2. *Bricklandia Comic*, no. 1, making light of Princess Leia's distaste for kissing Chewbacca. Credit: Ace Kim.

Princess Leia was cultural capital beyond playing *Star Wars* with the neighborhood boys. Becoming Princess Leia brought her white femininity. If two ice cream trucks arrived at the same time, with one announcing, "Ice cream for white people!" and the other announcing, "Ice cream for Jews!" they would run to the one for whites first. Such is the allure of masculinist, elitist, Anglo-Saxon whiteness for ethnicities further from its idealization. Then they would come back to the curb and wonder why I did not have any ice cream.

At age eight, even if our interest in kissing was as concrete as our interest in making money, we had been students of who was worthy of kissing and who was not in *Star Wars*. As chapter 1 shows, science fiction was part of this tutelage.

CHAPTER 1

The History of On-Screen Science Fiction Interracial Intimacy (1902–1987)

Introduction

Considered the first science fiction film, *A Trip to the Moon* (1902) follows a group of explorers who disembark from Earth. Led by Professor Barbenfouillis, they encounter a tribe of aliens, capture one, and return home. Utilizing techniques such as substitution splices, multiple exposures, and dissolves, French director Georges Méliès's *A Trip to the Moon* was a special effects extravaganza for its time. The image of their bullet-shaped rocket protruding from the right eye of the face on the moon is one of the most famous in film history. Like *Star Wars*, *A Trip to the Moon* wears its influences on its sleeve and offers a wealth of visual delights. But it also shows how the metanarrative from four hundred years of colonialism laid the foundation for the genre: white men explore, capture, and plunder other lands. From 1902 to the present, science fiction film would adorn that narrative with great imagination, technology, and allegory, leaving us to decode its relation to our society.[1]

The work of interpreting the relation of colonialism and science fiction really gets underway, then, by attempting to decipher the fiction's often distorted and topsy-turvy references to colonialism. Only then can one properly ask how early science fiction lives and breathes in the atmosphere of colonial history and its discourses, how it reflects or contributes to ideological production of ideas about the shape of history, and how it might, in varying degrees, enact a struggle over humankind's ability to reshape it. Through tropes of exploration, science fiction recasts colonialism as one of its central themes, but it also presents the by-products of colonialism: violence, inequality, and mixture.[2]

This chapter primarily argues that producers have been only so effective in hiding interracialism.[3] Second, it proposes that, during the past six decades (the post–civil rights era), disruption of monoracialism, whether symbolic or explicit, has clustered around certain years in specific ways. Third, it compares George Lucas's and Gene Roddenberry's choices regarding interracialism, holding *Star Wars* in contrast with *Star Trek: The Original Series* (1966–1969). I am not presenting these two works to praise one and chastise the other, but rather as cases to ply certain analytic questions. Both *Star Wars* and *Star Trek* offer material that is expansive and stimulating to the imagination.

Motion Pictures and the Common Sense of Anti-miscegenation

Several currents contributed to the concealment of interracial intimacy begun at the dawn of motion pictures: Social Darwinism echoed its Civil War–era predecessors in warnings against the ills interracial marriage would bring to society. Hoping to engineer the country's genetic fitness toward superiority, promoters of eugenics disdained interracial marriage as much as immigration. The Supreme Court's *Pace v. Alabama* decision in 1883 certified the state's law as constitutional because it punished both the man and the woman equally for their interracial marriage, completing the shift from censuring distasteful mores to criminalizing such behavior.

Released nearly simultaneously with *A Trip to the Moon*, *What Happened in the Tunnel* (1903) is a comedic, one-shot American film showing a Black woman sitting with a white woman and a white man in a passenger car of a moving train. The man intends to kiss the white woman after the train enters a dark tunnel. She must have switched seats with the Black woman, who is her employee, because when light returns to the cabin, we discover that he has made a move on her. The white woman has deployed the Black woman to give the sexually harassing male his comeuppance. Treating interracial intimacy as hidden, shameful, and ineffable, the film uses interracial intimacy as comic relief, a proposition as ridiculous as kissing a Wookiee. "Hence," according to Susan Courtney, "in this earliest film fantasy of miscegenation, we find a structure that at once allows for the expression of anxiety about the unstable state of dominant racial and sexual affairs but also offers, in its dovetailing of said affairs, means to negotiate its multiple anxieties. If there is one thing that binds together all American film fantasies of miscegenation, this is it."⁴ *What Happened in the Tunnel* does not bear directly on science fiction, but it is relevant to all genres of American film, offering two-thirds of a guidebook to depicting interracial intimacy that did not exist, even though its precepts were well established by 1915. The short film suggests that filmmakers can completely hide interracial intimacy by placing it off-screen; or they can make a joke of it, using humor to diminish its importance. *What Happened in the Tunnel* does both.

A Trip to the Moon only alluded to interracialism, and *What Happened in the Tunnel* gave a quick primer. But *The Birth of a Nation* (1915) was all about mixture. Based on Thomas Dixon's 1905 novel *The Klansman*, *The Birth of a Nation* tells the story of the Civil War and Reconstruction from the point of view of resentful Confederates. Before the war, two families from across the Mason–Dixon Line are friends, even though the Southern Camerons own slaves, and the Northern Stonemans are led by a Republican congressman. A seminal work of narrative filmmaking, *The Birth of a Nation* was our first blockbuster, and director D. W. Griffith's innovations—dramatic close-ups, tracking shots, and parallel action sequences—are commonplace today, especially in epics about war, fathers and sons, and overstated good and evil—like *Star Wars*!

Through one subplot, *The Birth of a Nation* provides the last third of the guidelines for depicting interracial intimacy: make a death out of it. The Southern daughter, Flora Cameron, goes alone to fetch water, and sparks the desires of Gus, a newly commissioned Black captain looking for a white wife. A chase ensues and, rather than appeasing the Black soldier, Flora throws herself off a cliff. Her death inspires the whites to establish the Ku Klux Klan. (In reality, the Klan was founded in Tennessee, not South Carolina.) The movie's climax follows their ride to bring vigilante justice to Gus, and the national birth of the title was the post-Reconstruction United States.⁵

With the centrality of mulatto villains and the preoccupation with interracial intimacy, the primary threat *The Birth of a Nation* targeted was not slavery, which the South fought to maintain. The problem was not even that the North won the war, nor was it that the South lost the war, because reunification solved that. Nor was it the production of mulattoes through white male sexual license, since they had existed before this period, and they remained innocuous until the breakdown in mores that Reconstruction engendered. I also say that the problem was not Reconstruction, but the interracialism it allegedly brought. The

Figure 1.1. Gus, played by a white actor in blackface, accosts Flora Cameron in D. W. Griffith's *The Birth of a Nation* (1915).

great challenge proposed in the movie was how to discipline racial mixture and racially mixed people. The solution, if not slavery, was vigilantism. Later in this chapter, we see this in action in what I call the symbolic interracial intimacy cluster.

The common sense of endogamy found expression in immigration laws as it did in marriage. For example, the Cable Act, passed in 1922, made women's citizenship contingent on their husbands' status, revoking the citizenship of any woman married to "aliens ineligible for citizenship," terminology that appeared in the 1790 Naturalization Act, the Immigration Act of 1924, and various states' land laws. In an effort to restore citizenship to women after the Nineteenth Amendment granted suffrage in 1920, the act claimed "that the right of any woman to become a naturalized citizen of the United States shall not be denied or abridged because of her sex or because she is a married woman," but it did discriminate against certain kinds of marriage, namely interracial ones with Asian men.[6] Even if such a woman renounced her marriage, she could not regain her citizenship. Currently, interracial marriage was illegal in many states. These forces influenced white feminism by countering the push for suffrage, demands for labor rights, and an expansion of sexual freedom against the pillars of citizenship, racial purity, and marriage. Why would anyone want to endanger those? Wouldn't women cherry-pick their battles from these, leaving issues related to other populations untouched?

In the culture wars of the early twentieth century, fundamentalists, conservatives, and nativists on a local level measured others by exacting standards of patriotism, morality, and loyalty. Subjects who fell short in any one of these areas would face disqualification from them all. Issues as far-ranging as education, prohibition, labor, the role of women, and decency became high-stakes battlefields. In response, in 1922, the fledgling movie industry created the Motion Picture Producers and Distributors of America (MPPDA), a precursor to the Motion Picture Association. Will H. Hays, a Presbyterian elder, former US postmaster general, and former Republican National Committee head, served as its president for twenty-five years. Rather than face regulation from the federal government, Hays suggested forming an industry-led committee to censor motion pictures. Along with Irving G. Thalberg of Metro–Goldwyn–Mayer (MGM), Sol Wurtzel of Fox, and E. H. Allen of Paramount, they constructed a list of "Don'ts and Be Carefuls" to satisfy local censorship boards in 1927. Miscegenation was number six on the list. Later, in 1930, studio heads, including MGM's Thalberg, found it more agreeable to submit to a code of standards constructed by Martin J. Quigley and Rev. Daniel A. Lord than to face government intervention in matters of censorship. They wrote the document, but they named it after the MPPDA head, who agreed to abide by the code. The Production Code Administration (PCA) launched in 1934, requiring all films to obtain a certificate of approval before reaching theaters. Again, miscegenation ranked near the top of the list, making "sex relationships between the white and black races" more than a regular crime to regulate.[7]

Newer anti-miscegenation laws of the early twentieth century continued the previous century's tradition of characterizing interracial intimacy as a threat to society, but they reached further than before, disciplining popular culture, leisure, and the sex industry. During the 1920s, "law enforcement authorities and sex trade workers alike had to establish that interracial sex remained inferior to same-race sex, that white men retained greater sexual liberty than nonwhite men, and that nonwhite women remained less appealing than white women."[8] A hierarchy of sexual practices aligned with the long-standing racial hierarchy, with hetero marriage on top, associated with whiteness; and casual interracial intimacy on bottom, associated with minorities. Dancing, drinking, and dating were acceptable if they remained within racial boundaries. Jazz music, zoot suits, and even single parenthood became associated with minorities, needing punishment. These associations were apparent on the streets and on the screens.

The concealment of interracialism in movies was about censorship, morality, and racial animus, but it was also about jobs. So, when studios refused to cast minorities in interracial relationships, they were consolidating opportunities for fellow whites as well as evading accusations of promoting miscegenation. Steady employment was important for actors, as well as crew members and creators. As with every industry, giving moviemaking jobs to whites effectively ensured that only whites succeeded. White decision-makers knew that, regardless of the profession, those who succeed are also the ones who influence the industry later. On the other side of the camera, they perpetuated strategies to keep casts all-white. Blackface minstrelsy gave roles representing Black characters to whites, and yellowface and brownface applied that model to Asian and Mexican roles.

As with other mores of Jim Crow, the rules of the Hays/Production Code were so rigid in protecting white privilege that bewildering choices ensued. Casting of mixed characters followed the casting of their minority parent groups. George Siegmann and Mary Alden played the two mulatto characters in *The Birth of a Nation*. Jeanne Crain played the title character in *Pinky* (1949), who was racially passing as white. Ava Gardner beat the incomparable mixed race American actor Lena Horne for the role of Julie LaVerne, a mulatto, in *Show Boat* (1951). Jennifer Jones starred as the Chinese doctor Han Suyin in *Love Is a Many-Splendored Thing* (1955). A white actor could play a white role, an unmixed minority role, or a mixed role. But no minority actor could play white. Nor could minorities play the spouse of a white person during the years of the Hays Code. For example, the whole cast of *The Good Earth* (1937), the bestseller adapted from the Pulitzer-winning novel, consisted of white actors in yellowface. Asian actors were available for roles, and Anna May Wong campaigned to play O-lan, the story's female lead. Producer Albert Lewin said that she was "not beautiful enough," but ultimately industry rules dictated she could not appear as the wife of actor Paul Muni.[9] In other words, her Asianness disqualified her from playing the wife of an Asian man because a white man played him. The role went to a white German actor, Luise Rainer, who won an Oscar for Best Actress.

But society's norms also caused a loosening of the Hays Code. Broadcast television offered home entertainment that met lofty standards of decency, and the movie industry had to offer something distinctive for the premium a movie ticket represented. The Supreme Court's 1952 *Joseph Burstyn, Inc. v. Wilson* decision declared that motion pictures constituted free speech. Audiences and critics made successes of movies like *The Man with the Golden Arm* (1955), which dramatized heroin addiction; *Anatomy of a Murder* (1959), which depicted the perspective of an accused murderer and rapist; *Some Like It Hot* (1959), which made light of cross-dressing; and *The Pawnbroker* (1964), which was the first major film to show exposed breasts. The first three on this list reached theaters despite failing to receive MPA approval; the fourth received a special exception. Audiences existed for this material, emboldening the studios to defy the board. The mass media may bend to demands of decency, but profits were their ultimate goal. At the end of the 1960s, the MPA developed the rating system that stands to this day. The freedom movements of the preceding years pushed societal norms in many ways that affected hiring, representations, and story lines in motion pictures. In 1967, the Supreme Court's decision in *Loving v. Virginia* deemed the remaining anti-miscegenation laws unconstitutional, signaling a shift in norms around race, marriage, and family making that would unfold in the decades that followed.

Symbolic and Explicit Interracial Intimacy

Symbolic interracial intimacy includes four types of nonexplicit representation: color-coding, innuendo, experimentation, and transformation. The concealment may be systematic, and viewers must figure out the code to understand the representations. Symbolic interracial intimacy can be versatile, presenting anything from flirting to casual sex, from marriage to child-rearing. Likewise, it is applicable to consensual or forced relationships.

Color-coding is first because it lays the groundwork for the visual language in the *Star Wars* movies, indicating the character of the items they dye, whether costumes, races, or sides of the metaphysical energy field known as the Force. As Jim Paul writes of George Lucas's "medieval mind," "Lucas' visionary way of working has ancient antecedents. In the Middle Ages, the illiterate masses received and stored their information in complex visual signs, or icons. In pictures of the saints, every detail had some prescribed meaning—the color blue for the Virgin, a dove for the Holy Ghost. The Dark Invader, Darth Vader, is an icon too—an effective visual sign, instantly familiar from our own cultural catechism, black and caped and evil."[10] *Star Wars* relies on archetypes recycled from previous ages. Newcomers to *Star Wars* recognize Leia as the damsel, Vader as the fallen, Luke as the hero, and Obi-Wan as the mentor. As J. W. Rinzler wrote of the color relations in the first film:

> The characters' costumes and design also play a part in the director's larger look. "Leia is dressed in white and is part of the technological world—black, white, and gray," Lucas says. "She has a spaceship, but she would've been a stranger if she'd gone to Tatooine, the natural world: tan, brown, and green. She would be like Artoo. I really liked the idea that when Luke, Ben, the Wookiee, Threepio, and Artoo are all together, everyone except Artoo blends into the real world, Tatooine; it works very well. But when you go to the Death Star, it works just the opposite. Artoo fits in with everything because everything is black and white, and he is primarily white. We made the stormtroopers white, too (also to mix things up, so not all the bad guys were dressed in dark colors)."[11]

Even the sounds of character names cue us to their moral qualities in terms of light or dark. A few exceptions buck this code, most notably stormtroopers. The sound of their voices and their station as law keepers, along with the predominance of white people in the first movie, suggests that they are racially white. But their armor signifies uniformity, and their grimacing masks recall the *mempō* war faces of samurai. They are colored white and racially white, but morally evil.

In American life, we call people white or Black, even though they are not literally white or black. But our history has rested on these labels and the qualities they convey. White people are normal, worthy of inclusion in "We the People." Black people are inferior, to be excluded. But in the world of *Star Wars*, characters are literally white, black, or gold, and their characteristics are set. So, while assigning racial classification based on the color of their surfaces is prejudicial in the real world, in *Star Wars*, the color names align with the characters' good and evil characteristics. Characters often think in either-or terms about themselves and their adversaries. There is rarely space for ambiguity. As Stuart Hall writes of racial identity, "Identity is always . . . a structured representation that achieves its positive only through the narrow eye of the negative. It must go through the eye of the needle of the other before it can construct itself. It produces a very Manichean set of opposites."[12] Characters' regard for each other is dyadic, polar, and essentialist, making the struggle between the Jedi and Sith monastic orders, the Rebel Alliance and the Empire, and the light and the dark resemble a race war.

As soon as the movie pulls in to show characters, *Star Wars* announces that it is all about white people. Aboard Princess Leia's ship, white rebel soldiers prepare for an attack by the Imperial forces. The first close-up is of one of these soldiers, with blue eyes and blond hair. C-3PO, the first character to speak, is a robot, but he has a British accent. This establishes him as a special kind of white, a real Anglo-Saxon. He is discussing a princess, evoking the royal family we recognize so well. The system is not so simple as white is good and black is evil. I propose that color-coding in *Star Wars* runs along three axes: The first is the literal color, especially when it pertains to black and white. The second is racial whiteness or not, reflecting the principal racial dyad of our history. The third is good or evil, which indicates respect or disdain for life. Almost every character can be coded along these three axes. Their initial appearances are most telling, especially if they debuted in the first *Star Wars* film. Often, being colored white also means being morally white (or light), and being colored black means being morally black (or dark). Dressed in white, racially white, and leading the efforts to protect life and liberty, Princess Leia is white along three dimensions of this schema. Luke Skywalker comes second with his dingy karate outfit. Han Solo wears black and white, and eventually commits to the good guys.

The racial homogeneity complicates the matter because all the humans are racially white. The homogeneous cast almost seems to be a strategy to avoid accusations of pitching minorities as negative stereotypes; however, as nonhumans, the droids and sentient humanoids serve as the benighted racial minorities. As Adilifu Nama writes, "In this sense, Star Wars carries on the tradition by using masks and exaggerated physical mannerisms to create the illusion of alien life-forms that signify people of color. This type of racial 'othering' on display in the cantina scene reaches its hyperbolic zenith in the figure of Darth Vader, the villain fully clad in black, with an obtrusive and foreboding wraparound black head mask."[13] Darth Vader is colored black—to the extreme. He is morally black—to the extreme. And his racial identity is up for questioning, mainly because of James Earl Jones's voice. It is the only African American presence in the movie. Darth Vader is either "a reminder that there are no other people of color in this film," or he is the only African American "presence in the film, and he is evil."[14]

The second type of symbolic interracial intimacy, innuendo, which is the most superficial and easy to miss, often hides in the serious, then becomes apparent and comical as viewers know more about mature topics. In other words, innuendo reveals hidden meanings and makes jokes of them, so that you do not have to make a death of them. So, Darth Vader provides the hint of racial Blackness audiences had learned to remove since *The Birth of a Nation*. This is a deadly serious business that needs comic relief, so it can be easier to laugh about how Darth Vader's helmet looks like a penis than it is to mark him for lynching.

The third type of symbolic interracial intimacy, experimentation, is common in science fiction because of the constant employment of technology. Its effectiveness relies on our conceptions of hubris, as used in foundational Western stories, like the myth of Icarus, the Tower of Babel, and *Frankenstein*, to assure that punishment awaits those who push science too far. Of relevance to the galaxy far, far away is cloning, featured most prominently in the second prequel movie. In science fiction, cloning is a sort of reproductive technology, making offspring from genetic parents, in a lab, rather than in a bed. I argue that there is a direct line from the American proslavery scientists arguing that racial mixing was unnatural to the depiction of mixture in cloning narratives. When white racial purity is the paragon, anything short of a white man and a white woman in a monogamous relationship producing offspring by traditional intercourse is an experiment.

The fourth type of symbolic interracial intimacy, transformation, also appears because of science fiction's wide employment of technology, sometimes depicting a character's change from being wholly human to some combination of human–cosmic entity super-being, human–alien hybrid, or human–machine cyborg. As LeiLani Nishime writes of cyborg cinema, "By questioning distinctions between man and machine, cyborg cinema asks the viewer to recognize that neither human nor machine is the true origin of selfhood and identity. This does not necessarily create a structure of equivalence. On the contrary, the loss of boundaries and origins inspires a conservative turn to nostalgia and melancholy."[15] Notably, once one is a cyborg, they cannot become human, and that shortcoming often becomes tragic. I follow Nishime in considering the "anxieties about the incoherence of the body of the cyborg as a parallel to the confusion and concern that centers on the body of the multiracial human."[16] But I also want to emphasize the process of transformation that many cyborgs undergo, because it gives them a mixed body and a new racial makeup. It also gives them a new identity that may or may not be mixed. Yes, I am arguing that makeup and identity are different, especially when the cyborg had a pretransformation life and knows it. Makeup is what goes into creating your body, while identity is what you make of it. Classification is different from these two and denotes what makeup others assign to you. And rarely do they acknowledge that makeup and identity are different.

The alignment of a cyborg depends on how much of the character's backstory is known. First, sometimes we know they were "born" cyborg. I place the first *Terminator* film (1984) in this category. As viewers, we know from the get-go that Arnold Schwarzenegger's character is a cyborg. Also, he never knew any other existence. Second, sometimes we do not know their backstory, and they *could* have been "born" cyborg. Following release order, Darth Vader fits this model, especially when his makeup was a mystery. Third are cyborgs we know used to be human. Following chronological order, which Lucas endorsed after the first six movies were out, Vader is the third kind of cyborg, one we know had been human.

Explicit interracial intimacy between humans, aliens, and robots is more frank and more infrequent, as opposed to the tropes of symbolic interracial intimacy, which present mixed characters, attraction, intimacy, and reproduction beneath layers of allegory. It is likely to appear in four forms. First, and least used, is mixture that happened long before the story the movie or show is telling, by ancestors. Here, as told in the backstory, a group of people came about from the interaction of two previous individuals or groups. Most prominently, the backstory of the *Harry Potter* franchise reveals that Voldemort, the principal villain, was of mixed descent.

Second, explicit interracial intimacy can happen off-screen, which is not necessarily taboo, but also not necessarily shown. This omission may be because of narrative exigency, meaning that it is not deemed necessary for the story. In *Firefly* (2002–2003) and *Serenity* (2005), Zoë and Hoban Washburne are a couple, and it is not necessary to show them intimately. I also include any "fade to black" suggestion of intimacy here, including those on broadcast television, where mature content may be regulated. The storytellers are not denying the intimacy or concealing it in symbolism. They are just bracketing it.

Third, the intimacy may be on-screen. Here, family making gets preferential treatment, as it does in treatments of mixed race in other genres as well as in nonfiction media. Following discourses on multiracial families, if a movie or show commits to utilizing an interspecies family, offspring often ensues. That offspring will likely become the key to interspecies peace. For example, the miniseries *V* (1983), its follow-up, *V: The Final Battle* (1984), and the subsequent network show (2009–2011) placed interspecies intimacy at the center. In the first, Robin, a human teen, falls for Brian, a Visitor. During Robin's pregnancy, which she attempted to hide, the resistance learns that the Visitors are reptiles hiding under a human disguise. In a moment seen by thousands on prime-time television, she gave birth to mixed twins. One, mostly human-looking except for its reptile tongue, became the savior of humanity. The second, mostly reptilian, writhed out of its mother in one of the most terrifying birth scenes since *Rosemary's Baby* (1968), another satanic impregnation story. It died soon after, and chemicals from its body became essential to a bioweapon used to defeat the aliens. Both of their appearances echoed folk knowledge claiming that mixed offspring could come out looking like the nonwhite parent and everyone would know.

Later, the 2004 reboot of *Battlestar Galactica* approached interracialism from multiple dimensions. The show echoed its 1978 inspiration by tracing the aftermath of the near annihilation of humans by their former robotic underlings. Much of this involved fleeing their inhuman enemies, the Cylons. However, the reboot introduced a complication: Cylons could appear to be human; they possessed intelligence, consciousness, and emotions to infiltrate the human ranks. In the case of Sharon and Boomer, both played by Grace Park, a Cylon could believe they were human until they were activated. The show explored the fact that little distinguished humans from Cylons. Even though great animosity fueled both sides, the Cylons sometimes showed great humanity, and the humans had to confront the fact that their historical cruelty toward their creations precipitated their own downfall. An intimate relationship between a human-appearing Cylon and a human facilitated the attack on humanity in the series-launching miniseries. Then, in season 2, it turned out that humans and Cylons could reproduce. Sharon, Helo, and Hera became an interracial family—there were racial minorities in-galaxy—and they had a mixed-race, mixed-species child. Their child becomes the key to both human and Cylon survival, coveted by both sides, and ultimately everyone's savior.

Fourth, a movie may present ambiguous bodies and provide little explanation for their presence. In the original *Stargate* (1994) motion picture, white American men cross through a portal to a parallel world populated by tawny, childlike people who labor (and condition their hair) daily for a man they believe is a god (Jaye Davidson's Ra). The original *Matrix* trilogy (1999–2003) presented brown-skinned people—the surviving humans—who come together for a rave at Zion, the last place on Earth free from oppression by the machines. Their governing body was diverse, as were the crews of the spaceships they commissioned. But very few adorn themselves with cultural signs from specific ethnicities around the world; they are merely brown and mixed looking. Since the movies did not make any explicit statement about race or ethnicity, the diverse cast is reduced to mere physical appearances. Both examples use ambiguous individuals (Ra and Neo) and ambiguous groups (inhabitants of the planet, inhabitants of Zion). Ultimately, the process of mixture is hidden. And the presence of ambiguous bodies provides a backdrop for white characters to stand out. In *Stargate*, the white men become leaders, objects of desire, and father figures because of the Indigenous people's unnamed, unexplained tawniness. In the *Matrix* movies, Neo seems whiter than many, and the white characters fulfill our expectation that white men rule.

Before *Star Wars*

Growing up in the 1950s, Lucas came of age when television sets became common in American households. Via a neighborhood friend's set stationed in the family garage, he became a fan of the 1936 serial *Flash Gordon*, which was originally shown in segments before main attractions in Universal-owned movie theaters. Later, in the early 1970s, Lucas hoped to adapt the films into a big-budget movie, but King Features, the company that owned the rights, turned down his proposal. So, he turned his attention to writing his own space opera. Lucas incorporated many elements from his childhood favorite into *Star Wars*, including the heroic story line, action revolving around laser guns and dogfights, an orchestral score, an episodic structure, and even the moving wipes that transition between scenes. But Lucas's movie also echoed characters and situations from the Buster Crabbe–starring original. Luke and Han sneak around an evil emperor's fortress by donning costumes of foot soldiers, just as Flash Gordon and Prince Barin infiltrate Ming the Merciless's planet, Mongo. Similarly, Princess Leia resembles Dale Arden, Flash's companion and love interest. *Flash Gordon* is an example from a specific genre and time, but its representations reflect wider norms from across popular culture in general, taking for granted that white characters are "powerful, brave, cordial, kind, firm, and generous," and minorities are, at best, "dependent, faithful followers to bolster the grandiose white self-image."[17] This tradition naturalizes the perspective of one set of people, and continues today even though society has changed. In imitating *Flash Gordon*, *Star Wars* continued the seeming naturalness of these norms. (Consider, for example, who gets medals after the first Death Star's destruction.)[18]

The invisibility of interracialism remained the norm because of society's norms. The decades of the Hays Code's prominence (the 1920s through the 1960s) indoctrinated two generations to adopt this as common sense. A Gallup poll in 1965 probed Americans' opinions on anti-intermarriage laws—48 percent disapproved and 46 percent approved. In the South, where these laws remained intact, approval for the laws stood at 72 percent for whites, while in other regions 42 percent of whites approved. Asking a broader question in 1968, Gallup found that overall, 72 percent of American adults disapproved of marriage between whites and nonwhites. So, shortly before George Lucas's film career began to take off, customs, laws, and attitudes toward interracial marriage were hostile, often considering it a crime.[19] The customs also encouraged generations of Americans to take for granted the interracialism taboo, including George Lucas.

Famous for depicting the choice to pursue an interracial marriage in a positive way, *Guess Who's Coming to Dinner* (1967) gestured to a broader reckoning between two generations; between social mores; and between engagement with social issues. Challenging assumptions about where the movie would succeed, *Guess Who's Coming to Dinner* was a hit across the country, including the South, where—regardless of subject matter—the studio had anticipated broad rejection of a movie starring the Black actor Sidney Poitier. Its director, Stanley Kramer, wanted to recruit counterculture directors like Lucas to do more projects like *Guess Who's Coming to Dinner*. But the young, rebellious auteurs Peter Biskind profiled in *Easy Riders, Raging Bulls*, which included Lucas, were not interested in creating message movies, leaving that work to scions of old Hollywood. In the end, the younger generation and looser social mores got a boost from the easy riders, but social issues did not. They were auteurs, buoyed by the notion that each was "the sole author of his work, regardless of whatever contribution the writers, producers, or actors may make."[20] This conception of an auteur emphasizes individualism, art for art's sake, and the ability to build a body of work. Most likely a man, this auteur is free to address or ignore issues, an attitude that requires a high degree of privilege to manifest.[21]

Black Power led to a more visible and outspoken presence for Black individuals in the public sphere, politics, and the arts in the late 1960s. Emerging poets, artists, dramatists, musicians, and writers emphasized their own brand of auteurship that would create art for African Americans, raise consciousness, and promote liberation. This Black Arts Movement also contributed to a change in representations in entertainment as well. It took Black, independent filmmakers like Melvin Van Peebles to answer the call of Black moviegoers, radically changing the portrayals of Black life in movies in the early 1970s. His *Sweet Sweetback's Baadasssss Song* (1971) set the model for Blaxploitation movies, which drew on changing mores, Black Power, and folk tropes. Unlike every decade of Black representation since the beginning of motion pictures, Black characters in these movies could be active agents at the center of the stories. They enjoyed Black, urban life. They flouted the respectable mores of the older generation. And they got away with it. Blaxploitation movies were highly profitable, saving an industry that had been in a free fall. After *Sweetback*'s success, all the major studios contributed their own entries into the genre and reaped the rewards. Some, like *Shaft* (1971), *Super Fly* (1972), and *The Spook Who Sat by the Door* (1973), had Black directors; the majority, though, including *Coffy* (1973), *The Mack* (1973), and *Black Caesar* (1973), were made by white filmmakers. Opportunities for Black actors increased and some, including James Earl Jones, Billy Dee Williams, and Glynn Turman, enjoyed the "spillover effect," moving into white films. Spillover actors from the 1970s had "Black" careers before they had "white" careers.[22]

Black productions with critical and crossover potential like *The Great White Hope* (1970), *Lady Sings the Blues* (1972), and *Sounder* (1972) resided beyond the urban crime drama pretense of Blaxploitation yet were allowed to flourish because of the genre's success. Movies outside the Blaxploitation genre like *Live and Let Die* (1973) showed that incorporating its elements could increase profits. A satire like *Blazing Saddles* (1974) featured a Black actor in a role created by comedian

Richard Pryor. *Silver Streak* (1976) showed that casting a Black costar could augment ticket sales. By 1974, the Blaxploitation genre had fizzled, but its impact in popular music, casting, and representations was irreversible.

Intentionality in *Star Trek* and *Star Wars*

Star Trek's original series ran from 1966 to 1969, ending less than a decade before the first *Star Wars* film. Its creator, Gene Roddenberry, had experiences as a World War II bomber pilot, a Los Angeles beat cop, and a freelance writer for the Western show *Have Gun—Will Travel* (1957–1963). From its inception, Roddenberry wanted to make the show about more than just space adventures—he wanted to put forth an image of our future. He later asserted that "the whole show was an attempt to say that humanity will reach maturity and wisdom on the day that it begins not just to tolerate, but to take a special delight in differences in ideas and differences in life forms. We tried to say that the worst possible thing that can happen to all of us is for the future to somehow press us into a common mold where we begin to act and talk and look and think alike."[23] Roddenberry believed seeing human diversity here on Earth as a positive was a prerequisite to exploring space, where even more diversity is likely to exist.

Now to compare Gene Roddenberry's and George Lucas's intentions toward interracialism in terms of three realms: The first, diegetics, covers the internal logic of the *Star Trek* and *Star Wars* galaxies. What are the rules? What is the internal logic? The second, stories, includes some of the plot lines treating with interracialism. Is there mixture? How does it happen? What are the experiences of mixed characters? The third, casting, deals with their efforts to populate their fictional worlds with actors from our world, including the use of minority actors. Are there many, or just tokens? How did minority actors' appearance shape the final product? What special considerations, especially regarding mixture, went into diversifying the cast? This approach resembles Daniel Bernardi's two-pronged analysis of *Star Trek: The Original Series*, which both "focuses on the conditions of production specific to the beliefs, goals, and practices of key decision makers" and "analyzes the project-in-the-text, or the representational and narrative forms of race—the signs and stories of race—in the broadcast texts."[24] However, I have parsed matters of casting from the real-world side into its own category. For example, choosing an actor to play Han Solo in *Star Wars* depended on George Lucas's willingness to engage in racial matters.

The interests of the United Federation of Planets in *Star Trek* are human-centric, like how the interests of NATO favor the former Allies. In Starfleet, there is no intrinsic hierarchy between individuals, except for the chain of command. Yet, the main function of the Federation, of which Starfleet is its naval instrument, is not militarism. Aliens are as worthy of rights as humans. They have their own lifestyles, which the Starfleet's Prime Directive holds inviolable. Aliens are different species from one another and from humans. In fact, we know *Star Trek* characters mainly through their ways of life, all of which are considered equal. (We know *Star Wars* characters through color-coding, which I discuss above.)

Attraction, romance, and sex are far more visible in *Star Trek* than in *Star Wars*. There is attraction between the wide variety of slightly distinguishable humanoids. If you are a human who can imagine being with a blonde or a brunette, you might be able to imagine being with someone with green hair or feathers. If you are from a species with ridges, you might fall for someone from another species with gills. *Star Trek* episodes have plenty of mixing, though. Captain Kirk's kiss with Uhura (played by Black actor Nichelle Nichols) was a landmark of television integration. Roddenberry's infusion of his beliefs can be seen in the Vulcan principle of Infinite Diversity in Infinite Combinations, stated several times in the original series. It argues that everything comes from the union of unlike elements. The show's official newsletter explained, "Concord, as much as discord, requires the presence of at least two different notes. The brotherhood of man is an ideal based on learning to delight in our essential differences, as well as learning to recognize our similarities. The circle and triangle combine to produce the gemstone in the center as the union of words and music creates song, or the union of marriage creates children."[25] Even when difference produces conflict or misunderstanding, it is worth taking on its own terms. Through the Vulcans' emotional detachment, Roddenberry was advocating "universal acceptance."[26] So it is no surprise that interspecies marriage is acceptable in *Star Trek*. Couples can produce mixed offspring, and those offspring can produce offspring.

What is it like to be a minority in this world? The *Star Trek* galaxy still favors white, human men, who are the most numerous. Most times, when an authority figure hails the USS *Enterprise*, a white male speaks. Other species are also humanoid. Nonwhites and nonhumans are generally tokens: Spock cannot sit with the other Vulcans in the cafeteria; Worf cannot go unwind with Klingons; and Sulu cannot commiserate with other Asians.

Through the prominence of the character Spock, the experience of being mixed permeates *Star Trek* lore. Likewise, the experiences of mixed characters in *Star Trek* featured the drawbacks of mixed people in the United States (as characterized by Gliddon and Nott and many early twentieth-century researchers of mulattoes). Hybrids frequently faced rejection from both sides. They often had to try twice as hard, partly because their traits were halfway between their parents. The most famous of these was Spock, whose father was Vulcan and mother was human. His character faced rejection from fellow Vulcans, and some humans—namely McCoy—constantly harped on his Vulcan ancestry. So, he identified mainly as Vulcan, and accepted the challenge of suppressing his emotions.

Since the initial run of the original series, Spock's mixture had held a special significance for racially mixed viewers. As a teen wrote to Leonard Nimoy in 1968, "I know that you are half Vulcan and half human and you have suffered because of this. My mother is Negro and my father is white and I am told this makes me a half-breed. In some ways I am persecuted even more than the Negro. The Negroes don't like me because I don't look like them. The white kids don't like me because I don't exactly look like one of them either."[27] Nimoy wrote an extended reply to the girl, telling her to have courage. Concerning popularity and finding friends, he suggested recognizing that the need for popularity can cause unhappiness.[28]

Over the years, Spock has served as a muse to racially mixed viewers, artists, and public figures, including President Barack Obama, who professed his love for the character when Nimoy passed away in 2015: "Long before being nerdy was cool, there was Leonard Nimoy. Leonard was a lifelong lover of the arts and humanities, a supporter of the sciences, generous with his talent and his time. And of course, Leonard was Spock. Cool, logical, big-eared and level-headed, the center of Star Trek's optimistic, inclusive vision of humanity's future."[29] A diverse cast was essential to Roddenberry's vision. Anecdotes from cast members George Takei and Nichelle Nichols illuminate how extraordinary this effort was during the mid-1960s, along with the pitfalls of such work.[30]

The History of On-Screen Science Fiction Interracial Intimacy 47

Figure 1.2. Leonard Nimoy's 1968 letter to a fan, encouraging her to persevere with her racial mixture. *FaVE*, May 1968.

Depictions of Sex

While sex is a part of social life in *Star Trek*, it is not for pleasure in *Star Wars*, even though Princess Leia engages in some noncommittal, pleasurable kissing. (More about this in chapter 3.) Sex is primarily for family making and the production of father–son relationships. (More about this in chapter 5.) Sex is not for diplomacy, or any reason Kirk used it. In *Star Wars*, there is always another tool to use, usually a blaster or lightsaber. In the original trilogy, sex is the prism through which the line between racial whiteness and racial nonwhiteness becomes clear, often through efforts to protect Princess Leia from perceived threats. Since the purpose of the prequel trilogy is to explain how Anakin Skywalker became Darth Vader, the parent of Luke and Leia, sex is for family making, not romance, intimacy, or matrimony. In the sequel trilogy, storytelling choices that veer the narrative away from Finn and Rey make human reproduction a matter of dynasty making, whether the Skywalker lineage, or the impromptu Palpatine lineage. As previously noted, sex is hidden, Freudian, symbolic, and some may even think it is not there. But it is, and so is mixture.

While cultural relativism is the rule in *Star Trek*, the cultures (as in ways of life) of nonhumans in *Star Wars* are portrayed only insofar as the human principals interact with them. Aliens menace at the cantina, Jawas sell stolen goods, Sand People attack settlers. Jabba is a crime lord, and his court just mills around his orbit. The Indigenous teddy bears on Endor are willing to fight the Empire, but they are also superstitious, primitive, and tribal. Some, like Chewbacca, R2-D2, and C-3PO, are honorary sidekicks.

We can ask Lucas the same questions we asked Roddenberry about casting: How did Lucas negotiate casting in the industry during his time? In the beginning of the casting process, Lucas imagined casting Toshirō Mifune, a Japanese actor who had starred in several samurai films, as Obi-Wan Kenobi. (He ultimately chose the white British actor Alec Guinness.) He had also entertained finding a mixed, white and Asian actor to fill Princess Leia's role, perhaps as a nod to his Japanese influences.[31] After all, she was loosely based on a character from Akira Kurosawa's *The Hidden Fortress* (1958). (The role was played by the white American actor Carrie Fisher.) Mixed characters can be markers for the colonial experience, and Eurasian characters often recall European efforts to colonize Asia, just as a "half-breed" recalls manifest destiny and a mulatto recalls slavery. Beyond that, female mixed characters suggest passivity, exoticness, and sexual availability. A Eurasian girl can symbolize racial unification, again between the colonizer and the colonized. Rarely is that unification equitable, especially when one character is female. Last, casting a mixed white and Asian actor would activate white narcissism, making it easier to identify with her. But if George Lucas had wanted white audiences to identify with her, why bother with the Asian part at all?

Lucas felt personally invested in the characters, and he also wanted lesser-known actors who wouldn't distract the viewers from other elements of his creation. He ignored the advice of 20th Century Fox to include bigger names in the lead roles, following instead the selection process he used with his film *American Graffiti* (1973). Since that movie was such a hit, and some of those actors were becoming stars, Fox's Alan Ladd trusted Lucas's judgment. Brian De Palma, who was working on *Carrie*, his 1976 horror movie, with a cast in the same age group, assisted Lucas with running cattle calls, the process of seeing thirty to forty actors a day for around five minutes each. Between the two, De Palma was the extrovert, while Lucas took notes and assembled a callback list. He called back around forty actors to do readings on videotape and then chose four sets of Leia, Luke, and Han, whom he shuffled to find the right on-screen chemistry.[32]

Lucas did interview several African American actors for Han Solo, and almost chose Glynn Turman, who had recently starred as Preach, the lead character in *Cooley High* (1975). Written by Eric Monte, who created the series *Good Times* (1974–1979), this movie also drew on his experiences growing up in Chicago. Turman's performance as a likeable proxy for Monte gained him attention in the following years, and he went to audition for *Star Wars*, not knowing what the role would be: "I was kind of on a roll. I remember going up to see Lucas for a picture they were going to do called *Star Wars*."[33] At the time (as today), roles usually specified what race the character was, but this one did not. "I was rather pleased because I was just being called in as a talent," Turman reminisced later.[34] He still did not know what role he was going for when *Star Wars* came out. Since no Black people appeared in the blockbuster, he assumed, "Oh, they cut the part of the black guy out."[35] Only years later, when Lucas's version of the casting process appeared in a book, did Turman realize how close he was to becoming Han Solo (who wound up being played by the white American actor Harrison Ford).

Casting Turman as the pilot would have implications for the directions Lucas could take the characters. Describing the early 1970s, Turman explained, "Those were the times—and he didn't want to get into that."[36] In Lucas's own words, "I didn't want to make *Guess Who's Coming to Dinner* at that point, so I sort of backed off."[37] This indicates a belief that if there is a racial matter in a movie, then the movie must be all about the racial matter. So, rejecting Turman and the other Black actors was a conscious decision, which is an acknowledgment that interracial intimacy matters. When prompted to consider interracial relationships, creators/producers responded similarly to the way regular Americans did.

Figure 1.3. Glynn Turman as Preach in Michael Schultz's *Cooley High* (1975). Credit: John D. Kisch / Separate Cinema Archive.

In December 1975, Lucas was imagining that Luke would passionately kiss Leia in the sequel. They would have a sort of *Gone with the Wind* (1939) love triangle, with Luke as Ashley Wilkes, Leia as Scarlett O'Hara, and Han as Rhett Butler. Elements of Scarlett and Rhett's dialogue resonate in *The Empire Strikes Back*'s first kiss between Leia and Han. Like the self-professed varmint from Charleston, Han would leave the scene. The romance between Leia and Han was uncertain and could have ended with each going their own way. So, even if Lucas wanted to avoid dealing with an interracial relationship, Glynn Turman could have worked in this role.[38]

During the period between the first two *Star Wars* movies, Harrison Ford was unsure he wanted to perform Han Solo past *The Empire*

Strikes Back, arguing that the character's death would complete his arc from selfish to self-sacrificing. Later, promotional images for *The Empire Strikes Back* strongly pushed the Luke and Leia romance. The extended version of their conversation on the planet Hoth featured more longing and desire. It was not until the revised drafts of *Return of the Jedi* that Luke and Leia's siblinghood was solidified. By this point, Lucas was burned out and willing to abridge his vision of Luke finding his long-lost sister, a new character, some point after events of the original trilogy.[39] In comparison, Gene Roddenberry strived for diversity in all three dimensions—diegetics, story lines, and casting. Just as Lucas's affection for *Flash Gordon* is a cornerstone of *Star War's* creation, depicting a functioning multicultural society was a key part of Gene Roddenberry's conception of *Star Trek*. So, if George Lucas did not allow for hybridity and relegated sex to reproduction, then most likely he was opposed to presenting interracialism. Ultimately, *Star Trek* was met with applause for its handling of diversity, while *Star Wars* faced grumbles.

The Symbolic Interracial Intimacy Cluster

During the decade after the original *Star Wars* film, symbolic interracial intimacy appeared in several prominent science fiction movies and television shows, including *Alien* (1979) and its sequel *Aliens* (1986), *Blade Runner* (1982), *The Terminator* (1984), and *RoboCop* (1987), some of the most enduring, successful, and popular franchises of the past forty years. On the small screen, *V: The Miniseries* (1983) and *V: The Final Battle* (1984) did the same. These examples do not make up all the sci-fi properties in this ten-year span, but they are enough to show consistent tropes of symbolic intimacy. *Alien* made the xenomorph a big, black, sexual predator who tears through Kane like he had sodomized him. Then, he menaces Ripley with his big head and erection–mouth, which made Vader's interrogation droid's proboscis, well, minuscule. The anatomy of the xenomorph in the original *Alien* was like a Swiss Army knife of phalluses, its newborn form dashing across the table, its tail sliding up Lambert's leg, its prehensile mouth extending beyond its jaws, its smooth yet hard skull pivoting toward its prey. The xenomorph was colored black, lurking in the alleys, and behaving like the African American criminals conjured by newscasts. Along with turning workers into credit-grubbing mercenaries, the commercial towing vessel *Nostromo*'s employers have delivered them into sexual danger. With its skirmishes between marines and xenomorphs, *Aliens* was different. Rival maternities replaced the threat of the lone Black antagonist (again, think *The Birth of a Nation*). Suiting up in the powerlifter, Ripley saves the nine-year-old girl Newt from molestation.

Story lines featuring experimentation typically exclude any elements of sexuality between characters, especially if the protagonist is a scientist. If intimacy in hetero, monogamous relationships is the natural way to produce offspring, cloning, reanimation, and extensive prosthetics are unnatural. Darth Vader must have gone through a transformation to become what he was, but that remained a mystery in the 1970s. Later, *The Terminator* placed viewers in a world where machine and man could mix to make a body without explaining how it happened. Except, this time they came from the future, where humans' machine overlords had perfected the technology. The Terminator is unnatural, unhuman, and unambiguously evil. *RoboCop* was the greatest example of transformation from the era because it did not cast aspersions on the cyborg Murphy merely because he was mixed. As LeiLani Nishime writes, "The film escapes the trap of defining mixed race as the corruption of once pure and unadulterated races. Nor does the film privilege human/white identity, since there is no single source of authority and authenticity for that identity."[40] The transformed Murphy, as distinctive as he is, presents a model of mixed identity unhampered by long-standing tropes.

Star Wars offers us another lesson: avoiding racial issues/themes was profitable. It was easier to produce stories with symbolic interracial intimacy than it was to cast progressive roles. Even with the PCA receding into the past, it was easier to produce symbolic interracial intimacy works than it was to allow interracialism on-screen. And with a shifting sense of what was racially offensive, it was easier to purvey veiled stereotypes than it was to reproduce *The Birth of a Nation*'s level of overt racism. Jim Crow had only ended twenty years before, and old ideas died hard. On some level, moviemakers and regular Americans still believed racial mixture was a weapon that could destroy society, and they were uncomfortable grappling with that. So, science fiction, like horror, helped them cope with these terrors. The prominence of symbolic interracial intimacy receded with the return of the *Enterprise* with *Star Trek: The Next Generation* (1987–1994), which continued Gene Roddenberry's philosophy of amalgamation. But that was on the small screen, where a combination of factors has resulted in a higher prevalence of explicit interracial intimacy: first, shows require less investment than movies, making experimentation less risky; second, television shows require more story lines, especially if they survive their first years, leading to experimentation; and last, audience rejection is less likely to be total and final if they dislike an on-screen relationship, unlike with movies. Throughout the post–civil rights era, even in small amounts, television has been the vanguard in matters of interracial intimacy that filmmakers could emulate.

CHAPTER 2

What Are You, Darth Vader? (1977–1980)

Introduction

I was not a sci-fi fan in 1977 when *Star Wars*' opening credits scrolled bright yellow text across the screen, but I became a Darth Vader fan. Shortly after a Star Destroyer captures a Rebel Alliance ship, stormtroopers blast through, easily overpowering, capturing, and securing the vessel. This sequence of events was suspenseful and scary at the same time. Then, through the smoke, enters Darth Vader. Every second thereafter establishes an important character development and gave me clues of who was behind the mask and the vital role Darth Vader would play as the story unfolded.

Heavy breathing, a black suit and cape, a commanding presence, and the voice of James Earl Jones—OMG! Darth Vader is Black!

Darth Vader did not fit the expectation of a Black superhero or villain. He didn't conform to cultural norms of a "Black" character in a certain type of Black movie. The bigger Black story challenged the narrative that a Black character could be complex and central to the movie plot and development. Translation—Darth Vader would not be killed within the first five minutes of the show.

My perspective on Darth Vader may seem excessive but, given my choices of Black exploitation films at the time and the history of cinema, what would you expect from a nine-year-old kid? The chance to center Black experiences outside the stereotypical setting of sports, slavery, and extreme poverty is no small thing. I celebrated the illusion for a bigger story.

These are the recollections of a friend of mine, an African American man in his early fifties, which he shared upon hearing that I was writing about race and *Star Wars*. He explained how he concluded as a kid that Darth Vader was an African American man. The sound of James Earl Jones's voice was instrumental to this, but my friend also referenced the character's swagger, his air of confident nonchalance. Many viewers remembering the first time they saw the movie refer to how the opening moments were like nothing they had ever seen, and my friend echoed this sentiment. After the imagery of the Star Destroyer flooding the screen, many were primed for anything; for him, this included the possibility of an essential character who was racially Black. My friend admitted that his interpretation was strident, but it came from a dissatisfaction with existing Black characters, Black narratives, and Black public figures. He indulged the "illusion" of possibilities to experience a richer, more sophisticated, more inclusive "story."

My friend was not alone in entertaining the possibility that Darth Vader was an African American man, even if millions of viewers of *Star Wars* movies would disagree, pointing out that Darth Vader was Anakin Skywalker, embodied by the white actors David Prowse and then Hayden Christensen. They would point out that Anakin received the black armor after fighting Obi-Wan Kenobi on the volcanic planet Mustafar. This knowledge comes from the movies, novels, comics, and television shows that have left no mystery regarding the character unturned. But all this information came out long after Vader first strutted through that smoky, white hallway in 1977. Since the movies came out in three trilogies—the original, the prequel, and the sequel—over forty-two years, most of our knowledge of the galaxy far, far away consists of retcons, or retroactive continuities, the literary device that changes the content of an established narrative. Arthur Canon Doyle provided an early example of a retcon after having killed off Sherlock Holmes in the 1893 story "The Adventure of the Final Problem." The uproar caused by the popular character's death led to an unforeseen sequel in 1903, which dictated that the death was an illusion. Retcons are also likely to arise when prequels are added, and many in *Star Wars* came about because of the 1999–2005 movies. As mentioned in chapter 1, Leia and Luke are siblings because of a retcon in *Return of the Jedi* meant to free a weary George Lucas from creating another trilogy to introduce a new character as Luke's sister. R2-D2's shift from a droid Obi-Wan had never seen to the companion of his best friend is one of many alterations made by the prequels to the original trilogy. In the sequel trilogy, Rey's supposed kinship with Emperor Palpatine is a retcon meant to bridge the three trilogies. But this book goes chronologically through the saga, revisiting an era when fans could not access answers for every question.

For the first three years of the *Star Wars* phenomenon, it was not wrong to say that Darth Vader operated as an African American man. Descriptions of him relied on his mystery, his powers, and his authority. Posters and other merchandise used the shadowy outline of his helmet to communicate his dark, phallic threat. But no one knew what his face looked like, so he could have been nonwhite, or even nonhuman. His bodily makeup clearly consisted of black armor, plus human body, plus breathing apparatus. In other words, he was a cyborg, man plus machine. Since the only clue about his body was that African American voice, some proportion of African American contributed to this cyborg. Asserting that we can hear racial makeup in voices can lead to a slippery (and unreliable) slope. Similarly, actors, who alter their voices by profession, complicate the matter of detecting race in a voice. However, while some characteristics of voices are willfully mutable, some are quite resilient, including gender, region, and ethnicity. Clues to ethnicity in voice can include the sounds of vowels and the range of pitch. So, it is possible to hear James Earl Jones's masculine, southern Blackness in his voice. Additionally, while some actors make vocal mutability part of their skill set, creating a set of distinct voices, Jones has a signature voice recognizable in all his roles.[1]

On the one hand, Sara Martín would censure us for dwelling on the question of Lord Vader's racial makeup, reminding us that reimagining his racial identity falls short of some deeper issues: "In my view, reimagining Vader as Black, symbolically or literally, is far less productive than exposing him as a white patriarchal villain."[2] I agree that he was down with white supremacy and patriarchy, forces as potent in the galaxy far, far away as they are in our society. On the other hand, Kwame Anthony Appiah describes what we get from reimagining the race of fictional characters: "What these fantasies ask is, who gets to tell you what you look like? It's not a representation of identity so much as it is a renegotiation of it."[3] Appiah places the conversation in the realm of play, but his renegotiation is really a form of oppositional reading that places oneself in unwelcoming realms of popular culture, the central mode of African American (and other minority) consumption of media.

For African Americans and other underrepresented groups, media criticism goes hand in hand with media consumption. Science fiction makes reimagining the past, escapism from the present, and hope in the future essential modes of thought, but these are all distinctively fraught activities for underrepresented groups, who have faced exclusion from the executive side of Hollywood as well as voting, employment, and property ownership. These temporal modes apply to the content of the entertainment they are partaking, but also the operations of that entertainment within the real world. Although it shouldn't be required, minority fans often must bear this complexity as a form of labor underappreciated by the mainstream, yet essential for enjoying science fiction, as well as any fan activities such as playing, dressing up, collecting, or projecting characters into deeper relationships.

After all, African Americans (and other minorities) had been involved with science fiction literature since Martin Delany's *Blake* (1859). Black musicians, including Sun Ra, George Clinton, and Afrika Bambaataa, have incorporated elements of science fiction into jazz, R&B, and hip-hop since the 1960s. African Americans have driven all consumerism since Madison Avenue first recognized them as a market in the 1970s. It follows that Black (and other minority) communities have enjoyed science fiction along with others. As Mark Dery stated in 1993, "Speculative fiction that treats African-American themes and addresses African-American concerns in the context of twentieth century technoculture—and, more generally, African-American signification that appropriates images of technology and a prosthetically enhanced future—might, for want of a better term, be called 'Afrofuturism.'"[4] Based on the paradox that African Americans have had their past "rubbed out," and that the future is "already owned" by those in power, the term has come to include a variety of activities undertaken by Black consumers when engaging with science fiction: Afrofuturist thinkers echo some aspects of Afrocentrism, namely an appreciation of African civilizations, a focus on self-determination rather than Eurocentric values, and a connection to people of African descent around the world. With a shallower well of Black creators to draw from, Afrofuturist artists often assemble the imagery they deploy from scratch. To feel the connections that whites take for granted, Afrofuturist fans must interject their perspectives when engaging with mainstream science fiction. Altogether, the labor of Afrofuturism is not just a matter of representation, but of acknowledging their often overlooked, omitted, and benighted perspectives. The roles have not been mutually exclusive, nor have they required certification by white institutions to practice.

This was the context for Black viewers critical of the first movie set in the galaxy far, far away, as they were critical of all other mainstream media. As Raymond St. Jacques, the star of *Cotton Comes to Harlem* (1970), realized after the fifth time he saw the movie, "I've ignored the obvious, and that is the terrifying realization that black people (or any ethic minority for that matter) shall not exist in the galactic space empires of the future."[5] He enjoyed the movie immensely but also realized its racial missteps. They knew representations of Blackness, whether African Americans themselves or the color black, were racial signs. So, emphasizing how Darth Vader operated as an African American was not so preposterous, given the color-coding in the movie, the movie's centering of white people, and his sheer uniqueness.

In considering the racial signs around the greatest movie villain of all time, this chapter first examines Darth Vader as a particularly classic villain, according to traditional creative writing instruction. But since these archetypes do not capture historical contexts or relationships to power, we will also match him with character types from African American traditions. Then, since his principal, symbolically interracial relationship was with Princess Leia—and since Darth Vader is cast as a sexual threat to her—this chapter will trace their interactions in the first *Star Wars* film. This section also serves as the beginning of a chronology of racially categorizing him, continuing into the period between the first two movies, considering both the responses of viewers between the movies and the proliferation of his backstory by print publications. Covering these two influences will introduce the world of fanship too. The chapter ends with a discussion of the casting of racially mixed characters outside science fiction from the late 1970s, suggesting that decades of hiding mixture and privileging whiteness resulted in representations that were inconsistent, contradictory, and indifferent to the realities of racial mixture.

The Man in Black Is Mixed and White

The first movie had portrayed Darth Vader as colored black and morally evil, but it did not offer much more about his personality or background. This made hating him "all the more fun."[6] However, some fans thought of him as colored black and morally ambiguous, wanting to know why he betrayed the Jedi Order. Many of these fans were female, and they debated the sexual aspects of his anatomy. They made jokes about "punching his buttons" and imagined his aloofness toward any sexual orientation at all.[7] By the time the next movie appeared, fans had been telling their own stories about Darth Vader for over two years.

Personally, I have come to think Darth Vader's racial identity was a matter different from his makeup: that he is biologically mixed and racially white. First, I am not saying that he is mixed and passing as white. There is no hiding the contradictory racial signs that compose his countenance, especially as the saga proceeded. He puts no effort into hiding the mixture of his body, even if we can imagine that the Empire has concealed his backstory. So, his attitude toward concealment is different from Anatole Broyard, the *New York Times* book critic and author who racially passed as white for many decades. It is also different from Jean Toomer, the Harlem Renaissance writer who maintained his multiethnic ambiguity throughout his adult life. Since he transformed from complete human into a cyborg at some time in the past, Darth Vader's identification also differs from Eston Hemings, the youngest of Thomas Jefferson's children with the enslaved woman Sally Hemings, who lived as white after his father's death, since only one-eighth of his background was Black.

Pulling from times closer to the present, it is possible to compare him to Keanu Reeves, who is mixed, white, and Chinese, but has identified as "middle-class white boy, a bourgeois middle-class white boy with an absent father, a strong-willed mother, and two beautiful younger sisters."[8] His physical appearance and society's tendency to ignore Asian descent made it easy to footnote his mixture. But the best analogy would be George Zimmerman, the rent-a-cop who shot and killed seventeen-year-old Trayvon Martin in 2012. Zimmerman's father was white, and his mother was Latina; some of the media tried to make something of it, casting him as multiracial. But the main indicators of his whiteness were the choices he made—shooting a Black boy, then using the system to exonerate himself. Before we even see Darth Vader, we already know from the opening crawl that he is a "sinister agent" of an "evil empire" that produces weapons that can "destroy an entire planet," in opposition to the Rebel Alliance's efforts to "restore peace to the galaxy." Just as Zimmerman's choices were about white supremacy, Vader's choices are in service of oppression, violence, and fear.

Titling this chapter "What Are You, Darth Vader?" evokes the quintessential, shared experience among racially mixed people: that of other people trying to figure out their racial makeup, often by candidly asking. The exchange is reductive, assuming that one's makeup is the whole of one's identity. It is also dehumanizing, requiring that a mixed person justify their existence as an object. Often, the question comes out of context, with a jarring effect. Sometimes it comes right after learning one's name (or even before), revealing that the inquisitor cannot proceed without knowing the answer to the question. Since physical appearance persists as the primary way Americans discern racial identity, the ambiguity of a racially mixed person can produce a mystery for many. In turn, this incites the wish to solve the mystery. The most eager of these new acquaintances holds racial identity as the primary way to understand another person. The question becomes a mystery to solve, while receiving an answer is very satisfying. On an interpersonal scale, this is how Americans praise ambiguity while preferring certainty. The mystery is exciting, but the solution is what they really want.

Often, the "What are you?" moment comes from a benign wish to get to know an ambiguous-looking person better. The speaker may consider blended features to be exotic and stories of mixed backgrounds especially interesting. Maybe people ask racially ambiguous people "*What* are you?" because they are nearly hardwired to categorize. Perhaps their biases need one tidbit before they can activate. In places like Hawaii, where mixture is more common, asking is as customary as commenting on the weather. But the real question is "Why do you need to know?" Answer this question, and you will understand something deeper than what my racial makeup is. I am plying the "What are you?" question to Darth Vader to uncover more: first, the processes of encoding and decoding; second, the disjoint between appearance, genealogy, and identity; and third, the slippages in George Lucas's construction of race.

White Villains, Black Villains

Leading guides to screenwriting offer advice on structure, characters, and genre. Altogether, they offer lists ranging from four to fifteen types of villains. Here we see the influence of New Criticism (which says only the text at hand matters) on screenwriting (which includes only the elements necessary for telling the story on the page). Screenwriting, as a skill, involves providing only the minimum, just as New Criticism teaches readers to consider only the minimum—except that screenplays are instructions for telling a story, while New Criticism is a way of reading a story, excising all context, identity, or ideology. In turn, conventional teaching of screenwriting tells writers to focus on characters' actions, imbuing them with individualism, privilege, and liberty from other social forces, a combination of gifts that considers characters free, white men. Comparing Darth Vader to some of these helps explain what kind of character he is and the actions he takes. But comparing Vader to these archetypes also traces mainstream viewers' ways of thinking about villains, themselves, and society broadly. In other words, these recognizable tropes reflect mainstream ways of telling, producing, and receiving stories.[9]

The first relevant to Darth Vader, the Machine, is often an emotionless robot, brutal in its murderous logic. From the first observations of Darth Vader, it is clear from the mechanical breathing and metallic voice that he is at least part machine. He is cold, calculating, efficient, and brutal. Underneath the suit, he could be anything from part machine to mostly machine. However, in *Star Wars*, robots have emotions, and the mysterious Darth Vader does as well. So, the narrow definition of the Machine character type is incompatible with the workings of the *Star Wars* galaxy. Examples of the Machine include the computer, HAL 9000, in *2001: A Space Odyssey* (1968) and the T-800 assassin in *The Terminator*. Second, the Henchman, while rarely the principal villain of a story, is usually the most visible, efficient, and lethal. Loyal to their liege, they are relentless obstacles for their stories' protagonists. The Henchman breaks rules, crushing the throats of ship captains and directing officers to cover up the taking of a diplomat's vessel. Often, the Henchman executes the will of the villain until the end of the second act, and then the hero must face the real big-bad in the third act. A good example is the character known as the Operative, played by Chiwetel Ejiofor, in *Serenity* (2005). Last, the Personification of Evil does bad things for the sole purpose of doing them, which prompts the hero to stop them. See, for example, Anton Chigurh in *No Country for Old Men* (2007). However, Darth Vader is an authority figure, especially in relation to the other Imperials. Order is what the Empire deals in, and all in its employ have a specific station in the hierarchy. In 1977, we knew Vader had been a Jedi like Obi-Wan and Luke's father, before he was lured into helping to wipe out the Jedi. But unlike most classic Personifications of Evil, his actions sprang from more than mere impulse. Within this framework, I would remove this label from Darth Vader.

But if you're a spectator with a different perspective, must you subscribe to these models to understand characters? Or, reflecting the skill you have developed for survival, do you apply models that pay attention to context and power? This project encourages exploring tropes beyond the "classics" to analyze character types from African American storytelling, blending storytelling perspectives. With these, the relationships to power are more apparent. Additionally, as a work of mixed race analysis, this book decenters white epistemology while drawing from Black thought.

The Trickster is the most familiar of African American folk figures. They are often disadvantaged, but get the best of greater adversaries by "indirection and mask-wearing."[10] What they lack in size, strength, or resources, they compensate for by "outsmarting or outthinking their opponents."[11] The most famous version of this Trickster folk character is Br'er Rabbit and his universally recognized adaptation, the Warner Bros. cartoon character Bugs Bunny. Equally famous among African American folk characters is another masculine figure, the Bad Man, who in some ways descended from the Trickster. While the latter negotiated his relationship with his white slaveholder during slavery by exploiting the disjuncture in their perspectives, the former staked his place as a free man after emancipation by challenging the systems that excluded him.[12] "Badman characters (or gangstaz, as they are known in gangsta rap)," writes Mich Nyawalo, "emerged as meta-juridical figures whose heroic depiction subverted the validity of an evolving legal system that has historically disenfranchised large segments of the African-American community."[13] The Bad Man maintained a disregard for criminal justice, voting, property ownership, and respectable entrepreneurship, all of which had disregarded him in the first place.

The most famous Bad Man is Stagger Lee, personified in the popular American folk song about "Stag" Lee Shelton, who murdered a man on Christmas Day, 1895. A pimp living in St. Louis, Missouri, Shelton was drinking with Billy Lyons, a fellow member of the local underworld and perhaps a political and business rival. A dispute ensued and Lyons grabbed Shelton's hat, refusing to give it back. In the song "Stagger Lee," the titular character ended the disrespect by shooting Lyons there and then with his pistol, picking up his hat, and walking out of the bar. Shelton was later found guilty of murder and served twelve years of a twenty-five-year sentence before being released, only to return to jail two years later for assault and robbery. Versions of "Stagger Lee" (or "Stagolee") date back to 1897, indicating that Shelton's story instantly became a folk inspiration. Later, Black Panthers cofounder Bobby Seale explained to his wife why he wanted to name their son Stagolee: "Because Stagolee was a bad nigger off the block and he didn't take shit from nobody."[14]

64 I'd Just as Soon Kiss a Wookiee

Figure 2.1. Lee Shelton shoots Billy Lyons in Timothy Lane's 2007 comic chapbook telling the story of the song "Stagger Lee." Credit: Timothy Lane.

In mainstream traditions, the Bad Man is like the Antivillain, who possesses qualities attractive to the audience and likely shines in the spotlight even more than the hero. During the original trilogy (especially before *Return of the Jedi*), since Darth Vader had a minimal backstory, it was easier to project on him and sympathize with him, making him an Antivillain. Lydia Millet wrote about how Darth Vader stood for all the confidence she envied as a teenager, and all the reserve she still lacked as an adult: "Darth Vader, dark *Vater, dark father*, unmistakably, was the most erotic figure in the *Star Wars* family and the only tragic one, and because of this he had a terrible beauty. . . . Vaders do not make inappropriate remarks at dinner parties, let down their guard in drunken moments to reveal the wanting soul within. The Vaders are too smart for that, and they know which side their bread is buttered on."[15] And he exhibited classic cool, the set of behaviors developed for survival in twentieth-century America. Darth Vader possessed "personal authority through a stylish mask of stoicism" while surrounded by the establishment.[16]

Following Stuart Hall's theory of encoding and decoding, let us say that white producers create "white stories" from a dominant–hegemonic encoding position. They have predominantly white casts and purvey age-old messages about whiteness. They may also use colors in moralistic ways, as George Lucas did. On the other hand, Blaxploitation movies were never encoded in the dominant–hegemonic way, making them more negotiated or oppositional than most white stories. When the protagonist was on the side of the law, Blaxploitation movies often expressed negotiated encoding positions about law enforcement; when the protagonist engaged in illegal activity, they expressed oppositional encoding positions about crime. Blaxploitation movies appealed to an oppositional decoding position, garnering disapproval from the more upstanding sections of the African American community—in other words, those who were more negotiated. Most importantly for this discussion, Blaxploitation movies complicated the decoding of villains along racial lines. Color-coding was disregarded: For example, John Shaft (*Shaft*) was a crime-fighting private investigator whose signature outfit was all black. Priest (*Super Fly*) wore all white and engaged in illegal activities. So, how one decodes a hero or a villain depended on one's racial perspective in relation to the hero's. It is easy to imagine a backstory for a character like oneself, and then sympathize with them, even if they operate as an antagonist.

I argue that, for those familiar with James Earl Jones's work, his résumé up to *Star Wars* influenced how they interpreted Darth Vader. In particular, he played roles in two movies made during the Blaxploitation era that inform facets of Darth Vader. The first approximates the Bad Man while dramatizing the life of a major Black icon, the 1910s boxer Jack Johnson. In both the 1970 film and the 1968 theatrical production of *The Great White Hope*, Jones played the protagonist, Jack Jefferson, modeled after the Black heavyweight champion who dealt with racially loaded antipathy. In the film and play, Jones endures the general public's clamoring for a "great white hope" to topple him from his position. As with the flamboyant and irreverent Johnson, they found this opportunity by targeting Jefferson's activities outside the ring, namely his relationships with white women. In Johnson's life, the United States Department of Justice indicted him under the Mann Act, which mainly punished prostitution, but also targeted vices like miscegenation. African Americans supported Johnson, not necessarily because he reflected their way of life, but because people gained affirmation from his accomplishments, recognized his challenges, and saw themselves in his struggles. *The Great White Hope* won the Pulitzer Prize for Drama, Jones won the 1969 Tony Award for Best Actor in a Play, and Jane Alexander—who played Eleanor Bachman, Jefferson's white girlfriend—won the 1969 Tony Award for Best Featured Actress in a Play. Jones and Alexander went on to win Drama Desk Awards as well, and then Oscar nominations for their performances in the subsequent film.[17]

66 I'd Just as Soon Kiss a Wookiee

The second of Jones's characters offers a type unforeseen in popular culture, but crucial to the 1970s and significant for the future: the Black Company Man. In *The Man* (1972), Jones plays Douglass Dilman, United States senator and the president pro tempore of the Senate. When an accident abroad kills both the president and the Speaker of the House, and the vice president's terminal health condition makes him decline the offer to take office, the line of succession ends with Dilman, making him the first Black president. Again, Jones's character must protect his

Figure 2.2. James Earl Jones as the Jack Johnson stand-in Jack Jefferson in the play *The Great White Hope* (1968). Credit: Bettmann / Bettmann Archive.

job from whites who do not believe he should be there, balance his personal wishes to protect a young African American from extradition to apartheid-era South Africa, and learn to trust his own judgment as a newly minted leader. The story, written by Rod Serling, who created *The Twilight Zone* (1959–1964) and wrote the first *Planet of the Apes* (1968) screenplay, follows those works in turning society on its head to critique power relations. By the end of *The Man*, Dilman comes into his own, decrying violence, flouting expectations, and committing himself to winning his party's nomination at their next national convention.

We have seen Darth Vader step over smoldering casualties, kill a detainee, and order a cover-up. This is a dramatic buildup for his actions in a scene where he vividly exhibits his combination of a Black Bad Man and a Black Company Man. After cutting from the scene where Obi-Wan teaches Luke about the Force, we are taken to a conference room in the Death Star, where some Imperial officers are discussing the capacity of the Rebel Alliance. When Governor Tarkin and Darth Vader enter the room, the administrator tells them, "The Imperial Senate will no longer be of any concern to us." An officer named Motti praises the space station they are on board as "the ultimate power in the universe," belittling Vader's "sorcerer's ways," "sad devotion," and "ancient religion." Vader's response places this scene as one of his most memorable—he uses the Force to choke Motti telepathically and quips, "I find your lack of faith disturbing." Like Stagger Lee, he responds with disproportionate violence to an insult cast at him in a public place. Motti's disrespect nearly proves fatal, until Tarkin implores Vader to stop.

Watching him crush Motti's throat is especially gratifying for anyone dissatisfied with their job, but even more so for those who suffer racial microaggressions in a corporate workplace. Following the civil rights gains of the 1960s and the affirmative action of the late 1970s, by the end of the decade, an increasing number of African Americans could appreciate Vader's combination of Bad Man and Company Man.

Seeing Darth Vader

In August 1977, readers learned that Darth Vader's voice was that of James Earl Jones, possibly complicating their understanding of the character. There was a chance Vader's face could match Jones's voice racially, making a Black man the blockbuster's villain. Lucas had considered the legendary director and actor Orson Welles but wanted a voice less recognizable. James Earl Jones's commanding bass was appealing, and he accepted $10,000 for the day's work, waiving being named in the credits for mere special effects work. But he was not chosen for racial reasons; George Lucas did not envision Darth Vader as an African American character. But as Jones says, "He picked a voice that was born in Mississippi, raised in Michigan, and was a stutterer," implying that his race, his place, his poverty, and his experience growing up with a speech impediment were part of the voice he brings to all his roles.[18]

The racial whitening of Darth Vader would continue in the second *Star Wars* film, *The Empire Strikes Back*. By then, fans knew of Vader's mixture, both in-story and in-production. Most went into the theater thinking of him as a white guy. This was confirmed at two points in the movie. First, seeing his helmet lowering onto his pale, scarred head. We had seen his armor, which was colored black. We had seen the actor in the armor, who was white. But that glimpse did not erase all the mixture associated with him. Sealing Vader's identity as a white person came when he told Luke, "I am your father." This bolstered Vader's racial whiteness through backward reasoning. First, if the son is white, the father must be white. This is a correlation–confirmation snafu that exists in our world. In fact, a racially white child can come from a mixed yet white parent. In this case, the mixed yet white parent, Vader, remains mixed, even though he has revealed the connection to Luke. Our understanding of Vader shifts, but that does not change the story. Until this moment on that Cloud City gantry, Luke Skywalker went through life believing his father was wholly human and white, and that he was too. Without knowledge of his parents' makeup, he thought of himself as purely, racially white, and 100 percent bodily human. By this point in the movie, with Darth Vader's racial whiteness established, it is easy to say that Luke Skywalker's pained reaction was because of Darth Vader's villainy, but Vader's moral darkness, black garb, and racial mixture are all bound together.

Additionally, if the young son has a human body that is racially pure and white and wholly organic, the father must have had the same when he was young too. But again, a mixed yet white parent can produce a nearly white child. If the parameters allow, the parent can live as white, present themselves as white, and further the causes of white privilege. Luke responded with shock and threw himself off the precipice. Just like Zoe, the titular octoroon in Dion Boucicault's 1859 play, he would rather die than be a racially nonwhite person; and like Flora in *The Birth of a Nation*, he would rather die than be intimately connected with a

Black person, whether in terms of color, race, or morality. Life is not worth living without purity. Vader's revelation began a process of transforming Luke's understanding of himself, his father, and their respective humanness. But Luke's initial response was denial. It did not instantly (bodily) transform him, but as viewers we can imagine it would. Would he join his father? Replacing his hand with a mechanical one did transform him into a mixture of human and robot. At that point, Luke's body becomes a mixed one. But as he is surrounded by the color white, the white princess, and the white droids, we are reassured that he will remain good.

Later, throughout *Return of the Jedi*, Luke wears black garb, hinting that he could turn to the dark side of the Force, fulfilling the notion of atavism. In the final duel between Luke and Vader, his mixed and white father suggests he will seduce Princess Leia, whom George Lucas had retconned into twinship with Luke. Again, she becomes the racial-sexual line in the sand that the good guys must preserve. James Earl Jones's iambic delivery of *sister* demonstrates the large pitch excursion prominent in African American Vernacular English. Again, Darth Vader recalls the racially ambiguous black predator in the first film, throwing Luke into a rage that nearly brings him to moral blackness. Luke recovers, then recognizes in both of their cybernetic hands his and Darth Vader's bodily mixture. Luke's coloring was black, his body was mixed, and he had come close to succumbing to evil. Then, his mixed and white father pushes the Emperor into a chasm, switching Darth Vader back to moral whiteness. Luke removes the elder's helmet, and the pale head of the English actor Sebastian Shaw brings the former Sith Lord back to the color white and racial whiteness. Yet, his cyborg body confirms my construction: Darth Vader is both mixed and white. If tragic mulattoes suffered merely because of their mixture, Darth Vader is no tragic mulatto. In fact, his return to goodness brought about his death.

I do not believe Darth Vader was racially passing, nor do I believe Luke Skywalker was. At the end of *The Empire Strikes Back*, five principal characters were nearby when the medical droid completed the installation of Luke's cybernetic hand. Although the matter of his paternity may not have been common knowledge among the Rebel Alliance ranks, the final movie of the original trilogy does not feature him hiding the fact. Luke differs from Peola or Sarah Jane, the racially mixed characters in the two versions of *Imitation of Life* (1934, 1959), both of whom enacted plans to racially pass as soon as the opportunity arose. Rather than forsaking "the ways that one recognizes oneself and is recognized as kindred," Luke sought a relationship with his father.[19] His trajectory resembles the contemporary real-life story of Bliss Broyard, who came to terms with her and her father's mixture after learning of it suddenly at age twenty-four. Hoping for "some kind of healing," she went on to connect with her previously unknown family, evolving "from being a sheltered, privileged white girl to, you know, someone I hope of a more sophisticated understanding about the role that racists played in our country."[20]

Now, when I encounter African Americans' reflections on their perceptions of Darth Vader, it is apparent they have pondered the matter for an extended period, perhaps since childhood. They are speaking about something personal and know that very few will see it the same way. During the publicity around the release of *The Force Awakens* (2015), Melissa Harris-Perry spoke of her feelings about *Star Wars* on MSNBC:

> I have feelings—good, bad, and otherwise—about *Star Wars*. I have a lot. I spent the whole day talking about the Darth Vader situation. . . . Yeah, like, the part where he was totally a Black guy whose name basically was James Earl Jones. . . . But while he was Black, he was terrible and bad and awful and used to cut off white men's hands, and didn't, you know, actually claim his son. But as soon as he claims his son and goes over to the good, he takes off his mask and he is white. Yes, I have many, many feelings about that, but I will try to put them over here.[21]

Several fans and commentators ridiculed Harris-Perry for this position, reflecting a refusal to entertain interpretations of the saga from perspectives other than their own. They readily cite knowledge that did not exist at the time of the original trilogy, showing their inability to see how a character may operate as something other than the white actors in front of them. They are so accustomed to the graces shown to their white perspectives that they don't know how to respond to a Black woman's perspective.[22]

Other white people have thought of Darth Vader as African American, and not just as a joke (e.g., the Black American character Hooper X in the 1997 film *Chasing Amy*). For its October 1983 issue lampooning *Return of the Jedi*, which had premiered five months earlier, *Mad* magazine put on its cover an illustration of the cast looking on while Darth Vader removed his helmet. Underneath was Mr. T, who starred

Figure 2.3. Mort Drucker's cover illustration for *Mad* magazine suggesting that Darth Vader was Mr. T's character in *Rocky III* (1982), Clubber Lang. Credit: *Mad* magazine.

as Bosco Baracus, a short-tempered demolitions expert, in *The A-Team* television show, which had premiered in January 1983. But his look here includes the feather earrings worn by Mr. T's character Clubber Lang in 1982's *Rocky III*. In that movie, Lang begins as the underdog, training with few resources and becoming the number one contender to

Sylvester Stallone's character through a series of knockouts. Lang wore these earrings at an event where he goaded Rocky, who was announcing his retirement. A provocateur, Lang also propositioned his wife, Adrian, in front of the assembled reporters. This interracial innuendo pushes Rocky over the edge, and he feels compelled to discipline this Black boy who came from Chicago and talked fresh to his wife. The humor in *Mad*'s cover lies in the suggestion that Darth Vader's physique, brutality, and cool came from the Black man in the suit, even if it is problematic to bind those characteristics to Black men. The humor is effective because we had a notion of this all along; the gasping, redeemed, white Anakin of the last act of *Return of the Jedi* does not jibe with the Darth Vader we saw, heard, and witnessed before that point.[23]

CHAPTER 3

Early Fanship, the Invisible Jetpack, and Black Fans (1977–1982)

Introduction

As an illustration of the role of reading in early fanship, as well as an example of the mystery of Darth Vader's identity in the early years, the second issue of *Star Wars Official Poster Monthly* described "a figure out of some galactic nightmare, Darth Vader dominates the dark side of the *Star Wars* universe. Gigantic in stature, robed in black and able to command powers beyond human understanding, the Dark Lord of the Sith is an evil force to be reckoned with."[1] This portrait relied on his mystery, his powers, and his authority, with no details about his body. However, this November 1977 article goes on to describe a lightsaber battle between him and Obi-Wan that leaves him scarred:

> Those who learn about the Force must be on their guard, however. As on earth where we have White and Black Magic, so the Force has its dark side and Vader, for reasons that are unclear, became consumed by it. It led him to that fateful day when, in a fierce battle, he killed Luke Skywalker's father.
> What is less well-known, is that Vader was then almost killed by Ben Kenobi, who was understandably enraged at his disciple's fall from grace. Vader's life might have ended then and there with a quick stab from a light saber; instead, during the fight, Vader stumbled backwards and fell into a volcanic pit where he was nearly fried alive.[2]

Now, we take for granted the similarity of this scenario to the climax of *Revenge of the Sith* (2005), the final film in the prequel trilogy, but at the time, it was a revelation. This author divined such vivid details of Darth Vader's backstory from *Rolling Stone*'s August 1977 interview with George Lucas, where he first mentioned the encounter between Darth Vader, Obi-Wan Kenobi, and the man who would be named Anakin Skywalker.[3]

Reading was the first prominent fan activity. Whether Fox- or Lucasfilm-produced publicity, or interviews with George Lucas and other principals, or condensations of such interviews, reading was the way fans learned more about *Star Wars* than the movie offered alone. The novelization of George Lucas's screenplay was published in November 1976, becoming a bestseller long before many had even heard of the movie. Comics published by Marvel followed in April 1977, with the first six issues adapting the screenplay. Without access to the film itself, Marvel's artists included artifacts that would not appear on-screen, like Darth Vader's coffee mug. Luke and Leia's two affectionate pecks were far more passionate. Later, children's magazines like *Pizzazz* (also published by Marvel) and *Dynamite* (published by Scholastic) featured the movie on their covers. Lucasfilm gave its license to companies like Paradise Press to publish the *Official Poster Monthly*, a series showcased at supermarket newsstands featuring articles and four-sheet centerfolds. Humor publications like *Mad*, *Cracked*, and *Crazy* parodied the movies, providing a model of satiric commentary that fans would use later in *Laff Tracks* (2018–2019), *Mystery Science Theater 3000* (1988–present), *Saturday Night Live* (1975–present), *Robot Chicken* (2005–present), and *Family Guy* (1999–present).

Star Wars fanzines began to appear within months of the first movie's premiere. The earliest were tributes to single characters: for example, Luke Skywalker, Han Solo, or Princess Leia. In fan fiction, fans began to create their own, original characters, since the one movie offered so few. *Star Trek* fanzines began to include *Star Wars* stories, even though some editors began to feel the new saga's popularity would drown out the elder, and others felt the movie was a fad. Lifelong fan writer Maggie M. Nowakowska named the first fanzine *Alderaan* (after Princess Leia's home planet), and its second issue reviewed other newcomers: *Hyperspace*, *SW Filks*, *Skywalker*, and *Against the Sith*. Before the end of the first year, fanzine editors started sending copies to Lucasfilm, out of adoration. The company welcomed the submissions, primarily to demonstrate the movie's popularity to 20th Century Fox. When the editor of *Hyperspace* sent his, he received a letter from Craig Miller, director of fan relations, calling it "quite a creative accomplishment."[4] He promised that they were working on a policy about copyright and fanzines that they would send with a press kit, guidance, biographies, and photos for editors to use.

Knowing that George Lucas wanted to protect the wholesome reputation of his creations, and that he would use the legal department to enforce his wishes, fanzine editors also sought Lucasfilm's guidance on sensitive material. Ships between male characters have a long history in fan fiction. The "slash" genre began with works pairing Captain Kirk and Spock from *Star Trek*, gaining its name from shared writing labeled "K/S" to indicate their subject matter to the fan fiction community in the late 1970s. Slash fiction can pair two women, but pairing two men has been more prominent. Fans knew as early as June 1977 that 20th Century Fox and Lucasfilm prohibited both selling unlicensed merchandise and using their characters in unsanctioned ways. Over the coming months, Miller did not deliver on his promise, resulting in suspicion and wariness among editors. His office collected fanzines but did not compensate the creators, leading to discontent. Fanzine editors continued waiting for guidance, mostly wanting not to violate it. Creations with sexual content began to circulate, but the organization's approach was to look the other way yet assure retribution for violations that crossed their desks. The threat of action led to both cautious writers, who shared physical copies with their closest friends, and brazen creators, who employed sexual content because of the attention it was getting. The issue of homosexuality reached a turning point in 1981, much earlier than the issue of interracial relationships.

Specialty magazines pushed readers into the more professional realm. *American Cinematography*, a professional trade publication, displayed *Star Wars* on its cover three times between 1977 and 1983, as did *Time* and *Rolling Stone*. Among celebrity news magazines, *Photoplay* featured Lucas's movies four times during the original trilogy years, and *People* showcased the galaxy far, far away six times. Focusing on science fiction shows and movies, *Starlog* placed *Star Wars* on its covers a dozen times between 1977 and 1983. Kids could obtain these printed items on a regular basis. While toys offered adventure, these texts solved mysteries about characters like Darth Vader, offered glimpses into the making of their beloved movie, and profiled its stars. Magazines, comics, photo books, and even trading cards bestowed a feeling of authority to readers, such as my childhood friend Michael from the introduction. Consuming as much print material about *Star Wars* as possible, Michael felt he knew best what was canonical, as in what truly happened in *Star*

Wars and what did not. He knew best how the *Star Wars* galaxy worked, including what would happen if the Empire were to show up at the medal ceremony. His rigidity about childhood play—including who could participate, whom they could portray, and what activities were allowed—would continue to resonate among fans throughout the twenty-first century.

To remedy this myopia, Rebecca Wanzo has recommended that "a new genealogy of fan studies is needed, one that includes different kinds of primary and secondary texts that have explored responses of Black fans."[5] Both kinds of sources have existed for ages, but scholars have ignored them, often because they are seen as pertaining only to a niche interest. Emphasizing the Black critical thought side of Wanzo's prescription, chapter 2 argued that, for African Americans and other underrepresented groups, media criticism goes hand in hand with media consumption. While it is hard to separate criticism from fan activity, this chapter emphasizes the Black fan activity side of Wanzo's prescription. I do not want to treat minority fans in a separate but equal way, thus reinscribing whiteness. Instead, I want this chapter to situate African Americans in the early years of fanship up to the 1983 release of *Return of the Jedi*, showing how the fanship privileged whiteness early in the original trilogy years. As in Peggy McIntosh's "White Privilege: Unpacking the Invisible Knapsack," I suggest that white fans are equipped with a sort of invisible jetpack that increases their mobility and lifts them above the concerns of others, making it easier to enjoy their diversions in a carefree way.[6] Then, I present a collection of African American fan practices pulled from conversations, reading, observation, and some personal experience. The common denominator among them is a retreat to the private, domestic sphere, where minority fans feel safe. Since attention to Black fan activities "complements and complicates current definitions and paradigms in fan studies,"[7] considering these activities sheds light on not only minorities, but our understanding of fan activities overall.

Early *Star Wars* Fanship

Far more than being an entertaining movie, à la *Close Encounters of the Third Kind* (1977), or one that amplified a subculture, à la *Saturday Night Fever* (1977), *Star Wars* became an all-encompassing sensation. Originally showing on only forty-two screens, owing to 20th Century

Fox's hesitancy, the studio quickly expanded to 1,750. Still, with lines forming nationwide at theaters showing it, *Star Wars* became the first modern "party movie." Kids cut school to see it, but adults also went for repeat viewings, upping the ante for bragging rights over how many times one had seen it in the theater.[8] Catchphrases like "May the Force be with you" entered everyday language. The silhouettes of Darth Vader, C-3PO, and R2-D2 became universally recognized icons. Merchandise, often marketed toward boys, gave kids the totems through which they imagined their adventures in the galaxy far, far away. Everyday household wares like bedding, clothing, and toothbrushes with *Star Wars* characters on them became children's favorites. Urged to collect them all, fans bought meals at Burger King to collect drinking glasses, bought packets of Topps trading cards to complete the set of sixty-seven, and hounded their parents to buy cereal with a *Star Wars* tie-in. Advertised in print, on television, and in catalogs like Sears, this merchandise was geared mostly toward children. The most legendary piece of *Star Wars* merchandising was the Early Bird Certificate Package, sold by Kenner, the underdog toy manufacturer that had obtained the license to create action figures based on the film. Since it took one year to produce these toys, Kenner did not have product in time for the film's May 25, 1977, premiere, so it sold a box—ranging in price from ten to fifteen dollars—containing a *Star Wars* Space Club membership card, a cardboard display stand depicting twelve *Star Wars* characters, and a sheet of stickers, as well as a return card to receive the first four figures (Luke, Leia, R2-D2, and Chewbacca) the following spring. This became a hot item during the 1977 holiday season, and customers who mailed back the card by January were promised to receive the figures in February.[9]

By 1979, fan-run conventions recognized *Star Wars*, and creators of *Star Wars* fan fiction and fan art won the first Fan Quality Awards. The summer 1979 issue of *Bantha Tracks*, the official *Star Wars* fan newsletter, introduced readers to Lando Calrissian, teased an image of the bounty hunter Boba Fett, and ramped up the anticipation for *The Empire Strikes Back*. A 1980 annual convention for fanzine producers and readers named itself "Mos' Eastly Con," a pun drawing from the first movie. *Star Wars* and *Star Trek* shared most of the panels, showing that the galaxy far, far away was as popular as the final frontier. Presence at the adult realm of conventions marked a shift in *Star Wars* fanship, making it more than just child's play. Entry into the adult realm also meant that associations with the stereotype of the nerd became applicable to *Star Wars* fans. Most likely, *nerd* came from Dr. Seuss's now-censured book *If I Ran the Zoo* (1950), which applied it to a small, grouchy creature. But the term took on the meanings of socially inept, not cool, and not fun-loving, insults within a teen culture that valorized socialization, leisure, and consumerism. *Nerd* became interchangeable with *dweeb*, *geek*, and *dork*, as illustrated by the 1974 poster in *National Lampoon* asking, "Are You a Nurd?" The writers associated a wide variety of "socially objectionable" traits to the characterization, from "pusillanimity" to (perhaps incriminating themselves) "using big words." Lack of self-containment (e.g., nose-picking) could reveal one being a nerd, but so could wearing the wrong brand of pants or completing assignments ahead of time. The poster instructed the reader to check themselves against the list to ensure they were a "cool guy." But if you shared too many of the traits listed, you should "check for a leper colony near you."[10]

Calling someone a nerd, or any of its synonyms, racializes them as a dysfunctional mutation of whiteness. Especially as a noun, but also as an adjective, *nerd* casts them as an abnormal strain of white, "deviating from the constructed-as-white norm of heterosexuality and employment through a 'childish' fixation on the object of their fandom."[11] Since those perceived as nerds do not measure up in terms of gender or culture, they also fall short in terms of race. The image of the white, male, cerebral enthusiast began to dominate the imagination of what *Star Wars* fans were. To be a nerd meant that your masculinity or your femininity were in question. Male nerds did not possess physical prowess or sexual know-how. They did not have the means to defend themselves or, if discussing the adult versions, the means to move out of their parents' home. Female nerds were far less visible but, given their bookishness, they were surely unattractive. Nerds and their interests were consistently racialized as white, so white that they were incompetent with the forms of coolness that hailed from Black culture. The racialization of nerds as Asian took off in the early 1980s, embodied in the characters Takashi (*Revenge of the Nerds*, 1984) and Long Duk Dong (*Sixteen Candles*, 1984). Ironically, in *Short Circuit* (1986), a white actor plays the film's Indian scientist.

Associations between nerddom and science fiction had begun in the fifties, as enthusiasm for pulp science fiction was an early characteristic. By 1968, enthusiasm for *Star Trek* became a characteristic of nerds, as they spearheaded the "Save *Star Trek*" movement, an effort to stop the cancellation of the series. With its rise in the mid-1970s, home

Early Fanship, the Invisible Jetpack, and Black Fans **79**

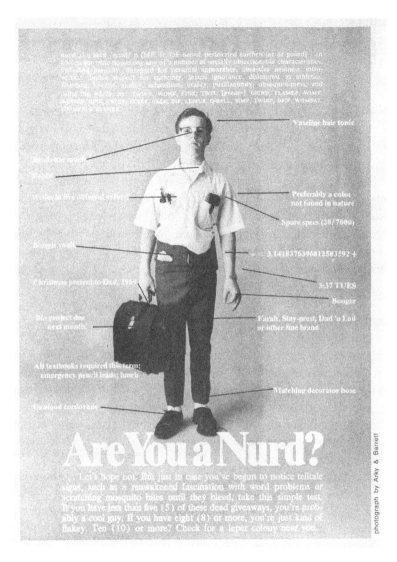

Figure 3.1. *National Lampoon*'s 1974 poster warning against showing the telltale signs of nerddom. Credit: David Arky and John E. Barrett.

computing also joined the realm of nerds. Role-playing games like *Dungeons and Dragons* became their imagined favorite pastime. Later, new wave music like Devo, Thomas Dolby, and Kraftwerk became associated with nerds, both because of its electronic sound and because its performers eschewed more masculinist rock styles.[12]

Could *Star Trek*, home computing, gaming, and new wave music survive on the socially inept alone? No, this was a stereotype. Everyone was familiar with these styles. Major motion pictures like *E.T. the Extra-Terrestrial* (1982), *WarGames* (1983), *Electric Dreams* (1984), and *Weird Science* (1985) featured youths proficient at these allegedly nerdy activities. Had nerds taken over the leading humor publications? No, but the slurs stuck; to be past puberty and into gaming, new wave, comics, or even *Star Wars* was an insult, even though thousands of nonnerds, women, and minorities enjoyed those things too. In fact, by the 2010s, psychologists and sociologists noted a blurring between adolescence, emerging adulthood, and full adulthood. This "life stage dissolution" merged these stages into a continuum where juvenile interests and adult concerns comingled, and abandoning one for the other was no longer taken for granted. Adults with geeky diversions like *Star Wars* became more normal.[13]

Black *Star Wars* Fanship

Still, minority fanship of *Star Wars* is hard to pinpoint. Their voices have been consistently hidden from the record for the past fifty years, for several overlapping reasons: first, the tendency of fanship scholars to think of fans in a colorblind way, which recenters white fans; second, thoughtlessness about the misgivings people of color might have about fanship, which leads to apparent nonparticipation; and third, a narrow conception of fan activities, which excludes anything beyond the most visible at the given moment (e.g., playing with toys in the 1970s, camping for tickets in the 1990s, making fan films in the 2000s, and cosplaying in the past two decades). Lastly, sometimes discussing racism along with the object of one's fanship gives the impression that a minority fan does not enjoy that object as recreation. Criticism can be mistaken for wholesale rejection, but it really points to something greater. Describing the expanded use of the term *Afrofuturism* in the late 1990s, Alondra Nelson credits this community of thinkers, artists, and enthusiasts, who not only shared their ideas but also collaborated on tangible outcomes: "The AfroFuturism listserv began as a project of the arts collective apogee with the goal of initiating dialogue that would culminate in a symposium called AfroFuturism I Forum."[14] Minority fans often prioritize anti-racist impact as their ultimate goal, with companionship as an intermediate goal and carefree pleasure as a secondary one.

Still, this chapter will present four overlooked areas of Black fan activity: childhood play, commentary by Black comics, participatory viewing, and hip-hop lyrics. More exist, but these illustrate how Black fanship is distinctive. Some of these are familiar, some are hard to observe. Some resemble predominantly white fan practices while also diverging from them. Some are marked by the experience of racism, and some may be common among other underrepresented groups.

Childhood Play

Enjoyment of *Star Wars* is often associated with childhood—the thrill of going to the cinema in 1977, the toys, the escapist role-playing, and so forth. But for minorities, childhood is also a time of encountering racism on a personal level. My story in the introduction dramatizes how children categorize and then express a possessive investment in racial purity by age eight. Ytasha L. Womack opened her seminal book *Afrofuturism: The World of Black Sci-Fi and Fantasy Culture* (2013) with a story of dressing as Princess Leia for Halloween in fourth grade. Not yet conversant in the monomyth, young Ytasha Womack was drawn to Leia's heroic qualities. But the details of the author's recounting reveal more: "It is a distinct memory, because wearing all white with a wooden sword on your hip in a rainstorm and trying to explain that you're a cosmic princess to candy-giving neighbors isn't a memory you forget."[15] She had to brave the weather, assemble the costume, and keep her hair dry. Most of all, she had to explain her choice to her neighbors, and play second to her chauvinist brothers, who owned real lightsaber toys. According to Womack, "The quest to see myself or browner people in this space age, galactic epic" inspired her to become the character she wanted.

Shawn Taylor's September 2013 essay "The Dark Side of *Star Wars*" tells how racial epithets hurt, and how grown-ups' incredulity can lead to sore feelings over *Star Wars* for the rest of one's life. In it, a white boy on the playground had just called young Shawn the N-word, but he had to carry on with the play (as in my story) and choose a character to be: "So my choices were to be either a big, furry, non-intelligible dog man, or to be the biggest, baddest, blackest source of evil in the entire galaxy. As you might have guessed, the choice wasn't difficult at all, 'I'll be Darth Vader.' With that choice, I turned myself in to a double minority. I was the only black kid playing *Star Wars*, and I was the only villain."[16] Facing five white kids with no allies, young Shawn retrieved a yardstick and returned to the playground. Their battle cry of "Get him!" turned out differently than they had imagined, and young Shawn laid his lightsaber on all of them. The boy using the slur lied his way out of trouble, but Shawn was suspended for his outburst. Over the years, Taylor continued to see the movies, but he also felt a "belly fire of rage" every time he associated with them. "Fuck *Star Wars*," he announces at the end.[17] While many associate childhood *Star Wars* play with innocence, for a minority child, it may have brought their first encounter with verbal abuse, escaping a mob, or limits on how they can enjoy the franchise.

Commentary by Black Comics

During the years after the civil rights gains of the 1960s, stand-up comedians served as the voice of the people even more than they do today. Across many topics, African American comedians have provided commentary the public might never formulate. But they also broadcast opinions from a Black perspective that outsiders otherwise would not hear. This role provides a glimpse into the other for whites and a validation for Black people, for whom criticism is a primary mode of reception. For example, in 1976, Richard Pryor reflected on the sci-fi film *Logan's Run*: "Hey Jack, saw *Logan's Run* the other day; twenty-third century, but there wasn't no niggers in it. Guess they're not planning for us to be around. That's why we got to make our own movies."[18] Within this brief takedown, Pryor covered representation, conventions of science fiction, indifference toward Black lives, and autonomy within the entertainment industry. White audiences delving into his characteristically Black humor needed to hear this, just as Black audiences needed the affirmation that their observations of these matters were valid.

Rising in popularity in the mid-1970s, Pryor got his own hour-long sketch comedy show on NBC the next year, and one of the four episodes that aired—before it was canceled abruptly—featured a skit sending up *Star Wars*. Thanks to Charles Lippincott, the same Lucasfilm publicist who had also allowed the *Star Wars Holiday Special* (1978) to air on network TV, the skit included masks and costumes used in the original film. Pryor plays the bartender at the Mos Eisley cantina, responding to customers, engaging in friendly teasing, and keeping drunk patrons in line. Writing about Pryor's development through the late 1970s, Mel Watkins praised the comic's ability to prove that "nearly undiluted African-American street humor—much of it expressed in

Figure 3.2. Scene from Richard Pryor's 1977 skit bringing his Black sensibilities to the *Star Wars* cantina. Credit: *The Richard Pryor Show*.

vernacular language and little of it cloaked by middle-class propriety—could appeal to all audiences, regardless of race."[19] At the same time, "for many blacks, his humor afforded a cathartic experience, a public purging of embarrassments and frustrations built up over decades of concealing real attitudes and cultural preferences, suppressing customs that largely defined existence for them."[20] Rather than chastise Lucas for excluding African Americans from *Star Wars*, Pryor's skit inserts one into the galaxy far, far away, inviting Blackness into that realm and asserting that it could have been present in the original.

Participatory Viewing

Because of the gulf that developed at the end of the nineteenth century between high and low culture, talking during movies became socially unacceptable with the birth of motion pictures. The cult of etiquette, which called for more reserved behavior in the realm of entertainment, paralleled other progressive concerns with the ways of the masses. Rowdy vaudeville gatherings that drew from many styles gave way to quiet appreciation and specialized performances. Later, between the 1940s and 1970s, suburbanization replaced nickelodeons with movie theaters, amplifying these mores, outlining the practice of moviegoing well before 1977. During these same decades, while many auditoriums subscribed to more reserved behavior, moviegoing remained a prominent arena for Black amateur comedic commentary. According to one stereotype (and confirmed by personal experience and monologues by comedians like Eddie Murphy), Black viewers in predominantly Black audiences talk to the movie screen. Does this come from the resilience of call-and-response oral traditions? Oblivion to proper manners? Aggression that comes from surviving urban poverty? I would say this is a stereotype that lives by confirmation bias. When we encounter people different from ourselves behaving differently than we do, it is easy to ascribe that behavior to their whole group. Talking to the entertainment, and to one another, had been the norm for a century, across racial groups. American audiences were more raucous, singing along, cheering, and heckling performers. However, while I pin the behavior on social forces, I would say that the contours of Black participatory viewing are distinctive, shaped by cultural practices.[21]

The comments made in Black theaters demonstrate other characteristics. First, a focus on survival, shown by admonitions to characters on-screen. This is a way to cope with terror, but it also expresses resourcefulness in hostile situations. Second, imbuing characters with values that make them more like the commentator. This increases empathy for white characters, who may remain less sympathetic otherwise. Third, criticism of the world within the movie, which shows the commentator's expertise of conventions. Lastly, oppositional reading, once again, results in a diminished reverence for the text at hand. The boundaries between extrovert, critic, and fan crumble, and it becomes clear that those talking to the movie may claim any of these identities. They offer an informal fan experience, not just what Karen Hellekson called "merely watching." Typical of the disregard for fan activities that do not fit the mainstream mold, she claims, "As I noted above, fans who, say, merely watch a particular TV show are not actually fans, who by this definition must actively engage in fandom. They are just people who watch a show; this is not an expression of the fan experience. The fan experience is fandom, which comprises people who post, engage, write letters, talk, meet face-to-face, dress up, or make vids. Central to fandom is this shared community."[22]

But what is "merely" watching? Does anyone only merely watch? Is Hellekson excluding classes of people from fanship? Where do you draw the line between merely watching and engaging? What ways are acceptable engagement? "Shared community" should be loosely defined to include strangers in the hall. After all, talking to the movie was ephemeral, a performance for the people present that wasn't archived or disseminated. Likewise, reverence for the text should not be a prerequisite.[23]

Star Wars first became available on home video in 1982, introducing the fan activity of watching at home. For fans of all races, this led to more viewing in private, where they could behave however they liked. According to another stereotype, personal experience, and research by Will Brooker, white *Star Wars* fans talk *with the movie* rather than *at the movie*. Brooker describes a get-together of adult fans watching *The Empire Strikes Back* on video, who make a game of reciting lines from the movie: "Much of the group's engagement with *Empire* consists of quoting lines of dialogue before they are delivered on-screen, usually in an imitation of the character's voice. Quoting in this way displays individual knowledge of the text, memory skills and imitative ability and is rewarded by the group's appreciative laughter."[24] Credit is given for reciting lines before the characters do so, in voices replicating those of the actors. This white gathering is far less improvisational, with a clear identification with both the white characters and the white creators. Also, their high degree of reverence for the text, combined with their identities as *Star Wars* fans, made their gathering an homage rather than a deconstruction.[25]

Ultimately, what is the primary influence on talking in the movies? "Certainly the context, and not the text," Janet Staiger has suggested. "Who is watching, what the occasion is, and whether the situation is serious or play—all of these seem pertinent. But audience identity or exhibition situation (such as mechanically synchronized sound) will not always match up with a listening or a talking audience."[26] Reverence for the text does matter, however, and comparing white fans who feel affinity with the creators with Black fans who feel opposition to the creators shows how different their practices may be.

Hip-Hop Lyrics

Looking back on how the *Star Wars* phenomenon changed merchandising, distribution, and visuals, Harry Allen compared it to hip-hop, the collection of cultural forms created by Black and Latino youth in the late 1970s that has become a recognizable style popularized around the world. As he wrote of the simultaneous development of *Star Wars* and hip-hop, "Perhaps by virtue of their mutually ignominious births, hip-hop and *Star Wars* also initially shared salient themes—that of principled innovators going up against entrenched opposition—that rang true for millions, resounding with unlimited cultural impact, leaving no one untouched."[27] This was especially true during the culture's first decade, before its mainstream popularity, when graffiti artists, DJs, and MCs felt the conflict between commercialism and artistic integrity, just as the Rebel Alliance and the Empire played out an unfairly matched war between good and evil on-screen.

However, the blockbuster amplified the connections between Black music and science fiction in songs we categorize as disco, funk, and R&B. During the same summer as its release, the music producer Meco had a platinum album and single with his "*Star Wars* Theme / Cantina Band," which reimagined several of John Williams's motifs as themes in a disco montage. Though three other disco artists did versions of the main theme, Meco's had the greatest success by far. The Black, British R&B group Real Thing asked, "Can you feel the Force?" in its song of the same name in 1978.[28] Lonnie Liston Smith serenaded an unnamed "Space Princess" in 1978. The next year, Instant Funk released an homage to Darth Vader titled "Dark Vader." The nine-musician outfit, which had backed up Bunny Sigler, Lou Rawls, and the O'Jays, made no qualms about considering him African American: "A tall Black man, entirely fearless / Came from the stars, we know that well / The universe commences to tremble / When they found out that he was there."[29] Even before *The Empire Strikes Back*, their song casts James Earl Jones's character as the messiah of the saga, prophesying, "He's coming back / He said he would!"[30] These musicians joined MCs in exhibiting a wide cultural literacy, mentioning historical figures, pop culture, and high culture in their lyrics. Rappers show their skill with words, their verbal toolbox, and their knowledge of life in the United States. They mention *Star Wars* and other cultural artifacts as throwaway lines that are easy to miss, but significant because their use indicates that the speakers are likely fans.

Notable references to *Star Wars* in rap music began a few years after the end of the original trilogy. Kool Moe Dee's "How Ya Like Me Now?" (1987) warned, "You took my style, I'm takin' it back / Comin' back, like *Return of the Jedi*."[31] Biz Markie's verse in Big Daddy Kane's "Just Rhymin' with Biz" (1988) imagined seeing *Star Wars* characters on the Brooklyn–Queens Expressway: "I watched *Star Wars* just to see Yoda / Or R2-D2 drivin' down the BQ."[32] As one half of DJ Jazzy Jeff & the Fresh Prince, Will Smith bragged, "That's when I snap and I'll attack and go mad like Rambo / Or maybe like Commando, or like Lando /

Calrissian, 'cause you know he was down with the Force / Fresh Prince is the source I feel no pain or remorse," in the title track to their 1988 album *He's the DJ, I'm the Rapper*.[33] The collective wish of minority children of Ytasha L. Womack's generation contributed to the surge of Afrofuturism in hip-hop of the 1990s: "Between the streams of college kids who wanted to debate *Star Wars* and the unearthing of P-Funk in '90s-era hip-hop, the brewing of an aesthetic was obvious."[34] After all, both George Clinton's band and George Lucas's movie presented escapist adventures in outer space. Before *Star Wars* opened with a giant spaceship filling the screen, Parliament opened concerts with one landing onstage. George Clinton's alter ego, Dr. Funkenstein, began teaching humanity the ways of the Funk in 1976, around the same time George Lucas was finishing the fourth draft of his movie.

In 2015, *Wired* magazine teamed up with the lyrics clearinghouse Genius.com to count *Star Wars* references in rap lyrics.[35] They found that Eminem had the most with twelve. All the members of Wu-Tang Clan followed with ten. In their survey, Darth Vader was the character most often name-dropped.[36] With his dactyl-plus-anapest moniker, Obi-Wan Kenobi followed.[37] Luke Skywalker came in third. A pun on the droid C-3PO's name has often been used in a bragging manner, referencing parole officers ("See three POs").[38] Lightsabers and the Death Star were a couple of the locations and items frequently mentioned. But rappers have been likely to name many others, and a good number of references slipped through the *Wired*/Genius.com dragnet.

Those who make simple allusions, perhaps used just for the sound, make up one level of references to *Star Wars*. Nas titled an outtake from his 1994 classic *Illmatic* "Star Wars," but its lyrics only went as far as claiming, "We call it *Star Wars* / What happens when the shots ring out, *Star Wars*."[39] Allusions like these show that a rapper recognizes prominent names, places, and artifacts, but as with many culturally literate Americans, they may not delve deeply into the lore. Demonstrating a higher level of *Star Wars* knowledge, some rap artists have referenced the movies' struggle between good and evil as an analogy for the struggle against the establishment. For example, in 1996 the Fugees offer the following: "Meanwhile the government brings *Star Wars* from Glock to glockers / COP has an APB out on Chewbacca."[40] In 2003, Talib Kweli shows he can name the movies, referencing a state of mind bent toward survival: "We sell crack to our own out the back of our homes / We smell the musk of the dusk in the crack of the dawn / We go through episodes too, like *Attack of the Clones*."[41] Busta Rhymes's verse in A

Tribe Called Quest's "Wild Hot" (1997) shows his understanding of the Jedi as martial arts savants: "Punishin' wack niggas for disagreein' / Did you see him? / No, 'cause he move like the wind, in flight / Counterattack like a Jedi Knight."[42] References to more obscure *Star Wars* characters indicate a deeper level of knowledge of the galaxy far, far away. For example, Kxng Crooked's verse in "Shady CXVPHER" (2014) recreates the conflict between a villain from the prequel trilogy and the soldiers fighting him: "And beaucoup, beaucoup, I'm cuckoo / I'm a star goin' to war with you clones like Count Dooku."[43]

Condensing a character's arc also indicates a deeper fanship. Jay Electronica warns in "Annakin's Prayer" (2008), "She ain't know, that innocent shit with Obi-Wan / Behind a Jedi back can turn Anakin to Vader, (bitch) / Your lack of faith in the Force is disturbin'."[44] While this song is named for the main character of the prequel movies, its use of Anakin Skywalker ends after the first verse. Songs with multiple references to *Star Wars* indicate more extensive fan knowledge. For example, in "Can't Wait" (1994), Redman compares himself to Luke Skywalker in one verse ("The fly guy with the Force like Luke Sky' / Down for a ménage à trois bitch if you're fly"), and then the bounty hunter Boba Fett in another ("I said I, catch the A train, to the left (aha) / Smoke the choc', I set shit off like Boba Fett (aha)."[45]

Are rappers ignored as serious *Star Wars* fans because they're nothing like the stereotype of the fan, which descends from the stereotype of the nerd? I believe this is part of it. The stereotypes assigned to them as Black men dictate how cerebral, awkward, and obsessed with pop culture they may be. While the question of African American *Star Wars* fanship is less grave than that of incarceration, education, health care, and labor, the legibility of Black male rappers does limit the ways our society interprets them. In popular culture fandom, as in more serious arenas, "black men are seemingly bound to and bound by their legibility."[46] Because fans, media, and scholars see rappers as physically masculine, African American, and urbane, characteristics distant from the galaxy far, far away, they are always outsiders to fandom.

"Black *Star Wars* Fans—We Do Exist!"

In the fall of 2018, my research assistant and I searched YouTube for "Black *Star Wars* fans" and discovered the video quoted above, an invitation by Amiyrah Martin and her husband to connect with others like them. "So today on May the Fourth we wanted to come to you guys and have a little discussion, because we are a *Star Wars* couple. . . . We have a little melanin in us and so far, we're the only African American *Star Wars* couple that we've met, yes."[47] Although produced forty years after the beginnings of *Star Wars* fanship, it expressed sentiments as relevant now as Black fans expressed back then, especially regarding interacting with other fans. They want to find fans with similar perspectives. They want to find fellow enthusiasts with whom they can feel comfortable without having to be constantly on guard due to fear of experiencing microaggressions: "You may be our color and may be married. We're looking for buddies. If you're out there, it's May the Fourth. Anything could happen. We'll be your friend."[48] One of two relevant results on YouTube, the video had fewer than seven hundred views and just over a dozen comments in its three and a half years online. This discovery showed what a disproportionately small sliver visible, Black *Star Wars* fans constitute.

Although this example is anachronistic for the period being discussed, Amiyrah's expressions of fanship are likely perennial. From the T-shirt and mug appearing in the video to the mention of toy lightsabers, she and her husband express their fanship through buying merchandise. They have watched the movies many times since childhood, making references to trivia like bantha milk. They enjoy analyzing the fictional characters from their real-world perspective, inviting viewers to join them in calling the scavenger Jawas "stealers." Most of all, they enjoy sharing *Star Wars* with their children, close relatives, and lifelong friends. Although posting this solicitation on YouTube is a public act relying on a popular social medium, all their activities existed in the preceding decades. Their ways of demonstrating fanship also exist within the home, which is safe from microaggressions, concealed from public scrutiny. Today, in the summer of 2024, her video is still one of two relevant videos, with just under 1,200 views and twenty-eight comments. Amiyrah's presence on the internet has grown, via her Twitter, TikTok, and featured appearances on other websites. Her extroversion makes her different from many *Star Wars* fans.[49]

Considering how the experience of racism pervades fan activities for minorities, it is worthwhile to consider the cultural differences in fan behaviors. When fans do not feel welcome, when they feel their contributions will not be taken seriously, when they must put in the extra

Figure 3.3. Amiyrah Martin and her husband offer their friendship to Black *Star Wars* fans on YouTube. Credit: Amiyrah Martin.

mental energy to protect themselves, they find other ways to enjoy the objects of their fanship. Many stay home. On social media, many limit their conversations to vetted friends and allies. They collect merchandise, maintain a personal shrine, and only their loved ones know about it. Without an invisible jetpack, they stay close to home. Their activities escape the public record, and Black *Star Wars* fans remain invisible.

CHAPTER 4

Princess Leia, Lando Calrissian, and Fan Imaginations (1977–1983)

Introduction

Along with enthrallment with the spectacle of the first *Star Wars* film, many critics linked its escapist action and thematic simplicity to unburdened childhood. After claiming *Star Wars* had "no message" and "no sex," *Time* said that the movie possessed "that innocence and that feeling for romance," making it so "fantastic."[1] Vincent Canby called it "fun and funny ... good enough to convince the most skeptical 8-year-old sci-fi buff, who is the toughest critic."[2] Roger Ebert praised how the movie operated on "an innocent and often funny level ... so direct and simple that all of the complications of the modern movie seem to vaporize."[3] Writing for *Newsweek*, Jack Kroll said that the movie was "without a smudge of corrupt consciousness, in these smudged times," adding that it was made for "the child in all of us."[4] Pauline Kael dissented, panning the movie and critiquing the critics: "The excitement of those who call it the film of the year goes way past nostalgia to the feeling that now is the time to return to childhood." She detected a tendency among her colleagues not just to archive the past in the movie's influences, but to wish, as a child would, for "a box of Cracker Jack which is all prizes."[5]

But the 1970s were a complex time full of adult concerns. In addition to the failure in Vietnam, which George Lucas had in mind while writing, Americans grappled with the expansion of personal freedoms and civil rights achieved by the previous decades' social movements. *Star Wars* offered an air-conditioned, Dolby-amplified escape from those concerns. But once you were out in the real world with real people, feminism, civil rights (including interracial intimacy), and sexuality resumed, even if the movie did not address them directly. Carrie Fisher's Princess Leia stands as a feminist icon, yet she also served as a symbol of sexual and racial purity in all three movies. Billy Dee Williams's Lando Calrissian was a sex symbol everywhere but the galaxy far, far away. And fans writing fan fiction that put characters in sexual relationships pushed Lucasfilm to reconsider what was suitable use of their intellectual property. This chapter brings together these seemingly disparate tales about gender, race, and sexuality to show that such issues were concurrent and to historicize them in the continuum of sexism, racism, and homophobia that has influenced the US context. I want to capture the moment when it seemed that movies were coming to an end, and to show how fans established their ways for years to come. Lastly, in an effort that will pay off in chapters 6 and 7, I want to dispel the novelty, acceptance, and visibility that interracial relationships seem to have gained when they reappear in the sequel trilogy.

Princess Leia, Symbol of Freedom

Conventional wisdom says that, in terms of politics, Darth Vader represented authority, militarism, and brutality, whereas Princess Leia represented the institutional dimensions of freedom. She works to restore freedom, which is implied to mean democracy, as legislated by the Galactic Senate. Darth Vader and Princess Leia are set up as opposites, and their political positions are made apparent using dyadic, moralistic ways of color-coding. As a reminder of the three-axis color-coding I introduced in chapter 1, Darth Vader is colored black, and Princess Leia is colored white; Darth Vader has a mixed makeup, and Princess Leia is racially white; Darth Vader disdains life, and Princess Leia is leading the efforts to protect life and liberty. While Darth Vader is a symbol of racial mixture who ultimately enforces white supremacy, Princess Leia is a symbol of political freedom, white in literal, racial, and moral dimensions. However, if we include personal matters like social equality, reproductive rights, and sexual freedom, we see through her courting exploits that she also obeys the boundaries of white racial purity.

This exploration of Princess Leia reveals how George Lucas preferred to address institutional aspects of freedom, not individual ones. We can see how she reflects these boundaries: first, through the choices he made in constructing her; second, through her relationships in the original trilogy; and third, through activities that occupied fans after

1983. These contributed to a feedback loop, ensconcing her whiteness even more. Lastly, by the time of Carrie Fisher's passing in 2016, it was clear how influential a role Princess Leia played, becoming a feminist icon. This chapter ends with an examination of how the strong female character can communicate antimixing messages just as readily as the damsel.

George Lucas's experiences and political views had an impact on the creation of *Star Wars*. Formations of Imperial troops resembled those show in Leni Riefenstahl's *The Triumph of the Will* (1935). Palpatine's ascent from senator to emperor echoed Richard Nixon's path from congressman to president. The depersonalized military resembled that of the United States during the Cold War. And the threat of a Death Star resembled the dread induced by our real-world weapons of mass destruction. Essential to the original trilogy was the belief that outnumbered yet committed fighters could foil the Empire. For Lucas, who was a young man during the Vietnam years, this culminated with the Ewoks imitating the Vietcong in *Return of the Jedi*. Just as color-coding made analogies of characters' moral worthiness, representations of political factions in *Star Wars* had one-to-one relations to real-world, twentieth-century history.

Along with the crawl at the beginning of *Star Wars*, a deleted scene that would have hobbled the narrative momentum established George Lucas's conceptions of freedom early on. The scene depicted Luke Skywalker interacting with his friends on Tatooine while Leia's ship was being taken over. His best friend, Biggs Darklighter, has visited his home planet on a break from the Imperial Academy. The two discuss his plans to desert and join the Rebel Alliance. Reconsidering this scene, along with the crawl and Obi-Wan's reflections, we know the following about the "period of civil war": The Empire is drafting cadets from the Academy, which seems to be an independent institution. And the Empire might "nationalize commerce," which sounds ominous, whether one dreads socialism or oligarchy. The Empire is "evil" and "sinister," mainly because of its willingness to destroy planets. Its rule is a period of darkness. This defines the character of all the Imperials we see, culminating in the blackness of Darth Vader's armor. At the same time that the Empire is suspending habeas corpus, torturing detainees, and covering up a political arrest, Luke's friend is advocating taking a stand against authoritarianism. The rebels, who are independent of the Senate, aim to bring back a more representational democracy, as legislated by that body. They call themselves the Alliance, which sounds like teamwork.

Biggs describes the process of joining them as secret, but also "the right side, the one I believe in," which takes for granted that his judgment is good since he is Luke's friend and dislikes the Empire. But *Star Wars* is not the story of finding out your convictions were wrong; rather, it's the story of learning "what really is important" and choosing sides in an institutional conflict.

Thinking of George Lucas's conceptions of freedom and his generation, strong parallels lie in the Four Freedoms that Franklin Delano Roosevelt expounded in his January 1941 State of the Union address: freedom of speech, freedom in religious worship, freedom from fear, and freedom from want. Roosevelt likened them to the Ten Commandments, the Magna Carta, the Emancipation Proclamation, and the Declaration of Independence, documents that reflected the core values of our society. After victory in World War II, these concepts were used to ascribe high-mindedness to the times. For example, they are found in the preamble to the Universal Declaration of Human Rights, adopted by the United Nations in 1948. With its relevance to military oppression, freedom from fear is the most salient in the *Star Wars* movies. The other three are tangential; neither censorship, repression, nor poverty are recognizable threats compared to what is immediately at stake throughout the original trilogy: planetary destruction.

Although George Lucas was of the age to participate in the expansion of personal freedoms on many people's minds during the 1960s, we do not see these reflected in the galaxy far, far away. Unlike *Star Trek*, his original trilogy lacks story lines related to civil rights, women's rights, or gay rights. Those movements altered the way Americans thought of their freedoms. Of particular interest for this chapter, the women's movement produced a "world split open,"[6] with new perspectives on fertility, sexuality, courtship, work, and marriage. Second-wave feminism, which maintained that institutional change was necessary to address a variety of issues, had a significant impact on women's societal roles and personal freedoms. The connection between the two was best articulated by the 1970 essay "The Personal Is Political" by Carol Hanisch, which argued that many personal experiences grow from one's relationship to power, particularly for women. On one level, dissatisfaction with life as a housewife seems to be an individual problem, but Hanisch encouraged readers to recognize that societal structures produced the conditions for sex relations, childcare, and exclusion from the public sphere; it would take political intervention to change these structures.

The saying has been deployed to rationalize how any personal choice is feminist—for example, to drop out of the workforce, without examining why the workforce was inconducive to a woman's success. As an example within popular culture, Stephenie Meyer, creator of the *Twilight* series of novels, in defending her lead character Bella's choice to be in a regressive relationship with a vampire, claims that "the foundation of feminism is this: being able to choose."[7] Meyer confuses antifeminist restrictions with unfeminist libertarianism, which cares more for individual choice over reforming society. Hanisch was more concerned with the root causes than just freedom for freedom's sake. She wrote, "Whether we live with or without a man, communally or in couples or alone, are married or unmarried, live with other women, go for free love, celibacy or lesbianism, or any combination, there are only good and bad things about each bad situation. There is no 'more liberated' way; there are only bad alternatives."[8] Freedom of choice would not fix the truth that "women are messed over, not messed up!"[9]

Still, Princess Leia's personal behavior is of political significance. Whom she kissed or did not kiss made political statements. But let us keep a fundamental aspect of the matter at hand: Princess Leia is a fictional character whose choices were constructed. Storytelling about interracialism is political, because the stories writers, filmmakers, and fans tell are products of their relationships to power. By analyzing her brushes with interracial intimacy, we can see the outlines of racial meanings, the borders of whiteness, the shadows of what's taken for granted: by suppressing potential relationships with anyone different, the strong female character can be a tool for racial purity as readily as her less assertive counterparts. By acknowledging this, we uncover these meanings in an ungiving text like *Star Wars*, or in an ungiving context like the United States, where choosing to love across racial lines has been a personal and political act since first contact, since slavery, since the civil rights era, during the 1970s as George Lucas created *Star Wars*, and up through the current moment.

"What Have We Here?"

Like James Earl Jones, Billy Dee Williams had a two-pronged career. Works that appealed to white audiences followed one path, and works appealing to Black audiences followed the other. In the mainstream, Williams had been a character actor appearing in various episodes of

Another World (1964–1999), *Mod Squad* (1968–1973), and *Mission: Impossible* (1966–1973), before his most well-known role, playing football player Gale Sayers, the faithful sidekick to the tragic figure in the television biopic *Brian's Song* (1971). But he was also known for playing a range of leading roles in Black movies: the no-good heartbreaker in *Lady Sings the Blues* (1972); the faithful, community-minded leader in *Mahogany* (1975); and the charismatic Negro League baseball pitcher in *The Bingo Long Traveling All-Stars and Motor Kings* (1976). He was a big enough celebrity to guest star as himself in an episode of *The Jeffersons* in 1978, in which Louise wanted a celebrity to speak to children at the Help Center. George cold-called Williams, pretending to be *Roots* novelist Alex Haley, but also got Ralph, the doorman, to find a lookalike in case that plan failed. Hilarity ensued when Williams himself came to their apartment and their housekeeper, Florence, assumed he was an imposter. While *The Jeffersons* was a universally popular show, the exchanges here are predicated on his being a Black heartthrob. Billy Dee Williams's fame worked on two frequencies: white and Black, but more so the latter.

Lucas's belief that "we are all the same under our costumes" had not led him to cast more minorities in the first film, so it was with hurt feelings after critiques of its all-white cast that he sought Williams, writing Lando as "a suave, dashing black man in his thirties" to incorporate Williams's sex appeal into the character.[10] As Elvis Mitchell writes, "Williams's fox-slaying addition to the *Star Wars* mythos—besides making one wonder if Lando kept Teddy Pendergrass's 'Turn Out the Lights' going on the *Millennium Falcon*'s in-dash eight-track player—went a long way towards removing the bad taste that *Star Wars* left in the mouths of African American filmgoers in 1977."[11] Lucas would consistently practice colorblind thinking throughout the coming decades, but Williams presented two tactics when discussing racism in the weeks following the release of *The Empire Strikes Back*. Responding to one white interviewer's question about the challenges facing Black actors, Williams explained how difficult it is to be a working actor in a society "built on western, European values." He described the challenge as one of navigating an industry where "you are tolerated but not accepted."[12] On *Brian Linehan's City Lights* in 1980, he shared how that frustration "contributed to a kind of hostility that was creeping into my brain, my heart, my system."[13] Ironically, in *Ebony* magazine, he denied the impact of race in his career: "So far color isn't a factor. That's why I was chosen as Lando, because the people felt that I was one of those people who could present themselves as something colorless."[14] Williams's messages contradict what he surely knew of the situation, but they are likely flip sides of the self-representation he may have been undertaking at the time: willing to discuss racial obstacles with the white press, and willing to cast them as surmountable with the Black press.

Written by Leigh Brackett, who had a career writing science fiction in the 1940s before coauthoring the screenplay for *The Big Sleep* (1946), the first draft of the *Empire Strikes Back* screenplay featured Leia confessing her love and Luke suggesting Han is a safer choice. In the next revision, Luke professes his love and goes in for a kiss, only to be interrupted by Han. Their near consummation remained in the movie, even after filming began. In a deleted scene from the first act, made public in 2015, Leia displays a more romantic affection for the recovering Luke, and their faces draw together for a kiss, but they are interrupted by the arrival of R2-D2 and C-3PO. Then, Luke shares that he must go away for a while but withholds that he is going for training with the Jedi Master Yoda. Disappointed, Leia wonders, "When am I going to learn not to count on anyone but myself? . . . You know, I was getting along fine before I met you two moon jockeys."[15] This was meant to be right before the infirmary scene that remained in the movie, in which Leia kisses Luke, telling Han, "Well, I guess you don't know everything about women." Without the cut scene, it appears Princess Leia kisses Luke just to make Han Solo mad, and her true affections lie with the smuggler turned rebel. With the scene, Luke is the one she truly loves, and Han Solo is merely adding to her day-to-day frustrations. Either way, it's up to her to choose.[16]

Just as Dale Arden followed Flash Gordon out of the flying plane, Princess Leia followed Han Solo onto his ship, the *Millennium Falcon*, a few scenes later. The running theme from then on is trust. What kind of men can Leia trust as romantic partners? Off they go, with Han Solo piloting into an asteroid field, overlooking that the hiding place is a giant slug, and having no idea how to fix the hyperdrive. Leia, a former galactic senator, somehow misidentifies "Lando" as a planetary system when he suggests they go there for help. Han, Leia, Chewie, and C-3PO fly to Cloud City, where Calrissian is Baron Administrator, and wait on the landing platform. A Black guy appears (the first of any prominence in science fiction since Jeff Burton's character, Dodge, died in the first twenty minutes of 1968's *Planet of the Apes*), and he is the boss! "You have some nerve," Calrissian scolds Solo, and then he ceases the charade to greet Solo with some characteristic African American warmth.

98 I'd Just as Soon Kiss a Wookiee

The theme of trust continues, spotlighting the trustworthiness of the devil (or scoundrel) we know with the one we don't know. Even more revolutionary, though, is that Lando Calrissian talks fresh to Princess Leia with impunity:

> **Lando:** Hello. What have we here? Welcome. I'm Lando Calrissian. I'm the administrator of this facility. And who might you be?
> **Leia:** Leia.
> **Lando:** Welcome, Leia.
> (*Lando bows before Leia and kisses her hand.*)
> **Han:** All right, all right, you old smoothie.

Han takes Leia's hand and steers her away from Lando, who dares to see her as a potential interest, even if it's just to ruffle Han, despite her rebuffing him. The dialogue shows some level of attraction between Lando and Leia. Knowing Leia is giving out kisses and the crew of the *Millennium Falcon* is in danger, who knows what will happen? White characters hook up under much more dire situations, so this is not unthinkable. Lando talks about himself in the halls of Cloud City, providing exposition and showing his good qualities to Leia. He is a leader and provider, responsible to many, and skilled at negotiating.

Most of all, their exchange is racially transgressive. Let's not forget that representing Black men as sexual predators had been the norm since the South lost the Civil War. Emmett Till lost his life for allegedly doing the same twenty-five years before *The Empire Strikes Back* was released. The mere impression of flirting with a white woman meant

Figure 4.1. Lando Calrissian (Billy Dee Williams) flirts with Princess Leia (Carrie Fisher) in *The Empire Strikes Back* (1980). Credit: Lucasfilm.

death. Gunnar Myrdal astutely described Jim Crow–era race relations: "This attitude of refusing to consider amalgamation—felt and expressed in the entire country—constitutes the center in the complex of attitudes which can be described as the 'common denominator' in the [race] problem.... This brings us to the point where we shall attempt to sketch, only in an abstract and preliminary form, the social mechanism by which the anti-amalgamation maxim dictates race relations."[17] The racial order was willing to take any means necessary to avoid amalgamation. This attitude was comprehensive, permeating every aspect of life, including popular culture.

Even in the post–civil rights era, the model had been established: Bill Cosby never touched the white girl in *I Spy* (1965–1968); Greg Morris didn't in *Mission: Impossible*; and Clarence Williams III didn't in *Mod Squad*. But Williams did more than those actors had, even if no kissing occurred. As discussed in chapter 1, there is no explicit rule in the galaxy far, far away that interracial intimacy must not occur, but its lack is taken for granted. Racial rules from the United States mirror those in *Star Wars*, so when Lando flirted with Leia, he disregarded both his station and hers, daring to imagine outcomes beyond the conventional. Since this was a realm where vehicles travel faster than light, martial arts mystics hypnotized officers of the law, and portable plasma swords lit with a flash, it might also be a realm where a princess and a guy like Lando could become an item.

Later, right before Han Solo is frozen in carbonite, he orders Chewbacca, "The *princess*. You have *to take care* of her. You hear me? Huh?" The doomed pilot declares her a possession, up for grabs, needing protection. Leia's character shifts again. Between this moment and when it becomes clear that Lando Calrissian wants to evacuate Cloud City, sacrificing his wealth, Leia is at risk of ending up in another captivity narrative. The end of the movie presents some contradictions: Leia senses Luke, and then kisses him again on the *Millennium Falcon*. On the medical frigate, her expressions do not match the context. She looks at Luke adoringly while Lando and Chewie depart to find Han, giving the impression that the apprentice Jedi is the object of her affections.

As Adilifu Nama wrote, "[Lando's] duplicity in the film—first extending refuge to Han Solo (Harrison Ford) and Princess Leia (Carrie Fisher), only to be discovered later as having made a deal with Darth Vader for their captivity—makes his character more complex and intriguing than that of a simple sidekick."[18] Like Darth Vader, Lando Calrissian operates like a Black Company Man, except that he is the chief executive. He has his own program and his own agenda—even more than Yoda, who was just sitting around until Luke Skywalker arrived. Lando is responsible and cares about doing the right thing for his people. He reflects the pitfalls of the post–civil rights era Black middle class: Lando Calrissian's a token, but he makes it!

His perceived untrustworthiness affected Billy Dee Williams's day-to-day life after the release of *The Empire Strikes Back*. White fans openly expressed their disdain to Williams when they saw him in public. In 1998, he recalled, "When the movie came out, I would pick up my daughter from school, and these kids would run up to me and say, 'You betrayed Han Solo!'"[19] He received similar treatment from female flight attendants, and he felt the compulsion to try to explain Lando's side of the story. "You don't understand—it was a very peculiar situation. I had to deal with Darth Vader, and also I had Cloud City," he pleaded.[20] Williams internalized the conflation of the actor and the character, just as fans had. White fans continued the trend of bounding Lando, producing fan works that did not pair him with anyone. The fan anthology *Organia* included him in a "Portfolio of Sensuous Men," suggesting that he was sexually attractive. However, that drawing was a faithful reproduction of a 1980 publicity still, while drawings of Kirk, Spock, and even Christopher Reeve's Superman offered full frontal nudity. Lucasfilm-sanctioned creators also deprived Lando of romantic story lines. The three novels by L. Neil Smith that make up *The Lando Calrissian Adventures* provided the character with adventures that demonstrated his conscience, intellect, and humanity. However, his most consistent relationship—with a droid named Vuffi Raa, who resembled a starfish crossed with a modern photographer's drone—was devoid of romance. From 1980 to 1997, neither fans nor Lucasfilm creators seemed to have considered Lando Calrissian a sexual being.[21]

Had it been left to Black fans, who had considered Williams a sex symbol, Lando would have been irresistible. Since 1976, some considered him the "black Clark Gable," which he considered a compliment, unless it indicated that the speaker did not consider him a serious actor who could play characters with great depth.[22] Regardless, Williams maintained his sex appeal well after crossing over. Between 1986 and 1991, he appeared in advertisements for Colt 45 malt liquor. This kind of higher alcohol content beverage was often marketed to African Americans, but I argue that Williams's success, as well as that of hip-hop, made him a spokesperson who appealed to white men as well. Colt 45's motto, "Works every time," voiced an aspiration held by men of many races. In 1990, a team of Black female marketing executives at Avon convinced the corporation to launch Undeniable, a scent built around Williams's image. Avon's first celebrity-endorsed fragrance succeeded with all segments of their customer base and surpassed competitors' products that featured Julio Iglesias, Herb Alpert, and Mikhail Baryshnikov. With its name, which seems to flip the script on the Colt 45 tagline, Undeniable reversed the recent trend of losses the company had experienced, proving that a figure like Williams had universal appeal. These two examples show that considering Lando a nonsexual being was a choice by Lucas, Smith, and white fans that disregarded the desires of both Black and white audiences. Applying Lando Calrissian's lesser characteristics on Billy Dee Williams broadened the realms where some fans could censure the actor at will. This practice would continue later with hostile sequel trilogy critics' policing of both Finn and the actor who portrayed him on-screen, John Boyega.[23]

The Innocence of Imperial Crew Members

Back in June 1978, the question of who was a sexual being was on fans' minds, especially writers of fan fiction. Fan fiction writers were likely a sliver compared to the whole, and probably consisted mostly of white women. It was a private hobby, but also a growing community through fanzines. Authors of slash and het romances circulated their stories underground, via hard copies lent to one another. Word of the existence of a Han/Luke slash spread among fan writers while its author waited for guidance from Lucasfilm. Jane Firmstone, author of a short story titled "Moon Silver," decided to send the manuscript to Lucasfilm in 1980. As she recalled in June 1981, "Idiot that I am, I offered to send them Moon Silver my ancient X-rated Han and Silver Lady complete with R-rated illos. Now, this is a bit of erotic fluff that only contains one dirty word. How upset could they get? You don't wanna know. I got a letter from the Vice President of Lucasfilm demanding that I send him a signed statement that I would never have that story published anywhere!"[24]

Firmstone had already said she had no intention of publishing it, nor did she have any intention of supporting pornographic material. She classified "Moon Silver" with the erotica that was circulating privately, not the more explicit writing that was becoming more common. She had hoped to show that she and authors like herself respected Lucasfilm's standards. The reaction to "Moon Silver" marked a change in the legal office's approach. Rather than giving fans the benefit of the doubt, it would pursue authors who violated its high standards of decency. In

July 1981, Howard Roffman, associate general counsel for Lucasfilm, sent letters to a dozen fanzines. *Guardian*, which had printed an erotic piece featuring Leia and Han, "Slow Boat to Bespin," received this warning:

> I think you should seriously consider your responsibility to Lucasfilm, the copyright owner of these materials, and to the many loyal fans whose high regard for the Star Wars saga is based in part on the wholesome character that everyone associates with it. Any damage that you do to this character hurts both Lucasfilm and the fans, and it would be irresponsible for you to act without a sense of duty you owe to both. Therefore, this letter is to put you to notice of our strong position against any x-rated treatment of Star Wars characters and to demand your written assurance that you will make no further use of the characters in this manner.[25]

Linda Deneroff and Cynthia Levine, *Guardian*'s editors, objected to Roffman's calling all erotica "x-rated." They had set out to write a "beautifully romantic story" that maintained high standards. The periodical's readers concurred. Yet, they assured Roffman that they would "make no further use of the characters in this manner."[26]

In a letter reprinted in *Comlink*, Deneroff criticized Lucasfilm's choice to use the most pejorative label and employ the most vigilant restrictions, rather than discerning "the gray area between PG and X."[27] "Yet they know that there are many adult fans of Star Wars (and by that I mean simple chronological age) and we create material of interest to ourselves," she continued. "Children want the buttons, toys, games and puzzles. Some adults collect these too, but we're also interested in the literature of ideas. Star Wars is a perfect universe for speculation. Like anything else, some of these speculations are not for children, either because they're about violence, sex, or because the concepts are beyond a child's understanding and would confuse him or her."[28] Either Lucasfilm only wanted children as fans, eliminating those with an adult perspective; they considered all the fans to be children, whom they had to protect; or they were demonizing creators to show the public the entertainment company was upright. Fans like Deneroff dared the corporation to state its aims explicitly: "The issue boils down to what is PG? . . . It comes down to taste and culture. And since Lucasfilm is holding all the cards, I firmly believe it is up to them to state their terms clearly—graphically, if necessary—so that we can follow them."[29]

During the summer of 1981, a fanzine called *Imperial Entanglements* sent a story, "Hoth Admiral," to Lucasfilm for review. The story's authors, Barbara T and Sylvia Stevens, wrote it as a nonexplicit romance between two Imperial officers set in the same time frame as *The Empire Strikes Back*. In August 1981, Maureen Garrett, who had taken over Craig Miller's position at the Official Star Wars Fan Club, continued Roffman's work by sending a pair of letters to all fanzine editors. The first accused some of printing "X-Rated, pornographic situations," despite "our word-of-mouth warning to the contrary."[30] The accompanying letter elucidated that, "as a general guideline, the publisher of questionable STAR WARS material should realize that, since all of the STAR WARS Saga is PG rated, any story those publishers do print should also be PG. Lucasfilm does not produce any X-Rated STAR WARS episodes, so why should we be placed in a light where people think we do? You may quote us on this, we can and will take action, starting today, against any and all publications that ignore good taste and violate this reasonable cease and desist letter."[31] Garrett continued the practice of considering all erotic content objectionable. In September, she communicated her office's decision on "Hoth Admiral," writing, "We're terribly sorry, but we cannot authorize homosexual expression of love among the characters created by George Lucas. This controversial subject must remain detached from the world created by Lucasfilm in order to preserve the innocence even Imperial crew members must be imagined to have."[32]

Imperial Entanglements editor Karen Osman made five points in reply. First, Imperial officers, who had committed acts of genocide, were not innocent. Second, within the short story, no physical expression of sexual activity appeared. Third, aligning heterosexuality with innocence and homosexuality with deviance was prejudicial. Fourth, allowing nonexplicit heterosexual fan fiction but prohibiting that of the homosexual variety was prejudicial. Lastly, the existence of tasteful *Star Wars* slash had not hurt the brand, but the official policy Garrett had spelled out likely would. Osman's arguments were commentaries on the real world. By reimagining the fictional "A long time ago in a galaxy far, far away" in ways that appreciate queer, feminist, or minority perspectives, editors, writers, and other fan creators also reimagined them for the real-world past, present, and future. In small ways, they were answering what José Esteban Muñoz would later call a challenge "to feel hope and to feel utopia."[33] Between then and Garrett's next communiqué, word that Lucasfilm might change its position spread through the rumor mill. Barbara T contacted the executive directly and got this reply: "This is to confirm our conversation that we do not object to fan-written stories involving homosexual characters, as long as they, too, remain non-explicit about sex and within the rather nebulous bounds of good taste."[34] In October 1981, "Hoth Captain," the first officially sanctioned *Star Wars* slash fiction, was published.

For more than four years, Lucasfilm had maintained a punitive stance, and it took a fan's drawing attention to the company's discriminatory position to loosen its grip on the brand's reputation. This group of women editors took up the question of sexuality via the issue of slash fiction, showing that the genre is also popular with nonqueer fans seeking variations of romance stories. As Henry Jenkins wrote of the common ground slash fiction stimulated between gay and women communities, "A literature that explicitly constructs a continuum of male homosocial desire also may bridge gaps within the continuum of female homosocial desire, acknowledging commonality between groups patriarchal norms work to separate."[35] They pushed Lucasfilm toward more inclusion, expanding LGBTQ+ visibility in the early 1980s.

On the other hand, any effort to depict Lando Calrissian's sexuality during the original trilogy years has yet to be unearthed, even though *The Empire Strikes Back* made canon the notion of a Lando/Leia relationship in his advances on her. Beyond whether it made sense that Leia would trust him, Lucas held the real say-so on whether the two could hook up. As Brandi Wilkins Catanese describes the crossover appeal of African American actor Denzel Washington in the 1990s, "Locating his success as a feat of transcendence rather than transgression allows the history of Hollywood film and its legislating impulses to remain unmarked as the thing against which Washington's appeal is figured."[36] When paired on-screen with white women, Williams, the actor, and Lando, the character, would face limitations with *Star Wars*, as had Sidney Poitier and John Prentiss in *Guess Who's Coming to Dinner*, rendering him asexual. Later, all the principals involved with *The Pelican Brief* (1993) utilized colorblind logic to keep Denzel Washington's Gray Grantham uninterested in Julia Roberts's Darby Shaw. Unless moviemakers intentionally transgress racial–sexual mores, the logic of colorblindness preserves them.

The Metal Bikini

Occupying the first third of 1983's *Return of the Jedi*, the messy rescue of Han Solo relies on the sexual threat the alien crime lord Jabba the

Hutt poses to Princess Leia. The rescue consists of many moving parts: Lando Calrissian has implanted himself among Jabba's security force, giving him access to the prison and (ostensibly) allowing him to gather intelligence. The movie opens with the two droids delivering a message from Luke, offering them in exchange for Han, a reminder that they are chattel—dear companions, but property suitable for barter, nonetheless. The crime lord takes them, with no intention of reciprocating. Immediately after that, Jabba the Hutt beckons a dancer named Oola to come to him, clearly for sexual purposes. She refuses, and he throws her down a trap door, where she will meet her gruesome death. Oola was played by Femi Taylor, a Black actor, a choice that brings associations with both the sexual exploitation of Black women and their exoticization, without critiquing that legacy. Oola's doom foreshadows what will happen to Jabba's next sex object. In other words, a nonhuman woman played by a Black actor dies to raise the stakes for the white woman who enters the scene next—Princess Leia—who shows up disguised as a bounty hunter submitting Chewbacca for the reward Jabba has offered. Again, nonwhite nonhumans are chattel. The Wookiee gets thrown in the brig.

Then, even though Lando is better situated, better trained, and better armed, Leia sneaks into the throne room at night to free Han from the carbonite. Jabba catches her and puts her on display in a metal bikini. As Brad Ricca later wrote on the StarWars.com blog, "It hit me that when we first see her at Jabba's feet (tail?), she is the only human in the frame. Everything else is a puppet, a droid, or a prop. Nothing else is human; we don't even know for sure if Salacious, Bib, or Jabba are even male! The only thing real in that shot is Leia—in the forefront of the frame and luminous. She has all the light."[37] Right, she is the only human, full of light. She had whiteness on three axes, and now only on two. She is the border, the line in the sand. She ups the ante of the rescue mission, crystallizing the mess of a plan. Jabba is now the nonwhite sexual predator from whom Luke (a newly trained, full Jedi Knight, now certifiably white) must wrest the princess. He shows up, misses a potshot at Jabba, and gets dumped into the rancor pit. Then, befitting a James Bond villain, Jabba gathers all the heroes together to execute them in some spectacular, yet inefficient way. At the last moment, Luke retrieves his lightsaber, which he had hidden in Artoo at some point, practices the gymnastic skill he lacked earlier, above the rancor pit, and executes everyone in Jabba's party, including the crime lord himself, his henchmen, and his musicians. That's a lot of nonwhite nonhumans who bite the dust!

Thing is, any plan could work, because they are heroes. Instead, we must watch lots of miniplans fail, and these schemes don't even connect, as they do in, say, *Ocean's Eleven* (2001). But perhaps this disarray reflects the intentions of screenwriters Lawrence Kasdan and George Lucas. One, it gets all the main characters together for the viewers' delight. Two, it further characterizes Jabba as the Asian pasha, while Luke is the Western hero. But most of all, it puts Leia into the metal bikini. Leia in a metal bikini is contradictory and uncanny. She is strong but nearly naked. She is available for Jabba's visual pleasure as well as ours. As Noah Berlatsky later wrote in *The Guardian*, "The sequence is a bit of soft-core porn dropped in the middle of a kids' adventure story. Throughout the original trilogy Leia is irascible, tough, empowered and notably, completely covered. Then, suddenly, she's a vulnerable, objectified sex toy."[38]

Altogether, the three sources of Leia's predicament as the captive of Jabba cast her as the racial line in the sand nonhumans and nonwhite males must not cross. First, the imagery of Jabba's palace comes from depictions of the imperial harem, which housed wives, female servants, eunuchs, female relatives, and concubines of the Ottoman sultan. The architecture of his palace, the social relations, the degree of control Jabba exerted over his court members, echoed depictions of the Eastern world created by Western writers and artists. Described as a set of conventions only loosely based on fact, Edward Said established that the Orientalist way defined whiteness as developed, rational, and superior, while Asianness is secretive, despotic, and inferior.[39] Jabba is these things to the extreme. The Orientalist imagery in the first act of *Return of the Jedi* draws on this characterization.

Second, captivity narratives that placed white women with American Indian captors offered one kind of servitude of white people to racial others. But similar narratives set in North Africa became popular in the United States even earlier, dramatizing whites' fears of capture and enslavement. Paul Michel Baepler suggests "a reciprocal influence between the representation of Indian and Barbary captivity in which Africans are viewed as Indians and natives of North and South America are pictured as Africans."[40] Whites captured by North Africans faced the vengeance of potential Black masters, a fate doubly terrifying because they experienced what they had inflicted on African slaves, and triply terrifying because a slave revolt in North America could in fact bring such retribution. These stories conformed with the pattern Said traced for European works: the captors' qualities served as foils for the captives'.[41] Yet, they complicated the relationships by placing the power with Africans. The same is true for Leia's insertion into Jabba's court.

Third, the metal bikini had appeared before in popular culture; for example, Myrna Loy wore one as a Moroccan dancing girl in *The Desert Song* (1929), which was adapted from a hit musical play. In the 1930s, Dale Arden was often in a bikini, fighting with other women in bikinis. *Slave Girl*, the 1947 comedy set in Tripoli, put Yvonne De Carlo in a similar dancing girl costume. Maria Montez appeared several times in such garb, most notably in *Arabian Nights* (1942). Barbara Eden appeared as Jeannie, the scantily clad, wish-fulfilling captive of Major Tony Nelson in the sitcom *I Dream of Jeannie* (1965–1970). Through his mid-1960s book covers for the *Conan the Barbarian* series, illustrator Frank Frazetta offered a visual iconography, including half-naked females, that would affect depictions of Robert E. Howard's sword and sorcery character, the fantasy genre overall, as well as heavy metal music. Raquel Welch wore a fur bikini in *One Million Years B.C.* (1966), and Jane Fonda's Barbarella wore a metal one in 1968. Debuting in a February 1973 issue of the *Conan the Barbarian* comic, Red Sonja became the most popular metal bikini–wearing warrior. Presaging women cosplayers' adoption of metal bikini Leia, Red Sonja quickly gained popularity as a cosplay character at fan conventions. Along with comics, *Dungeons and Dragons* propelled fantasy imagery during the years of the original *Star Wars* trilogy. As a role-playing game that involved mostly planning, talking, and rolling dice, much of its imagery came from its core handbooks (*Player's Handbook*, *Dungeon Master's Guide*, and *Monster Manual*), Red Sonja comics, and *Heavy Metal* magazine.[42]

Neval Avci is correct to point out that the dualism does not fully describe "the anxiety in the face of creolization" that stories of Barbary captivity articulated.[43] Regardless of their locale, captivity narratives could lead to a sort of hybrid identity. At stake for Barbary captives is the loss of their pure, white identity. Will they go native? Will they forget where they came from? Leia's change in garb hints at her impending transformation, as well as her molestation (which may or may not have already happened). Even though Darth Vader had been a better drawn, better equipped, and better acted villain six years prior, all he could do was violate her with his pointer finger or needles. Besides, his shift in priorities neutralized him as a threat in *Star Wars*. Jabba was a threat to Leia distinctive from Darth Vader: His command may transform Leia into something hybrid, no longer racially pure, morally innocent, or colored white. But I would not call this hybridity a means of resistance. It only challenged the homogeneity and hegemony of colonial discourse and power by replacing it with something different. The gang was not going to leave Leia there to explore a new identity, nor to suffer molestation by the pasha. She returned to her role as soon as possible, and the racial, sexual, and moral order stayed intact. In *Return of the Jedi*, Edward Said's theorization of the East in relation to the West remains essential.[44]

Leia ends up a captive again with the Ewoks, childlike teddy bears who also have a social structure, folklore, and industry. Although she once more wears clothes some other species chose for her, the Ewoks are not a sexual threat. The interactions between Leia and the Ewok named Wicket resemble those between a primitive and a colonial explorer, a street urchin and a privileged tourist, and the United States' "little Asian brothers" we engaged with fighting communism.[45] But look at the macho puffery Wicket performs. It's like he's a child playing *Star Wars* with a babysitter. Look at how the Ewoks have a dress for Leia at the Ewok village, and how they revere her. They don't want to eat her; they want to keep her. Perhaps we're supposed to get the impression that her maternal side is showing, proving her a suitable mate for Han Solo. Rather, having the Ewoks adulate Leia shows how preposterous it would be for her to be intimate with any of them. Leia could have seemingly exclaimed, "I'd just as soon kiss an Ewok as I would kiss a Wookiee."

Upon the release of *Return of the Jedi*, Carrie Fisher gave her interpretation of how Princess Leia ended up in the metal bikini:

> She has no friends, no family; her planet was blown up in seconds—along with her hairdresser—so all she has is a cause. From the first film [*Star Wars*], she was just a soldier, front line and center. The only way they knew to make the character strong was to make her angry. In *Return of the Jedi*, she gets to be more feminine, more supportive, more affectionate. But let's not forget that these movies are basically boys' fantasies. So the other way they made her more female in this one was to have her take off her clothes.[46]

Fisher's analysis of her appearance followed Laura Mulvey's critique of the "image of woman as (passive) raw material for the (active) gaze of man."[47] The actor also described the experience of filming those scenes: "This was no bikini. It was metal. It didn't go where you went. After the shots, the prop man would have to check me. He'd say, 'Okay, tits are fine. Let's go.' So I started checking for any bounce or slip after takes. Then it was, 'Cut. Hey, how they doin', hooters in place? Tits all right?' I was embarrassed at first with a hundred guys going crazy over my revealed self. Dignity was out of the question."[48]

The fantasy of Leia's stoicism was nothing like the reality of Carrie Fisher's discomfort. Beneath her wit lie embarrassment and indignity. With her bestselling 1987 novel *Postcards from the Edge*, Fisher added author to her extensive résumé. Called on to roast George Lucas at his 2005 American Film Institute life achievement award ceremony, she joked, "George is a sadist. But like any abused child wearing a metal bikini chained to a giant slug about to die, I keep coming back for more."[49] In her one-woman show *Wishful Drinking* (2006), she told the story of Lucas stipulating that there was "no underwear in space" and that was why she had to go without.[50] In 2015, she urged Daisy Ridley, who played Rey in the sequel trilogy, "Well, you should fight for your outfit. Don't be a slave like I was. . . . You keep fighting against that slave outfit."[51] Fisher did not feel like a sex symbol, and she admonished the young actor to resist that label early on. Around the same time, an Instagram post by Colin Hanks, son of actor Tom Hanks, led to discussion of the "slave Leia" moniker, as well as the lack of empowering merchandise for girls. Hasbro slowed the production of slave Leia figures but did not increase production of any other female Lucasfilm characters. Still, commentators abandoned the moniker, moving toward alternatives. For example, "Huttslayer" was suggested by *Star Wars* novelist Claudia Gray and *The Last Jedi* (2017) director Rian Johnson.[52]

Princess Leia killed Jabba, so it all turned out okay. What was a little objectification along the way? But there was scant reflection by Lucas, later writers, or fans on the historical roots or racial symbolism of the three minutes Leia appeared as a slave. Similarly, Lando Calrissian was a racial token who made it, but his characterization has received little scrutiny regarding its limitations, including the notion that he is inconceivable as a viable mate. Slave Leia served fans much longer than she served Jabba. The character endeared countless fanboys too young to face the subtexts. Many young men reflect on slave Leia as a turning point in their adolescence. Prominent references in the sitcom *Friends* (1994–2004), the series *Chuck* (2007–2012), and the indie film *Fanboys* (2009) presented Jennifer Aniston, Yvonne Strahovski, and Kristen Bell in the famous costume. Later, each of them was included in men's magazines' lists of sexiest women.

The website LeiasMetalBikini.com became a clearinghouse for all things related to the character's appearance. Founded sometime around

2002, it collected photos of women in cosplay, linked to merchandise depicting Princess Leia in the metal bikini, and gave tips on how to construct one's own costume. It featured news on the topic, artwork, and a mailing list. The metal bikini's significance has been much different for women fans, who see it as a symbol of strength and physical beauty, leading to it becoming a popular choice among women cosplayers. Worn by women of many physical appearances and ages, the costume is a mainstay of conventions and websites. According to Amira Sa'id, "I saw the movie when I was seven and I was absolutely thrilled by Leia—what a wonderful character. Jabba put her into the outfit to humiliate her, but Leia was such a strong character, her will made the costume empowering."[53] Sa'id went on to put the costume at the center of her belly dancing act, celebrating the sensuality of the look. Her choice also takes the costume partially back to its 1940s motion picture influences.

Taking agency with the erotic side of the metal bikini costume, Hannah Foxx, a licensed sex worker at Carson City, Nevada's Moonlite Bunny Ranch, further reflected the appeal of the costume among male customers. Role-playing as slave Leia has become part of her repertoire. She shared that some of the appeal is generational; early teens in 1983 were now men with income to spend on their fantasy. She admitted that some men did want BDSM elements in the role-playing and, as a licensed specialist in those practices, she could engage with her clients that way. Slave Leia was her "most requested role" and "the modern day taboo men just gotta have."[54] Even if these women have different interpretations of the metal bikini, objectification, whiteness, and male pleasure remain.

I believe that, because for all fans knew *Return of the Jedi* was the final *Star Wars* movie, this image resonated as we entered a new phase of fanship. From 1983 to 1997, fans began making *Star Wars* material for the next era, often drawing from the Expanded Universe texts; these creations filled their needs, including those that reaffirmed their racial identities. Well before the prequels approached, fanship had become predominantly white, male, and nostalgic. A feedback loop developed across three arenas: protecting white privilege, solipsism, and narcissism. First was the three-film original trilogy, the product of George Lucas's world-building, casting choices, and storytelling conventions. Second was the Expanded Universe, which added new storytellers' biases, tendencies, and associations to the canon established by the movies. Third were the fan activities, already gelling around cosplay and fan fiction, areas more leisurely for those with the invisible jetpack. The

Figure 4.2. Hannah Foxx, here with another licensed sex worker at Carson City's Moonlite Bunny Ranch, attests to the popularity of the "slave Leia" fetish. Credit: Moonlite Bunny Ranch blog.

results of this feedback loop are fourfold: (1) George Lucas's myopic tendencies in terms of race, gender, and intimacy remained unexamined; (2) other creators' reliance on traditional science fiction tropes was canonized; (3) a wall was built around what is and is not fanship; and (4) a mastery of *Star Wars* trivia was demanded as a badge of authentic fanship. All these criteria allowed white ways of thinking to continue, even if unintentionally.[55]

Within the galaxy far, far away, it is unlikely characters like Princess Leia and Lando Calrissian could become an item, because she doesn't trust him. Then again, why should she trust Han Solo, with his returning to Yavin at the last moment of the battle, his flying into asteroid belts, and his ignorance of the habitats of giant space slugs? For a woman like Leia, Lando is just as viable. Behind the scenes, we already know George Lucas didn't want to go there regarding interracial relationships. But we're also seeing confirmation that the freedom to engage in interracial relationships is one of many individual and sexual freedoms George Lucas doesn't want to engage with. In the end, romance in *Star Wars* is like going steady. Luke has received the most kisses, while Han has received one. Lando remains at zero, which puts him in the same bunch as Chewbacca, and we know how she feels about kissing a Wookiee.

What does it matter if fan fiction remains endogamous? As a reflection of the times, the attitudes of the fans, and what they can imagine in a genre bound only by imagination, it does matter if fan fiction remains endogamous. The stories we ignore are the stories we will stifle, reject, and oppose, perhaps in supposedly colorblind terms of "not canon," "not right," or "preachy." The stories we imagine are the stories we will tell, incorporate, and seek. In fan fiction (and shipping), this is where we can see the tension between racism and inclusion. The unlikeliness of Princess Leia ending up in a romantic, interracial relationship reflects our limited imaginations as fans, as well as the limited imagination of her creators.

Praised for her bravery, resilience, and self-reliance, Princess Leia's sensibility echoes in Sigourney Weaver's performances as Ellen Ripley in the *Alien* franchise (1979, 1986, 1992, 1997). Joss Whedon disassembled her in *Firefly*, disbursing her characteristics to Zoë, Inara, Kaylee, and River. Leia's influence permeates Hermione, Buffy, and Katniss, strong females primarily looking out for one group—those like themselves. Princess Leia is associated with the idea of home. She wants to save her people. As the princess of a planet, she must have a whole planet of people. Did Lucas imagine them homogenous and young, like in *Logan's Run*? Or were they predominantly white with a few tokens, plus a benighted Indigenous species, like in *The Phantom Menace*? Or perhaps all the leadership is white, and minorities chime in from the masses, as in the later visions of Asgard in *Thor* (2011). After Leia's planet is destroyed, it is a mystery whether they are related by kinship or affiliation. The impression remains that a character like Princess Leia might believe she is fighting for everyone, but she also holds condescension for the people they call "everybody." Some heroes' worlds are so white that their saving "everybody" is just saving white people. By having her look out for only those like herself, by limiting her relationships to other whites, by following the racialized associations with chastity, cleanliness, and moral goodness, the strong female is as antimixture as the damsel. These choices lie with the creators, resulting in white parochial feminism; and later the audiences reinforce the values embodied by the characters.[56]

CHAPTER 5

Don't Ask the Prequels Where Babies Come From (1999–2005)

Introduction

By the end of *Return of the Jedi*, mysteries about fundamental human relations remained: romance is cast mainly as Leia's ability to run around with the boys; explicit intimacy is limited to Leia bestowing kisses on either Luke or Han; and kinship is a surprise revealed, not a relationship that comes from the other two themes. Although Princess Leia is charged with the expectation of finding a spouse, marriage was also a mystery. Luke's Uncle Owen and Aunt Beru were the only married couple, and it was unclear how they were related to Luke at all. Since Owen is often the foil to Obi-Wan, perhaps he is Darth Vader's brother? Or perhaps Beru is Darth Vader's sister? Or maybe they are related through Luke and Leia's mother, a woman whom Leia described as "very beautiful. Kind, but . . . sad." As Ahuva Cohen jokes, "'I am your mother, Luke,' said no *Star Wars* character ever."[1] The many homosocial relationships in the galaxy far, far away indicate that paternity was more salient. Even though marriage is society's most favored way of becoming kin, and even though the family serves "the primary metaphor of the nation" as the "the primary ideological apparatus," George Lucas was as stingy with these themes as he was with race.[2]

One of the reasons interracialism is the central theme in this book is because it complicates conventional, intraracial kinship. And kinship is built on conventions of inclusion (with whom we associate), romance (how we choose mates), and intimacy (the sexual act). Elisions in one theme often follow elisions in others. For example, in the prequel trilogy, Lucas's treatment of women is so underdeveloped that it draws attention to the male chauvinism that permeates the franchise, just as his treatment of diversity is so thoughtless that it draws attention to the pervasive whiteness. He offered his characters few options, and he offered us, the fans, few official ways to explore their relationships within these. In turn, fans found their own pathways within the established canon and filled in gaps according to their preferences. However, when the prequels expanded on these themes in unexpected ways, many fans rejected the explanations.

So, this chapter focuses on kinship in the prequels, to consider a deeper theme that is close to people's beliefs, cannot be denied ("I'm not racist"), and cannot be rationalized away ("That's not about race"). Three kinds of family/kinship making appear in the 1999–2005 movies: (1) Social family making includes forms like those in our society that also appear in the prequel trilogy: namely adoption, but also Naboo's nonhereditary monarchy. (2) Technological family and kinship making is most notable in the prequels, drawing from the diegetics of the *Star Wars* galaxy: the explanation of midi-chlorians, Anakin's virgin birth, and the cloning of Jango Fett into an army (and into a copy of himself whom he raised as his son, Boba Fett). And (3) natural family making appears in Padmé's pregnancy with the twins Luke and Leia. This chapter continues with an exploration of these three categories, but in chronological order of the events in the movies.

George Lucas is a notoriously reticent person who shares little about his personal life. However, facets of his relationship with his first wife likely affected his thinking about family making. Marcia and George Lucas had infertility challenges during much of the original trilogy years, and they decided to adopt a child (Amanda) in 1981. After their 1983 divorce, he adopted two more: Katie (1988) and Jett (1993). These are deeply personal choices that vary for the individuals and couples experiencing them. Adjusting from expectations to conceive a child of one's own genetic makeup to the realities of bringing in an adoptive child takes a leap. Whether the creator of the galaxy far, far away was the kind of person to make that leap easily or had to wrestle with the disappointment, it is possible that the imaginative thinking about his own family making seeped into the stories of the prequel trilogy, resulting in a multitude of social, technological, and natural means of making relations.[3]

This focus on family making reveals how the prequel movies clashed with more than just movie conventions (as in, the prequels were not very well-made), more than nostalgia (as in, they fell short of expectations), and more than racism (as in, they featured more minorities). Examining the distinctive features of the prequel trilogies shows that the movies challenged viewers' conceptions of nation by including a vast array of beings created in new ways. By introducing other methods of forming relations, the trilogy threatened their conceptions of romance, intimacy, and kinship like no *Star Wars* story had ever done before.

Ultimately, this chapter argues that the backlash against the prequel trilogy had, in part, a racial basis. The betrayal fans felt mirrored their distaste for multiculturalism, affirmative action, and demographic shifts of the real world interjected into the *Star Wars* galaxy. Lucas's new movies depicted a galaxy with bureaucracy, globalization, and diplomacy. Fans who had never questioned the primacy of white characters now had to accept more minority ones than ever. The movies also cast some favorites—who many fans had presumed to be white—as people of color. These were not the movies fans had hoped for in their heads. But I also want to follow another path to this backlash, one that addresses the themes left unexamined in the original trilogy: intimacy, romance, and kinship. With George Lucas's introduction of various reproductive technologies, the prequel trilogy is all about family making. He filled in several familial relations, presenting a society that was multicultural, decentering white people just enough to hurt their feelings. Critics were correct to point out the middling filmmaking ferrying these additions, but some elements were just different from what fans liked, leading to reactions ranging from distaste to sheer hatred. This chapter explores some of the racial stereotypes George Lucas purveyed in *The Phantom Menace*. Then, I explore the feelings of betrayal, acceptance, and refusal from some fans concerning the prequel movies, presenting the ways they expressed them. Some had a reasonable amount of distaste and expressed it with well-tempered analysis. Others made personal attacks on the cast that crossed the line from criticism toward racism. Toxic fans attacked Ahmed Best, who played Jar Jar Binks, the hapless sidekick of the two principal Jedi, with such virulence that he entertained suicide.

Some consider the reactions to *The Phantom Menace* as the beginning of a new mode of expression, not just for *Star Wars*, but for pop culture in general—the creation of toxic fandom. The first characteristic of toxic expressions was authority, in that they knew the object of their fanship more than anyone else. I have discussed how that developed over the decades prior to the prequels. Second was possessiveness, or the feeling of owning it. In toxic statements, any change is a violation of their property, as if someone came and handled their yard gnome. Third was entitlement, or the feeling that they are owed. When fans have a sense of entitlement, they feel their expectations are unduly jilted when things are not done the way they expected. These three are flip sides of nostalgia, a term coined in 1688 by Swiss physician Johannes Hofer, combining the Greek *nostos* (homecoming) and *algos* (pain). The condition described the malaise exhibited by mercenaries fighting abroad. Or as the actor, writer, and celebrity *Star Wars* fan Simon Pegg says, "Nostalgia even sounds kind of like a medical condition. It's a tendency to drift into the past as if the past was something that it wasn't, and dwell there because it feels safer."[4] Like hysteria, which was associated with women, nostalgia had many symptoms and causes. In addition to longing for artifacts from home, nostalgics long for the way things were, whether clinging to preferences from their own youth ("Pearl Jam was better than Nirvana") or valorizing one era over others (as in Peter Biskind's *Easy Riders, Raging Bulls*). Sometimes nostalgic, historical thinking is reasonable—for example, mourning people and places lost in war. Sometimes it focuses on the good and leaves the bad underexamined—for example, asserting that the "greatest generation" populated the World War II era. Sometimes it disproportionately privileges the careers of leaders (as in the label "Camelot" applied to the John F. Kennedy administration after his assassination). And sometimes nostalgic, historical thinking provides a whole perspective meant to distort the truth, making the losers winners and the reformers oppressors— such as the Lost Cause myth valorizing the Confederacy after the Civil War, which was most famously articulated in *The Birth of a Nation*, perpetuated in historiography for decades, and continually imitated in contemporary politics.[5]

I argue that fans exhibit both the individualized sense of nostalgia and the historical sense. They are aware of the big currents going on around them (e.g., multiculturalism), and when that reached a critical mass in the realm of their beloved, they reacted badly. This leads us to persecution, which follows authority, possessiveness, and entitlement as the fourth characteristic of fan expressions after *The Phantom Menace*. Fans who felt that their authority, possession, or entitlement had been disregarded believe that they are in the minority, beset by the things they don't like. From there, they mobilize their communities, purvey their messages, and personally attack fellow fans or the creators of the very works they claim to adore.

In Pegg's sitcom *Spaced* (1999–2001), cocreated with Jessica Stevenson and Edgar Wright, he played Tim, an illustrator who works at a comic shop. A quick cut in series 2, episode 2, brings us face-to-face with Tim as he argues the superiority of the original trilogy to an unseen customer: "You are so blind. You so do not understand. You weren't there at the beginning. You don't know how good it was, how important. This is it for you. This jumped-up firework display of a toy advert. People like you make me sick. What's wrong with you? Now, I don't care if you've saved up all your fifty P's, OK? Take your pocket money and get out!"[6] The scene reveals that Tim is talking to a child who wanted a Jar Jar Binks toy, but Tim is the one who feels beset upon. "What a prick," Tim remarks after the child runs out of the store, as if the customer had initiated the attack instead. We see all four characteristics here—authority, possessiveness, entitlement, and persecution. Technology, via the internet—which was rapidly becoming more central in people's daily lives—gave toxicity free rein. Even in this earlier era of the internet, users already took extreme positions for shock value. Under the cover of anonymity, they said hateful things with impunity.

Perhaps the appearance of Jar Jar Binks (and other nonhumans) triggered an irrational, racist reaction. It is true that some *Star Wars* fans reacted with expressions of racism when encountering the far more diverse world of the prequels. But I want to make a distinction on this

Figure 5.1. Tim Bisley (Simon Pegg) berates a child fan of Jar Jar Binks in a 2001 episode of *Spaced* (1999–2001). Credit: *Spaced*.

notion: visible diversity did not cause the reaction—their preexisting racist beliefs did. US history has featured a long parade of racist notions that were the foliage, not the seeds, from the Three-Fifths Compromise, to proslavery arguments, to manifest destiny. In the 1920s, eugenics modernized expressions of racism by arguing that whites were threatened by "the rising tide of color."[7] But these trends did not make Americans racist, nor did they trigger people.

In the 1990s, demographers observed the changes in immigration and interracial marriage that had occurred since the 1960s, when immigration laws removed racial restrictions and welcomed many from Latin America and Asia. Additionally, it had been a generation since the Supreme Court declared state laws against intermarriage unconstitutional. "Even more startling," Steven Liss wrote in *Time*'s fall 1993 special issue, "sometime during the second half of the 21st century the descendants of white Europeans, the arbiters of the core national culture for most of its existence, are likely to slip into minority status."[8] Anticipating the switch where whites will have to adjust to a more diverse culture, he claimed, "That prospect hardly pleases everyone."[9] But again, these are rationalizations. Racist whites were already racist, and they reacted in kind to social trends. They had those beliefs all along, but it went unnoticed, perhaps even to themselves. Having a negative reaction to diversity is not like sorting socks, where discrimination (in the form of "Dress socks go here, gym socks go here") is harmless, and prejudice ("I prefer wool to cotton") does not affect another's life. Racial discrimination is a rational choice that our society has rewarded. They did not go crazy; rather, they showed the beliefs they already held, assuming they would not have to change. So, when *Star Wars* fans react badly to Jar Jar, to all the extra, computer-generated aliens, to characters different from Luke, Han, and Leia displaying heroism, they are showing their true selves. And that true self was racist and/or sexist. As an analogy, I present parents who suddenly appear to be racist when their child brings home a significant other from another race. They were not suddenly racist about interracial relationships—they just never had to deal with it. Again, endogamous marriage choices are not a happy accident. They are shaped by society and beliefs, so when the child brings home someone different, they are going against the established order, which the parent held onto all along—just as eugenics, fear of white diminution, and rejection of interracial relationships shows the leaves of racism, not the roots. Toxic fandom shows that interracial relationships are litmus tests of racial attitudes, not triggers.[10]

1997: A New Hope

As the twenty-year anniversary of the original film's debut, 1997 was a landmark year in *Star Wars* fanship. Lucasfilm released the Special Editions of the original trilogy between January and March. The company had invested $10 million into the rerelease of *Star Wars: Episode IV, A New Hope*, which matched its original production budget. The Special Editions of *Empire Strikes Back* and *Return of the Jedi* cost $2.5 million each. These rereleases pulled in $252 million in the United States and $220 million overseas in box office alone, not including the unprecedented merchandise and home video sales. By giving everyone an opportunity to see the movies on the big screen, they renewed fervor for the older fans and introduced the movies to younger ones. They also primed everyone for the 1999 release of *The Phantom Menace*.[11]

Lucas made three kinds of changes in the Special Editions: tweaks, illuminations, and retcons. The first group included background elements, like buildings on the horizon. The second inserted sequences that clarified the narrative flow, such as the *Millennium Falcon* blasting out of the spaceport on Tatooine. The third, retcons—an abbreviation of *retroactive continuity*—changed the stories. The most discussed of these was the alteration of the exchange between Han Solo and Greedo, the bounty hunter who had come to retrieve him so he could answer to Jabba the Hutt, the crime lord Solo had stiffed. In the original, Han shot Greedo first. In the 1997 Special Edition, though, Lucas had Greedo shoot first, missing at close range. Then, instantaneously, Solo shoots. The added effects exonerate Solo from manslaughter, but they do not match the actors' motions, nor do they follow the characters' reputations, built up from twenty years of fanship. As a slogan, "Han shot first" has become shorthand for distaste for changes in the 1997 versions that alter story lines and characterizations, or unduly complicate the workings of the *Star Wars* universe. It has appeared on stickers, mugs, and T-shirts—one of which was worn by Lucas himself, a choice seeming to express contrition to the fans. Preserving Han Solo's initiative preserves his characterization as a quick thinker, survivor, and bad boy. A Han Solo with a quick trigger finger is a slayer of gibberish-speaking aliens who nonchalantly throws the bartender a coin for the trouble of cleaning up the mess. It ties him to famous gunslingers like Clint Eastwood's Man with No Name from director Sergio Leone's *Dollars Trilogy* of spaghetti Westerns (1964–1966). This original portrayal also shows that Han Solo is willing to go to great lengths to suppress the truth Greedo reveals: that he might give up Luke, Obi-Wan, and the droids at the first sight of Imperial cruisers.

In August 1997, Kevin Rubio released his seminal fan film *Troops*, which retold the first act of *A New Hope* from the perspective of minor characters, like Tom Stoppard's 1966 play *Rosencrantz and Guildenstern Are Dead* retold *Hamlet* from the point of view of the prince's two hapless friends. The film's visual style and its mockumentary dialogue imitate the Fox crime show *Cops* (1989–2021). *Troops* follows Imperial stormtroopers stationed on Tatooine and charged with finding R2-D2 and C-3PO. Unaware of the events unfolding in the main narrative of *A New Hope*, these stormtroopers police the area, encountering Jawas, Aunt Beru, and Uncle Owen. *Troops* displays the stormtroopers as Texas Rangers in the Wild West, disciplining inferiors, protecting property, and shooting suspects. Presented as everyday heroes, the troopers are unaware of their brutality, condescension, and bias. They already had white-sounding voices in the movies, and in this short film, they speak with Upper Midwestern accents, making them sound even more racially white. *Troops* was a showcase for Rubio's technical skills, his deep knowledge of both *Star Wars* and *Cops*, and his ability to direct amateur actors. Fan films became a major part of fan activities, endorsed by Lucasfilm itself, which cosponsored annual honors between 2002 and 2010. Fans tuned in via the internet to screen the nominees, vote, and view the awards ceremonies.

Meanwhile, the visibility of explicit interracial intimacy seemed to increase in science fiction entertainment in the late 1990s. Such popular culture shifts arrived alongside discussions of including a multiracial identifier on the 2000 Census, the attempt to cast in a cheerful light the prediction that white people would become the minority in the United States, and the visibility of mixed figures like professional golfer Tiger Woods. On the big screen, *Species* (1995) warned against producing unnatural alien–human children. *Blade* (1998) praised the main character's hybrid advantages, while condemning the sexual violence that brought about his creation. *Splice* (2009) warned against intimacy with unnatural offspring.

On the small screen, Joss Whedon's *Buffy the Vampire Slayer* aired from 1997 to 2003. Starring Sarah Michelle Gellar as Buffy Summers, the show followed her adventures as the latest in a series of slayers who hunted evil beings in Sunnydale, a fictional town in present-day California. The principal target of her hunting were vampires, a variety of undead demons whose weaknesses followed established vampire texts:

sunlight, crosses, holy water. They could exist outside the demonic realm only by possessing human corpses, which happened when they mixed blood with their victims. Vampires needed to consume fresh blood to nourish their bodies, much like in Bram Stoker's 1897 novel *Dracula*. In the realm of *Buffy*, vampires were hybrids, hated by more pure demon species. In a way, these vampires are mixed and white, like a certain black-clad villain from *Star Wars* who was the subject of chapter 2. The series characterized mixture as evil and made Buffy the antimixture executioner. In both the show's story lines and its casting, minority representation ultimately joined in purveying traditional whiteness.[12]

Lucas's Stereotypes, Fans' Racism

Choices made by Lucasfilm shifted the population of the prequels radically from the original trilogy. Some of these are achieved through the new technology available—for example, computer-generated droids, humanoids, and creatures in the background—thus filling the world of the prequels with many more kinds of beings. Lucas had dabbled in these for the Special Editions of the original trilogy, but he made them far more common in the prequels. Positive minority representations abound in *The Phantom Menace*, which introduced low-profile, helpful, and agreeable characters like Mace Windu, Captain Panaka, and Adi Gallia. But as part of a mise-en-scène that may have irked fans, those characters were unlikely to win them over. If Lucasfilm needed to appeal to minority and international markets to increase profits, its casting choices in the prequel trilogy indicated a half-hearted effort.

Shortly after *The Phantom Menace* was released, viewers made connections between the depictions of other alien creatures and past racial stereotypes. Nute Gunray and the Neimoidians who blockaded the planet Naboo echoed effete villainous Asians; Anakin Skywalker's master, a junk dealer named Watto, resembled a Jew from historical propaganda; and Jar Jar Binks resembled "a Rastafarian Stepin Fetchit on platform hoofs, crossed annoyingly with Butterfly McQueen."[13] These evoked an era when stereotypes abounded, little regard was paid to their potency, and minorities were widely excluded from the industry. Some noted the similarity between the characters in *The Phantom Menace* and racist caricatures in animated features of the thirties, forties, and fifties. As Todd Boyd explained, it is easier to detect racist live-action characters in dramas set in the real world: "But if you were to suggest that 'Roger Rabbit' had issues that were problematic racially the response would probably be, 'It's a cartoon.' The assumption seems to be that if something is geared for children then it couldn't be sophisticated enough to carry those sorts of messages."[14]

As with *A New Hope*, *The Phantom Menace* offers scant information about human proliferation throughout the galaxy. Along with a few tidbits of exposition given by Obi-Wan Kenobi, viewers must draw from their storehouse of associations to understand the intergroup relations in this movie set one generation before the 1977 original. George Lucas continued his aversion to world-making, preferring to cast us in medias res into a world inhospitable to mixture, dependent on servitude, and deferential to whiteness. The Jedi Knights Qui-Gon Jinn and Obi-Wan Kenobi land on Naboo, meet Jar Jar Binks, and inadvertently save his life. He declares that he owes them a life debt, a trope used broadly in various genres (usually with all the parties being men). In these relationships, the rescued debtor becomes subservient to the debtee and that person's companion for the rest of the adventure. Often, the rescuer has no idea about this bargain he has entered. Also, often, the debtor's belief in a life debt is cast as a primitive/superstitious surprise sprung on the debtee. This can be played to comic effect, depending on the debtor's prowess in relation to the debtee. If the debtor has greater qualities, he can question the other's worthiness. If the debtor is equal, the pair may become "brothers," a process that may involve mutual fondness, an even exchange of heroics, and sometimes, literally, blood. If the debtor is neither as smart nor as strong as the debtee, he will be a burden. In that respect, Jar Jar operates as a sort of child to the Jedi. Though he guides them to the Gungan City, he needs disciplining, speaks out of line, and often puts himself in danger. Qui-Gon offers child-rearing to Jar Jar Binks. In other words, the Jedi have adopted him. The trio comprises a sort of family. Jar Jar Binks becomes a great warrior by the end of *The Phantom Menace*, a common path toward manhood in *Star Wars*. But Jar Jar does not reciprocate the Jedi's rescue, leaving the resolution of the debt up in the air. Perhaps he is freed by Qui-Gon's death, or maybe he becomes an adult through his performance in the final battle.

These are some of the substantive critiques of the relationship with Jar Jar Binks. But if you feel a visceral (racist) hatred toward the character, despising his inclusion in the galaxy, you might wish him and his kind dead. You might recoil at the seemingly forced adoption, like you might recoil at arranged marriages or becoming a foster parent to a disadvantaged child. Jar Jar Binks was a sort of refugee, but you might see him as a burden on the system, unworthy of inclusion or protection by the high, mighty, and white Jedi. And similarly, your hate for the movie might match your lack of love for the kinship George Lucas proposed.

Apologists for the stereotypes most often relied on three frames. Some argued that detecting stereotypes is small-mindedness itself. As one letter writer to the *Los Angeles Times* wrote, "The fact that some viewers perceive Lucas' creations to be ethnic stereotypes in our own world shows how biased they are. If you're going to be that way about it, you might as well complain that the only evil characters in 'Star Wars' movies happen to be white males."[15] This attempt at reverse victimization is a typical strategy used to derail conversations about privilege. Second, some—like conservative talk show host Larry Elder—admitted to not seeing the movie, but vilified those who did. Elder deemed *Star Wars* fans who identified these similarities victocrats, "people who go through life looking for slights . . . people who go through life with race-tinted glasses, looking for some sort of offensive statement, offensive image, offensive gesture. When in fact, maybe it's just a character."[16] Here we see the decades-old strategy of considering cultural pluralism, political correctness, and cancel culture to be sowers of division. His portmanteau recalls bureaucracy, as well as the Democratic Party. Third, some doubled down, attacking those who brought the stereotypes to our attention. They cast critics as neurotics unfit to reproduce: "Making such wild accusations . . . only makes more rational folks fearful that these nabobs of negativism can not only vote, but they can breed as well."[17]

Lucasfilm emphasized that the director's intentions were innocent, and that *The Phantom Menace* was a work of fiction: "There is nothing in 'Star Wars' that is racially motivated. 'Star Wars' is a fantasy movie set in a galaxy far, far away. To dissect this movie as if it has some direct reference to the world we know today is absurd."[18] Here was a willful denial that movies are products of the real world, regardless of how fictional they are. Lucas himself responded, "This whole issue of racial stereotyping in Episode 1 is completely absurd."[19] He accused the *Los Angeles Times* of having an agenda to sell more newspapers by pointing out irrelevant stereotypes. He did not believe that anyone took the accusations seriously, especially organizations he favored, like the National Association for the Advancement of Colored People or the Anti-Defamation League. Lucas suggested that leading critics in dozens of publications didn't know what a stereotype was: "They can't; otherwise, they wouldn't be using [the term] that way."[20] He argued that Jar Jar's accent was completely made up, thus showing the delusions of the complainers. Since complaints were coming from journalists and gay people, but not Jamaicans themselves, they must be invalid. Rather than acknowledge that critics might have a point, Lucas became defensive, then denied.

Continuing his self-defense, he asserted, "I mean, he's orange, and he's clumsy in the same way that Buster Keaton, Jerry Lewis or Jim Carrey is. He's a comic orange amphibian stereotype!"[21] He described the process of creating a character as "fashioning them out of some kind of human personality traits, and a lot of people speak with accents. . . . We've done that in all of the movies, and nobody seemed to notice, except with this one—which is just bizarre."[22] When white actors like Keaton, Lewis, or Carrey are clumsy, they can just be characters. But thanks to the widespread use of racist imagery, when a minority (or nonhuman) is clumsy, there's a chance that character is evoking some racist image. It was astounding that George Lucas, whose films are pastiches of past works, didn't know any history of stereotypes, nor did any bells go off telling him to steer clear. His are liberal, but not anti-racist, expressions of good intentions, yet weak convictions, as Martin Luther King Jr. laid out in *Where Do We Go from Here: Chaos or Community?*[23] Michael Eric Dyson, who immediately recognized the "stereotypical elements to this character," suggested, "Maybe this time around in reaching back to borrow from old movies, maybe Lucas or his people had trouble separating stereotypes from the sort of things that would help strengthen the movie."[24]

Will Brooker's 2001 article "Readings of Racism: Interpretation, Stereotyping and *The Phantom Menace*" points out that one's cultural framework, their prior knowledge, and the presentation of unfamiliar analysis affect whether viewers agree on, or even detect, racial stereotypes in popular culture. He walks a narrow line between excusing ignorant bliss and allowing reactionary denialism. But he does point out that once you know, it is hard to go back. And once you know, what do you do? As with knowing when you have crossed the line with racial jokes (Could you be hurting someone's feelings?) or cosplay (Are you trying to be Black?), I offer this guideline for disliking a movie: Are you attacking a person? Is your problem with the movie or the people in the movie? Those who oppose Jar Jar, deny the presence of stereotypes, and criticize the excessive use of computer-generated characters in the new movies, along with attacking the creators and their fans, demonstrate that they want to go back to a white galaxy far, far away.[25]

Brooker's 2002 book *Using the Force: Creativity, Community, and "Star Wars" Fans* forefronts the feeling of betrayal, then explores the different expressions of it, organizing fan respondents to *The Phantom Menace* into various groups, starting with the rehabilitators, who tried to see the best of what the movie had to offer, often by watching it repeatedly, finding its strengths, and forgiving its weaknesses. In contrast, gushers claimed to accept the movie as George Lucas's vision, something we should be grateful for. And finally, bashers were unforgiving toward the movie, its apologists, and Lucas himself, whom they characterized as naive, greedy, or corrupt. Brooker calls the bashers' humor "jocular," letting them off the hook. He focuses on hatred of Lucas, but does not go near racial hatred or animosity directed toward Jar Jar Binks, the prequels' diversity, or the different modes of relationships in the movie.[26]

At least two webpages appeared in 1999, collecting swipes at Jar Jar from movie reviewers and offering Special Edition–type improvements to scenes to remove his presence. These sites' creators were building communities with others who felt similarly. "Stop this insanity," wrote one commenter. "Please write to your congressman and ask how you can help," they pleaded. Another, the Jar Jar Job Hunt site, solicited job opportunities for the fictional Gungan, to "find gainful employment for Mr. Binks somewhere outside the 'Star Wars' universe."[27] Statements against Jar Jar Binks quickly and undeniably took on a racially violent tone. One group, the National Association for the Extermination of the Gungan Race, imagined the cleansing of Jar Jar's species. Hundreds joined the International Society for the Extermination of Jar Jar Binks, which also offered a JarJarMustDie.com email address upon sign-up. MindSpring, the web hosting service, had to deactivate one "Jar Jar must die" site, not because it fell short of community standards, but because it exceeded the company's traffic quotas. This led the page's owner, Joel Reeves, to pay for a unique URL (DieDieDieJarJar.com) and upgrade the page's capacities. Others looking to create anti–Jar Jar communities snatched up IHateJarJar.com, KillJarJar.com, and other similar URLs. In turn, the online index Yahoo! started a new category just for anti–Jar Jar pages.[28] One of these sites, titled KILL Jar Jar Binks NOW, was most active from August 1999 to April 2003, and remains available to peruse to this day. Jar Jar Binks had become a racial scapegoat for the faults of the movie, joining the ranks of welfare recipients, immigrants, and Asians in other moments of US history, and some fans used attacks on Jar Jar Binks as a coded way to oppose the growing representation of diversity in *The Phantom Menace*.[29]

Later, actor Ahmed Best recalled the racial hatred he received after all the work he had put into the role of Jar Jar Binks. "I was called every racial stereotype you can imagine," Best recounted, stating with certainty that racist fans had targeted him personally: "The hardest part for me in that entire situation was all of the criticism that came from a racially motivated point of view. Growing up, being Black, and wanting to be an artist—which is a very challenging and brave thing to do, it's not easy—we're always faced, as Black artists, with this idea of being a sellout. We have our guard up when it comes to being portrayed as an Uncle Tom, a racist stereotype, or anything that makes you, as a Black person, look less than."[30] He had focused on one aspect of being a Black artist, but the ensuing response surprised him: "I faced a media backlash that really made me feel like my life was over." He didn't know how to respond, and the targeting made him feel isolated. Depression followed, and he felt "broken" from the experience. In 2018, he tweeted that after the film's release he contemplated suicide, bracing to throw himself from the Brooklyn Bridge.[31]

The second element of *The Phantom Menace* that gained fans' ire was midi-chlorians, the microscopic life-forms measured by Qui-Gon to estimate young Anakin's connection to the Force. Lucas had previously depicted the Force as a metaphysical power, an essence like the Holy Spirit, chi, or extrasensory perception that could be used for either good or evil. Reflecting Asian influences on his thinking, one perfected their use of the Force through meditation and practice. The most extensive tutelage in the ways of the Jedi came in *The Empire Strikes Back* when Yoda advised Luke Skywalker that he would understand the Force better when he was "calm, at peace, passive." The young man returns with more questions, and the master snaps, "No, no, there is no why. Nothing more will I teach you today. Clear your mind of questions."

Even-Keeled, Technical Evaluations versus Strident, Personal Attacks

Anti–*Phantom Menace* rhetoric has cooled since 1999, but the pattern remains: critiques of the movie's technical aspects avoid taking a hateful tone, while those opposed to the new relationships make personal

Figure 5.2. Image from Ahmed Best's 2018 tweet sharing his suicidal depression following the racist backlash against him. Credit: Ahmed Best.

attacks. For example, Peter Travers's May 19, 1999, review in *Rolling Stone* opened, "The actors are wallpaper, the jokes are juvenile, there's no romance, and the dialogue lands with the thud of a computer-instruction manual," yet he stuck to matters of writing and character development when chastising the movie.[32] He praised Ahmed Best and gave newcomer Jake Lloyd the benefit of the doubt for his depiction of young Anakin. Travers's chastisement of Lucas draws from things we had known about him as a director since the 1970s: He is motivated by the profits made each time we buy merchandise and rewatch the movie. He has "a poet's eyes and tin ears." The virtual universe he created plays like "the video game supreme," with peaks of excitement that make audiences cheer out loud. Of course, this is classic film criticism, as detached as New Criticism, privileging the perspective of the auteurs over us amateur viewers or the betrayed and persecuted rank and file.

On the other hand, in J. Hoberman's review in the *Village Voice*, published on the movie's May 18 premiere date, the abundance of nonhuman creatures is his most discernable complaint. Hoberman describes Jar Jar Binks as "a rabbit-eared ambulatory lizard whose pidgin English degenerates from pseudo-Caribbean patois to Teletubby gurgle." The critic names the stereotype that Jar Jar Binks resembles, but he does not condemn the inclusion of the caricature. It is one of several stereotypes he mentions: "Although Jar Jar can be construed as grotesquely Third World and the fish faces talk like Fu Manchu, the most blatant ethnic stereotype is the hook-nosed merchant insect who owns young Anakin." He considers other forms of nonhuman life less valuable; they are just "pesky critters." By asserting that "Jar Jar and his fellow Gungans suck the oxygen out of every scene; their human costars seem understandably asphyxiated," Hoberman applies murderous intent to their presence. He is pointing toward George Lucas as the source, but this race of nonhumans receives his immediate blame.[33]

In Todd McCarthy's review for *Variety*, *The Phantom Menace* is "neither captivating nor transporting, for it lacks any emotional pull." However, McCarthy equated the lack of "freshness and a sense of wonder" with its replacement of humans with computer-generated imagery: "Beyond that, the new CGI characters are notably lacking in charm or interest other than on the design level; they bring nothing new or special to Lucas' universe, and in a sense overpopulate it." In terms echoing supporters of eugenics, McCarthy complained, "This is truly a world of extraterrestrial diversity gone berserk: There are hundreds of droid warriors, all manner of animal-like creatures, and enough spaceships, fighting machines and vehicles to supply an entire toy store."[34] Rarely did complaints about merchandising bemoan a surplus of Obi-Wan, Qui-Gon, or Anakin figures; they often revealed a distaste for diversity.

Even years later, mild-mannered reviews such as WatchMojo.com's 2017 video focus on the technical aspects.[35] "Top 10 Reasons Why the

Star Wars Prequels Are Hated" equivocates between labeling the feeling "loathe," "hate," or "tendency to dislike." The ten reasons revolve around Lucas's choices and his direction. When they get to "Too much CGI," the creators point out how artificial the effects look rather than damn the inclusions. At number one is Jar Jar Binks, but this is a reporting of the opinions they have observed rather than a damnation of him as a character. Overall, the list is like Travers's in content, but delivered in a voice less like a professional critic. On the other hand, strident, personal attacks on Lucas, Binks/Best, and other elements of expanded kinship have continued to be racist in tone. For example, the 2015 video "The Top 5 Things the Star Wars Prequels Did Horribly, Horribly WRONG" reflects the model of distaste for *The Phantom Menace* that points its hatred at stupid kids, stupid robots, and too many aliens. Again, the rhetoric of ruination, especially in assertions that "This is not *Star Wars*." The name of the channel (I Hate Everything) is supposed to be humorous, but it's not.[36]

Attack of the Clones

Upon the premiere of *Attack of the Clones* (2002), *Late Night with Conan O'Brien* (1993–2009) sent its recurring character Triumph the Insult Comic Dog to roast *Star Wars* fans waiting to be admitted into the Ziegfeld Theater in Manhattan. A rubber puppet of a hound on the hand of staff writer Robert Smigel, Triumph cast sharp barbs at its human subjects. In this case, *Star Wars* fans made easy targets: "It's premiere night here for *Attack of the Clones*, but outside the Ziegfeld Theater is the real show, Return of the Dorks. Thousands of thirty-five-year-old men, waiting days, even months, for just a taste of George Lucas's table scraps. Lonely men, who had never had sex, not even with a Catholic priest."[37] Three years after the hype of *The Phantom Menace*, *Star Wars* fans were ready to show their enthusiasm, and the general public was ready to consume more representations of "fandom as a sort of failed nonheteronormative whiteness that serves a regulatory function, positioning the supposed inadequacy of fans as the result of bad—but correctable—decisions, reinforcing rather than challenging privilege as a natural property of white, heterosexual masculinity as it produces fandom as a racialized construct."[38] Triumph's jokes did not spoil their fun at all; rather, the humor augmented it. Writing about it thirteen years later, one of the participants reflected on the two-day process of filming the skit: "Everyone there was a fan and if you watch the video, people are hunched over laughing in the background in basically every shot. We were glad to let him mock us. In fact, we helped." During filming, Germain Lussier realized they were working to promote a specific image of *Star Wars* fandom: "In the middle of the crowd was a young man who looked exactly like Jude Law. Meaning, he looked like he would be more comfortable on a runway than a *Star Wars* line." This fellow fan was too conventionally attractive to appear in the sketch. Moreover, he was too affluent and rugged, having flown in from Australia to catch the debut. "And that's when it hit me how specific the vision for this whole skit really was," Lussier reflected.[39] The skit was in good cheer, but it deploys the stereotype of fans as unmasculine, white, and childish, without questioning the construct.

Attack of the Clones returns to Anakin Skywalker ten years after the events of *The Phantom Menace*. The Jedi Council tasks him and Obi-Wan to investigate two attempts to kill Padmé Amidala (the former queen, now a senator), who had come to the galactic legislative body in Coruscant to oppose a military creation act. Anakin escorts the young senator back to her home planet, Naboo, where he senses his mother's abduction by Sand People on Tatooine. Because of its resuscitation of captivity narrative tropes, I must mention Shmi's capture. Her situation also fits what comics writer Gail Simone has called "fridging," in which a woman character must receive gruesome treatment and then die, just to inspire a male protagonist to action. After getting the details at the Lars homestead, Anakin rides off on a speeder bike to do what his stepfather could not. He shows up at the Indigenous savages' camp to find his mother in a tent, tied, dying, and clearly abused. They have an exchange, and she passes away in his arms. This pushes him over the edge, turning the petulant teen and Padawan prima donna into a genocidal maniac. He kills everyone in the camp. This situation ties Shmi to white women held captive in the past, thus making an object of her whiteness, and in turn Anakin's. Again (as with Spike and Buffy and Anakin and Padmé), the love of a good, pure, white woman makes the man whiter: "The death of Anakin's mother and his brief romance with Luke's mother function as fulcrums in the transformations of both Darth Vader's pathology and the political economy of the *Star Wars* universe."[40] The image of ravaged Shmi is one of the closest glimpses of intercourse in the *Star Wars* franchise, more explicit than any longing gaze, any kiss, or any phallic interrogation droid. In this case, sex is nonconsensual and traumatic. Evoking ideas of captivity narratives to inspire young

Anakin, it is supposed to make his turn toward evil sympathetic, rather than a failure to adhere to the Jedi way. As interspecies intimacy, it is supposed to repulse us. As in the cases of Luke Skywalker learning of his paternity and Flora's suicide in *The Birth of a Nation*, the possibility of mixture is meant to shock viewers. However, unlike American chattel slavery, enslaved women in *Star Wars* are not forced to produce offspring, nor are they separated from their offspring, nor do they have to abandon their loving relationships. This is because Shmi is a white woman who, even in fiction, must be protected from the brutality of slavery. However, it is acceptable to portray her as a sexual victim, since that served as an inspiration for Anakin.

Revenge of the Sith

More faults of the prequels reveal themselves in the treatment of Padmé Amidala, the young queen from *The Phantom Menace* who becomes the mother of Luke and Leia by the end of *Revenge of the Sith*. Even in 2002, Lucas's character development choices drew criticism because they shifted her from a proactive character in the first movie to merely Anakin's love interest in *Attack of the Clones*. Having children with Anakin became Padmé's prime function, so the films depict her series of choices that contradicted her formerly mature, independent, and brave personality, as well as the fact that she is eight years his senior. In *Attack of the Clones*, Anakin's persistence with Padmé keeps the romance going, rather than a mutual feeling. This portrayal leads to her acceptance of his increasingly bad behavior, from his tantrum over Obi-Wan's guidance, to his toying with authoritarianism, to his murder of Sand People. Echoing the original trilogy, the pair ends up in enough adventures together that she reciprocates his sentiments when it seems they are moments from death. Padmé is bound to Anakin without the opportunity to examine how a grown woman thinks, feels, or acts.

Since the Jedi Code forbids romantic love, Padmé and Anakin marry secretly at the end of the second prequel film. She reveals to him at the beginning of the next episode that she is expecting a child. From then, her activity mostly involves asking him what is bothering him, and he conceals from her his seemingly prophetic dreams about her death in childbirth. Although boundless fuel, lasers of all sizes, and interstellar travel abound in the galaxy far, far away, birth control is never mentioned, prenatal care is unknown, and it comes as a surprise that she is having twins. How are we supposed to believe this in such a technologically advanced society? The answer is simple: because George Lucas had deemed this matter of women's health unworthy of developing. Padmé's only matter where she exercises her choice is in keeping her pregnancy. But then, just as no one had noticed her relationship with Anakin, no one noticed she was pregnant. She travels in a social set with some observant individuals, yet none of them says anything. Some of these people are magically perceptive, and none of them notices either. No one whips out a midi-chlorian counter!

Darth Sidious, the Sith Lord who has been manipulating events since the first movie under the guise of Naboo's own Senator Palpatine, has gained Anakin's trust, using the young warrior's anxieties about Padmé to lure him to the dark side. Her pregnancy has come to term when she decides to sway Anakin from following the Sith Lord. Despite her efforts, she gives up the will to both live and continue preserving democracy, proving Anakin's dreams to be prophetic. In the end, Padmé dies not of a crushed trachea or even uncontrollable hemorrhaging, but of a broken heart. By introducing Padmé, a major character never seen in the original trilogy, the prequel trilogy activates several pitfalls of employing retcons. First, her fate is bound by the original trilogy, where she is already dead. Second, her characterization is bound by how seldom she is mentioned in the older movies. That came in *Return of the Jedi*, when Luke asked Leia if she remembered her mother, and she responded, "She was very beautiful. Kind, but . . . sad." Third, her biological role as mother of Luke and Leia limits her potential. Ultimately, this major character introduced sixteen years later bears George Lucas's choices from when he was writing the first movie, so his clumsiness with women in the 1970s affects this female character three decades later. Again, one can argue that this is kids' stuff, and that's why sex is hidden. But for decades, prime-time television shows had hinted at how babies are made. By the late 1990s, plenty of sitcoms had featured twins and explained how they came into being. *Episode III* was bound to receive a PG-13 rating for its violence, so why couldn't Lucas acknowledge her pregnancy in a more substantial way?

Revenge of the Sith runs through a kill list of characters it must dispose of (basically, anyone who is not in the original trilogy). The story also compels characters to make choices that fit the original trilogy. So, baby Luke must go to Anakin's stepbrother, and Leia must go to Bail Organa, two characters introduced in the prequels. Both children could go to Padmé's family, but that would have complicated the story of their upbringing, as told by the original trilogy movies. Lucas treats adoption with such inconsistency that it seems unnatural, as contrived as midi-chlorians, virgin birth, and cloning. The adoption of Princess Leia was a retcon hinted at in *The Phantom Menace* when Palpatine mentions his fellow senator Bail Organa in passing. The retcon is deepened in *Attack of the Clones* when we see Jimmy Smits, a medium-complexioned, Puerto Rican and Surinamese actor, portray Organa. The retcon blooms in the closing scenes of *Revenge of the Sith* when he agrees to adopt Leia: "My wife and I will take the girl. We have always talked of adopting a baby girl. She will be loved with us." There is no talk of why they want to adopt—whether infertility, having many children already, or openness to a new experience.

In the closing shots of *Revenge of the Sith*, we see Bail present the baby to his wife, portrayed by the Australian actor of Filipino and German descent Rebecca Jackson Mendoza. A prominent family adopting a child out of the blue is rather conspicuous. Whether one imagines Alderaan as a homogeneous or a mixed society, Leia's different complexion is also conspicuous. As viewers, we had to just go with it as the end music swelled. But this racial retcon makes it even more notable and, for some, challenging to reconcile.

Luke's adoption placed him on a more marginal planet, supposedly to hide him from Darth Vader. It is an intraracial placement, with his uncle and aunt. Until *Attack of the Clones*, it was unclear who his uncle was. From the dialogue in *Star Wars*, he seemed to be a paternal relative with a larger role to play in his father's story. Since Luke, his uncle, and his aunt appear racially similar, their nuclear family raises fewer questions from audiences, requiring fewer in-universe explanations from the writers.

Clues from George Lucas's Life

George Lucas and Mellody Hobson met in 2006 at a conference that brought together film and finance people. After graduating from Princeton University, Hobson joined Ariel Investments, a minority-owned, multibillion-dollar investment company, and became its president in 2000. She appeared as a regular contributor on *Good Morning America* (1975–present), *CBS This Morning* (1987–1999, 2012–2021), and the ABC television movie *Unbroken: What You Need to Know about Money* (2009), which she executive produced. By 2012, she had served on the boards of JPMorgan Chase, the Chicago Public Education Fund, the Estée Lauder Companies, and others.[41]

A few years later, Lucasfilm produced *Red Tails* (2012), a film about the Tuskegee Airmen, which Lucas had been trying to make for a long time. All the studios kept saying no, revealing their racial prejudice against Black films, or even films with Black topics produced by one of their most successful creators. Through Lucasfilm, he financed the $58 million budget. And when studios said they couldn't promote it, he pitched in for that too. *Red Tails* stands as an example of how the industry estimates potential projects' success based on how other, similar works fared, thus reentrenching presumptions about Black films' profitability.

A product of the white racial frame, George Lucas may be liberal and well-intentioned, but he also reveals feelings of superiority over minorities at the same time. He elaborated on the stakes at hand with *Red Tails*: "I realize that by accident I've now put the Black film community at risk. I'm saying, if this doesn't work, there's a good chance you'll stay where you are for quite a while. It'll be harder for you guys to break out of that [lower budget] mold. But if I can break through with this movie, then hopefully there will be someone else out there saying let's make a prequel and sequel, and soon you have more Tyler Perrys out there."[42] But during the same years, Black filmmakers were making historical dramas about Black people's experiences, including Lee Daniels's *The Butler* (2012), Ava DuVernay's *Selma* (2013), Ryan Coogler's *Fruitvale Station* (2013), and Steve McQueen's *12 Years a Slave* (2013), which won the Oscar for Best Picture. While the industry retained racial disparities, it also released Black biographies told from a Black perspective that did not need the heroics of white men like Lucas. These films' financial successes also indicated that such stories could be told outside the big-budget model.

However, Lucas laid on the table his attitude toward his status, Black films, racism, and his interracial relationship when he referred to Hobson in the same interview promoting *Red Tails*. He explained, "My girlfriend is Black, and I've learned a lot about racism, including the fact that it hasn't gone away, especially in American business. But on a social level there's less prejudice than there was."[43] Throughout history, whites have used their acquaintance with minorities as proof that they are not racist. Similarly, they have flaunted their interracial relationships as credentials of their own progressiveness. In recent decades, minorities have been more vocal about their displeasure in being used this way, pointing out that white self-congratulations can ring hollow. Yet, as 75 percent of whites have zero minority friends, they continue making this faux pas, sometimes ending up with hurt feelings when criticized for their superficiality.[44]

From Michael Harriot to Robin DiAngelo, advice on interracial friendships begins with knowing the line between appropriate and inappropriate, between professional and casual, and between camaraderie and condescension. Yet, Lucas carted out his interracial relationship, his still-fledgling knowledge of racism, and his narrow set of experiences to make an arguable point about race relations. As for interracial relationships between nonbillionaires, though, Lucas essentially showed how much he doesn't know when he tried to show how much he knew. He also confirmed what had likely been true for forty odd years: that he was woefully clumsy in matters of race and gender. After seven years of courtship, Lucas and Hobson—at the ages of sixty-nine and forty-four, respectively—married in June 2013 at his home in Marin County, California. The celebrities Oprah Winfrey, Robert De Niro, Glenn Close, Harrison Ford, Calista Flockhart, Quincy Jones, and Rashida Jones were in attendance. Francis Ford Coppola, Bill Moyers, and Jett, Katie, and Amanda Lucas participated in the ceremony. Former New Jersey senator Bill Bradley walked Hobson down the aisle.[45]

Chinyere K. Osuji's concept of "romantic careers"—or "the ways that people draw on prior romantic and dating experiences to understand their ethnoracial preferences or (lack thereof) for romantic partnership and marriage"—is instructive in understanding Lucas and Hobson's coupling.[46] Theirs was her first marriage, but Lucas's second. Their lack of public statements reflects their personalities as two individuals who generally retreat from the public eye. But it also indicates the general tendencies of the Los Angeles couples whom Osuji had interviewed, who rarely discussed the actual process of developing their ethnoracial preferences in dating: "Instead of a romantic career, they discussed ethnoracial preferences. This was taboo, however, given US society's false attempts at color blindness. This resulted in less discussion of preferences overall as well as more silence or hedging around the topic."[47] So, when George and Mellody say, "We are extraordinarily open-minded people, open to what the universe brings us," they are telling a simple version of their relationship built on the myth of romantic individualism.[48] Ultimately, ethnoracial preferences do exist and play an active role in contemporary interracial couples' courtships, even with the silences. Because romance is a private arena where discrimination

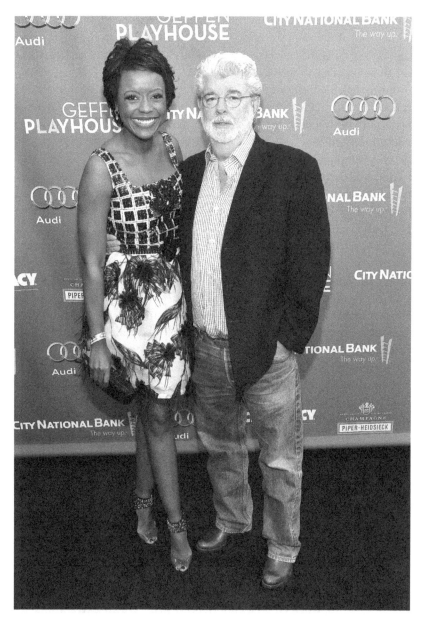

Figure 5.3. Mellody Hobson and George Lucas attend Backstage at the Geffen on March 22, 2015, in Los Angeles. Credit: Alberto E. Rodriguez / Getty Images.

is permissible, many people begin interracial relationships "without upsetting the status and privileges associated with whiteness or the stigma associated with blackness."[49] As opposed to resembling soldiers who are "conscripted into a quiet revolution" challenging "long-held notions about the biological, moral, and social meaning of race," most of them leave boundaries intact.[50] Lucas and Hobson are likely among those numbers.

CHAPTER 6

Four Ships Sailed. Which Would Land? (2012–2016)

Introduction

In 2015, the infosphere around the new *Star Wars* movies consisted of three groups: gatekeepers, big players, and small players. All three are likely to use various social media platforms simultaneously to disseminate their content; those with more resources are more likely to coordinate efforts across Twitter, YouTube, Instagram, and Facebook. With the rise of Web 2.0, gatekeepers and big players no longer held exclusive control of reviews, how-to guides, and think pieces. First, gatekeepers primarily comprise the producers: in this case, Disney, Lucasfilm, and their licensees. They are most likely to purvey dominant readings befitting their corporate statuses. Second, big players consist of media outlets—whether print, video, or social media—with large followings and editorial staffs. The gatekeepers and big players are useful for explicating the conventions that moviemaking and storytelling craft, so I will be drawing from them when giving a quick sketch of the critical reputations of *The Force Awakens*, *The Last Jedi*, and *The Rise of Skywalker*. Some on YouTube taught viewers how to be critical viewers. For example, the web series *How It Should Have Ended* (2005–present) presented humorous animations taking down various movies, suggesting resolutions that challenged the final product, but made sense based on what the works offered. This sort of humor, which appealed to fans' critical consumption of media, worked precisely because viewers could sense such takedowns were warranted.

Screen Junkies (2011–present) is the YouTube channel owned by Wikia, the open-source, user-created, pop culture encyclopedia, which became Fandom in 2016. As opposed to the animations of *How It*

Should Have Ended, videos on Screen Junkies' popular *Honest Trailers* web series imitate the structure of movie trailers, using humor to critique the works, which have already been released to theaters. *Honest Trailers* mixes footage from the film with a voice-over that points out plot holes, well-worn tropes, and social contexts. Their videos are longer and more detailed than those produced by *How It Should Have Ended*. Again, its humor works because it gives voice to criticisms that the original producers probably don't want consumers to think about. Descendants of *Mystery Science Theater 3000*, these outlets brought humor, pop culture knowledge, and a critical eye to viewers. In a way, fans' attentive gaze resembled bell hooks's oppositional gaze in that it challenged what producers had dealt them and concurred with what the works offered.

Small players, the last group of voices in the infosphere, consisted of individuals on more independent platforms utilizing fewer mechanisms of promotion and reflecting perspectives beyond the mainstream. They were also vulnerable to the impact of big players and gatekeepers, either drawing from them for information, competing for attention, or even harassing them. Although harder to find and exercising a narrower reach, the small players became accessible to those looking for them. Almost all minority voices sharing their perspectives on the sequel trilogy were small players.

Among fans' reactions to the sequel movies, three patterns arose. First, fans positioned themselves politically through their support of an intraracial "ship" between the white characters Rey and Kylo Ren or an interracial one between Rey and the Black character Finn. Second, polarization on this issue reflected that of the United States broadly, with the more conservative position enjoying an advantage over the more liberal one, and social media amplifying the animosities between them. Third, a conclusion of the trilogy confirming a romance between Finn and Rey seemed just as likely as one confirming a romance between Rey and Kylo Ren. After four years of competition, anticipation, and obsession over how the characters' relationships would unfold, fans went into the last installment of the Skywalker saga unsure which way it would go. The increased visibility of interracial relationships in popular culture made Finn and Rey ending up together a real possibility.

Focusing on shipping demonstrates which stories fans ignore, stifle, reject, and oppose, often in colorblind terms of not adhering to *Star Wars* canon, but sometimes in terms of bringing in racial politics or antagonizing minorities. Focusing on shipping also spotlights which stories fans imagine, share, incorporate, and seek out. The ships fans nurture are not bound by consequences, personal identity, or even realism, so they are a matter of free choice. (The same is true for fan fiction, a related fan activity.) Yet, the reach of racism and the limits of inclusion show themselves even more readily when examining attitudes toward interracial ships. On the other hand, sensationalism, absolutism, and reactionism became means to gain clicks. This was a realm mastered by right-wing media, but also practiced by seemingly reputable outlets as well as content farms—companies that pay droves of freelance writers to produce what search engines will drive web users to. This created a sort of "vortextuality" around the *Star Wars* movie debuts. As coined by Garry Whannel, this term describes how various media echo each other at an accelerated pace, thanks to electronic and digital technologies: "Certain super-major events come to dominate the headlines to such an extent that it becomes temporarily difficult for columnists and commentators to discuss anything else. They are drawn in, as if drawn in by a vortex."[1] Whannel used the term to describe how coverage of certain events quickly consumes our attention. Because it focuses more on the supply side than the demand side, I want to lace Whannel's concept with another, "ambient awareness," which Andreas Kaplan defined as "awareness created through regular and constant reception, and/or exchange of information fragments through social media."[2] Seen as an increase in empathy, this feeling came with Web 2.0's participatory content creation. Clive Thompson describes it as "the return to small-town life."[3] They are talking about the interpersonal, but I believe it applies to fans' interactions with both their avocations and the popular culture they follow in general.

The constant supply of information they follow leads to a state of all-consumption. I mean this in two ways. The first is the act of consuming everything. All these dots of information result in an outline of the times in terms of interracialism. The second reflects how engaging with this vortex of information can be all-consuming, especially because fans adore their objects. The information adds to fans' knowledge but also contributes to their longing, and even depression. That longing is a by-product of their emotional investment in their avocation. As an activity involving heightened emotional investment, shipping became a high-stakes game, especially as new movies approached. But beyond mere romance, they imagine the world as they would like it to be, a utopia, just as slash writers, fancasters, and visual artists had before them. The real world they wanted featured feminism, queer love, and interracialism.

Again, utopian thinking collapses time, recalling forebears, indicting the present, and shaping the future, simultaneously.

Through most of the sequel trilogy years (2015–2020), Reylo, the ship between two characters played by white actors (Daisy Ridley as Rey and Adam Driver as Kylo Ren) was far more popular than Finnrey, the ship between characters played by a Black actor and a white actor (Finn, played by John Boyega, and Rey). It was the subject of far more fan fiction, more art, more tweets, more coverage by essayists, and so on. The first of the sequel movies clearly set up Finn and Rey as a couple, yet fans were more interested in Reylo. The popularity of Reylo reflects the racial identity of *Star Wars* fans, most of whom are white. It indicates their aversion to interracial relationships, even at a time when Gallup claimed that 87 percent of Americans approved of Black–white marriages (96 percent for Blacks and 84 percent for whites).[4] The aversion to interracial relationships indicates the political standing of fans, both white and Black. Conventional wisdom denying my propositions says: One, spotlighting racial matters is neurotic. A few bad apples are getting an outsized amount of attention. Two, this is a free marketplace of ideas, and the Reylo idea is just more popular. Fans' choices may contradict the material given to them. And three, storytelling conventions make an intraracial ship like Reylo more popular. But these explanations are superficial, leaving the deeper motivations unexamined.

Figure 6.1. "Only in the Darkness Can You See the Stars," fan art by Heidi Hastings depicting Kylo Ren's abduction of Rey as a bridal carry. Credit: Heidi Hastings.

Increased Visibility for Minority Fans

The second decade of the twenty-first century marked an increase in the visibility of minority fans and their positions, primarily in terms of on-screen representations. The blog *Angry Asian Man*, which covered Asian American popular culture, was founded in 2001 and continues to point out biases in popular culture to this day. In 2010, Philip Yu, its founder, expanded its mission to addressing hate crimes against Asians in the United States.[5] In 2009, the Media Action Network for Asian Americans led a boycott against the movie *Avatar: The Last Airbender* (2010). The source material, an animated show on Nickelodeon that ran from 2005 to 2008, featured many Asian characters and hired Asian American consultants for matters of representation. But the movie was set to have all white actors, except for some of the villains.[6]

In 2010, Bao Phi, a Vietnamese American poet, published an op-ed in the *Minneapolis Star Tribune* stating the principles of the nerds of color. He focused on the challenge of being a minority in a predominantly white subculture:

> And you'd think that fellow nerds, regardless of race and gender, would understand given that our status as freaks and geeks and outcasts would give us some humility and common ground to stand on. Unfortunately, this is not often the case. Try bringing up issues of race, class, gender, and homophobia on a video game message board and see the vitriolic response you get, no matter how diplomatic you try to be. Bring up issues of representation and race to fans of *Battlestar* and *Firefly* and get told that you're a killjoy or one of the "PC police" who doesn't understand what their favorite show is trying to do.[7]

Phi engaged in wishful thinking, mistaking fandom as racism-free, and ended up with reminders of the outsider status cast on him.

In 2012, the portmanteau *Blerd*, which described African Americans comfortable with geek culture, provided a label to describe nerdy Black activities that had existed long before—for example, Malcolm X's "horned-rimmed glasses and insistent intellectualism recall the earlier figure of the egghead."[8] The visibility of Barack Obama, Skip Gates, and Neil deGrasse Tyson led to recognition of some bookish, Black males, at least. But it was also a label Black nerds proudly applied to themselves, following the historical pattern of creating "spaces for ourselves where we are made visible, can commune, and celebrate our accomplishments."[9] Whether interested in comics, science fiction, STEM, gaming, or cosplay, Blerds care about representation, inclusion of their perspectives, and supporting one another. They acknowledge that their interests set them apart from conventional markers of cool Blackness like toughness, urbanity, and athleticism. The disparagement of their masculinity or femininity plays out in ways distinctive from how it does for white fans. Meanwhile, in predominantly white geek spaces, Blerd perspectives are denigrated, especially when they want to discuss racial matters. In fandom, some Black nerd figures became household names in the 2010s: actor–writer–comedian–rapper Donald Glover became a favorite for fans wishing to recast a Spider-Man movie. Keegan-Michael Key and Jordan Peele produced a sketch comedy show deploying characters from the margins of Black "cool." Ta-Nehisi Coates wrote commentary for *The Atlantic*, won the National Book Award for his 2015 autobiography *Between the World and Me*, and took the helm of Marvel's *Black Panther* comic book for a series. The blog *Very Smart Brothas*, the comedian W. Kamau Bell, and *The Daily Show* (1996–present) host Trevor Noah capitalized on their intellect to mix humor with social commentary. Discussions of the Blerd phenomenon often contrasted it with the television character Steve Urkel from *Family Matters* (1989–1998). But as Eric Deggans pointed out, no one wanted to be that "walking punchline."[10]

Omar Holman and William Evans, authors and founders of the blog *Black Nerd Problems*, argue that the qualifications for being a nerd are loving something and wanting to share it. To them, being a nerd had a negative connotation, à la the 1974 *National Lampoon* "Are You a Nurd?" poster (see fig. 3.1), *Revenge of the Nerds*, or the Triumph the Insult Comic Dog *Star Wars* sketch, but the mainstreaming of geek culture brought more kinds of people to the subculture. However, "If you're a Black or POC nerd, then you're in a subculture within a subculture (*Inception* shit)."[11] Holman and Evans observed that gatekeepers, who are now facing calls to share the scene, follow by saying that minority nerds did not measure up to their standards. The authors illustrated this argument with an analogy echoing Yoda's speech about the dark side of the Force from *The Phantom Menace*: "All this from a fear of a loss of identity. See how fear is the path to the dark side? Fear leads to anger. Anger leads to hate. Hate leads to ~~suffering~~ gatekeeping. Nerds gatekeeping other nerds to see if they're 'nerdy' enough for the nerdy club looks like Anakin Skywalker cuttin' down them Jedi younglings."[12] Elitism, elevating mastery of trivia, sexism, and racism hurt the scene. I argue that those standards are based on preserving white privilege, white representation, and white solipsism/narcissism. Fandom gatekeepers don't want to lessen the special value of their white identities by sharing *Star Wars* with others.

In 2014, Tumblr became the forefront for social media platforms for fandoms, and several accounts began giving fans of color a forum to discuss the prejudice they experienced in their avocations. *Fandoms Hate People of Color* launched in May 2014, discussing the representations of South Asian men in popular movies. *Fans of Color* followed in August, acknowledging the "ridiculous fandom racism" that made Tumblr a perilous space.[13] Focusing on a specific franchise, *MCU Fandom Hates People of Color* started in October. Its first post critiqued mainstream fan interpretation of the *Agents of S.H.I.E.L.D.* (2013– 2020) character Skye, played by the mixed, white and Asian actor Chloe Bennet: "Skye is played by Chloe Bennet a biracial WoC, the fandom pretends she's white and her being biracial doesn't matter to her character and they ship her with the main bad guy Grant Ward. In doing so they've ignored the fans of color who want to protect a young WoC in a central role in what is a canon abusive relationship, where Skye is constantly being manipulated by Grant Ward."[14] The tendency of the series' fans to consider Skye this way revealed the low regard they had for minority and queer characters. Dictating what relationships characters may or may not enter is a colorblind way to express this antipathy. Even though minority fans utilizing social media to build community came from different ethnicities and followed an array of franchises, their concerns were common: minority fans wanted affirmation of racial perspectives, freedom from microaggressions, and respite from intersections of race, class, and gender that make engagement with geek culture a site of racial labor. When the subject arose, they were supportive of interracial relationships.

Following the purchase of Marvel Entertainment for $4 billion in 2009 and Pixar Animation Studios for $7.4 billion, the Walt Disney Company acquired Lucasfilm from George Lucas for $4.05 billion, including all consumer products and merchandising in October 2012. Half of this amount was paid in cash, and the rest in forty million shares of stock. Kathleen Kennedy, formerly cochair of Lucasfilm, cofounder of Amblin Entertainment, and producer of eight films nominated for Best Picture Oscars, became its president. She would also lead Lucasfilm, Industrial Light and Magic, and Skywalker Sound.[15] She quickly established the Lucasfilm Story Group, which would coordinate the development of narratives across all media. Rather than preserving Lucas's canon, they worked to expand the notions of whom the galaxy included. In January 2013, the company announced that J. J. Abrams would be directing the first sequel film. Known for his successful big-screen reboots of *Mission: Impossible* (2006) and *Star Trek* (2009, 2013), as well as for his strong female television characters in *Felicity* (1998–2002), *Alias* (2001–2006), and *Fringe* (2008–2013), he also planned to make John Boyega one of the three main heroes in the new trilogy. Kennedy also made the executive staff more equitable; by the end of 2016, half of the company's vice presidents were women. Meanwhile, led by screenwriter and producer Kiri Hart, the Story Group grew to eleven members: five were people of color, and four were women.[16] Their gains included a quantifiable increase in dialogue spoken by women in the Disney-era movies, plus the newfound prominence of characters like Ahsoka Tano, who had begun as a child sidekick in the animated *Star Wars: The Clone Wars* (2008) movie, but who became a linchpin between eras of the saga, played by Rosario Dawson in two recent Disney+ live-action series, *The Mandalorian* (2019–present) and *Ahsoka* (2023–present). Their mission reflected conversations surrounding the entertainment industry, where "a self-conscious moral duty in matters of identity, of inclusion and representation," had become the norm.[17] While politics in the original trilogy offered analogues to Nixonism and the prequels commented on bureaucracy, politics in the new movies were cultural politics "bound up in the franchise itself and in commercial considerations."[18]

During the same years, retrograde positions wielded the internet against progressives, using tactics like personal attacks, pathologizing criticism, and the amplification of their positions. In fall 2014, it was suggested that Zoe Quinn, developer of the game *Depression Quest*, traded sex for publicity from *Kotaku* contributor Nathan Grayson, a friend of hers. It was untrue, but men in the gaming community used the allegations as a rallying call to hack Quinn's personal information, threaten her, and share her private photos. She was an early victim of this kind of treatment, but the men participating in this activity targeted more women in the industry, whether journalists, developers, or critics. They used the term *Gamergate* as a label for their cause, but its tenets remained vague. This was not the exposure of the wrongdoing of men in power (Watergate); nor the passing of cheap wine as genuine Bordeaux (Winegate); nor the uncovering of President Bill Clinton's sexual relations with White House intern Monica Lewinsky (Monicagate). The possibility of corruption was the supposed target of these men's actions, regardless of whether the corruption happened. It all seemed like noise, something that would blow over, rather than a groundswell. The ephemeral -*gate* suffix also added to this impression. Although no one explicitly codified the movement's aims, philosophy, and impetus, Gamergate's expressions of resentment within the gaming community were more organized than anyone had noticed. Its mobilization revealed how white supremacists, sexists, and extremists had been recruiting from online gaming communities for years.[19]

In hindsight, Gamergate was an indicator of a major political shift and was employed as a tool of the conservative apparatus. The term gained major traction when it was tweeted by the *Firefly* actor Adam Baldwin, along with a pair of videos repeating allegations against Quinn and Grayson. In September 2014, Breitbart, the news service run by future Trump adviser Steve Bannon, announced in a headline, "Feminist Bullies Tearing the Video Game Industry Apart."[20] Its author, the alt-right provocateur Milo Yiannopoulos, claimed he became sympathetic of the stereotypic "dorky loners" because "an army of sociopathic feminist programmers and campaigners, abetted by achingly politically correct American tech bloggers, are terrorising the entire community—lying, bullying and manipulating their way around the internet for profit and attention,"[21] even though bullying was not the modus operandi of women in the gaming industry. Deploying the movement's favorite catchall pejorative, "social justice warriors," Yiannopoulos addressed their tendency to "bang on about equality, respect and ethics all you like. But don't expect to be treated as an oracle when your personal behaviour is utterly reprehensible."[22]

In November 2014, Lucasfilm released a two-minute teaser trailer for *The Force Awakens*. Its opening shot featured John Boyega, whose inclusion in the cast had been announced along with the others in April, as a stormtrooper who has removed his helmet, panicked, perspiring in a desert landscape. A later shot showed him with Anakin and Luke Skywalker's ignited lightsaber, intimating a character arc that would take him from stormtrooper to Force wielder. Many fans uploaded reaction videos celebrating the release, some created fan art, and others recreated it with Lego bricks. But some viewers reacted negatively to his presence after the teaser trailer. For example, asserting that the movie "didn't need some black Jedi." Or announcing, "Dear Black People, We are forced to include you into everything awesome we do."[23] Or "Thank you Disney for ruining and destroying the much-loved series star wars,

Figure 6.2. Anti-Semitic image from 2014 asserting that the pairing of Daisy Ridley and John Boyega was part of a Jewish conspiracy. Credit: Kate Wilson.

by adding racial politics."[24] Or purveying slurs: "Great, they gave a n****r a lightsaber. Well, this movie is ruined."[25] Or "Multicultural, diverse Jewish filth," suggesting that setting up interracial intimacy was part of a degenerate cabal.[26] They also complained that his presence was not canon, invoking their narrow, conservative authority through the language of ruination and accusations of racial politics. Would Disney discourage some fans' weaponization of their knowledge as a sign of authenticity over other fans? Would it see this division as an impediment to their outreach to younger, more diverse fans? As the company released the sequel trilogy films, would it bow to the wishes of older, conservative fans? Would Lucasfilm react as if these responses to a Black male lead were a new phenomenon, even though they echoed both the responses to the prequel movies and the methods of Gamergate?

Boyega responded on Instagram, thanking fans for "all the love and support," the fan mail, and the fan art. He expressed his excitement over the upcoming movie as a fan, and added, "To whom it may concern . . . Get used to it."[27] Instead of engaging racists in a discussion they would likely aim to derail, he let them know his presence was their problem, not his. He indicated that increased diversity in the saga was here to stay. This was only the first in a series of incidents in which John Boyega had the constitution to fight back. Not that he was stronger than his colleagues, whom trolls also targeted, but he was the kind who could go toe-to-toe with them. But they are not going to sit down, talk, and come around. The adage "Don't feed the trolls" is not working. So, Boyega's example encouraged the rest of us.[28]

In October 2015, the final trailer was released, just two months before the movie's debut. Again, a portion of fans complained, this time calling for a boycott of *The Force Awakens*. On Twitter, they said things like "If white people aren't wanted in Star Wars, then our money must not be either." And "SJWs [social justice warriors] complain about White artists 'misappropriating' culture created by blacks but then celebrate a non-White Star Wars." Most notably they called the movie "PC anti-white diversity crap" and "anti-white propaganda promoting #whitegenocide."[29] Removed by decades from eugenicists like Lothrop Stoddard, yet connected by sentiment, these racist fans updated the 1920s language of white replacement and applied it to their beloved piece of popular culture. Knowing that overt statements of violence, exclusion, and racism meet with disapproval, the US alt-right prefers to evoke the "self-determination and self-preservation" that white nationalism inspires over the historical violence that white supremacy recalls.[30] This maneuver also casts veils of culture, heritage, and individual choice over the group racial identity they want to privilege. Yet, their aims are the same: whites on top with every advantage, and everyone else on bottom with nothing whites would prefer for themselves.

The list of things this generation's white nationalists oppose shows the connections to past generations' white supremacists, revealing a fixation on controlling the trends that lead to demographic diminution: immigration, women's reproductive freedom, multiculturalism, census enumeration, and minority voting rights. Although invoked less often, opposition to interracial marriage is one of their historically perennial tenets. After all, along with violence, exclusion, and miseducation, controlling interracial intimacy has been one of the prime ways to protect the white way of life. Past eugenics advocates and contemporary white nationalists have targeted racial mixing because it lowers the proportion of racially white children and potentially builds relationships between racial groups. As the popular white supremacist "Fourteen Words" slogan states, "We must secure the existence of our people and a future for white children."[31]

Contemporary so-called white nationalists add a new twist, believing their demographic diminution is part of a conspiracy enacting white genocide. Moreover, in using the term *genocide* to describe the process by which whites are becoming extinct, white nationalists imply that those who support integration, multiculturalism, and diversity are deliberately promoting this regulated change, not forces of natural selection. From their point of view, anything that expresses distasteful values can be part of a conspiracy, as demonstrated by the wide variety of things they call "white genocide," including the prospect of interracial intimacy as depicted in Cheerios ads and the pairing of Finn and Rey in the sequel trilogy. These twenty-first-century alt-right supporters broke out their Gamergate playbook, utilizing the media to broaden their views and denigrate the anti-racist message. It has been suggested that uncivil antiracists produced "bad people on both sides." This argument engages in bothsidesism, asking us to show sympathy for a group that is always predatory.[32]

The challenge for Lucasfilm, moreover, was how to satisfy the silent, casual fans who came from many backgrounds while appeasing the vocal, predominantly white fans. The former made up most of the ticket (and merchandise) buyers and were more likely to accept the galaxy far, far away's left-leaning politics. The latter had a conservative vision of what the saga was about, which they built on whiteness, masculinity, and assertions of authority grounded in knowledge of the *Star Wars* canon. They had proven themselves more likely to reject diverse casting, overtures to real-world politics, and interracial relationships, and some of them were very vocal about it.

I agree with Mel Stanfill's argument that "fans are more important to media industries than ever, and they are increasingly seen as a resource to be managed whenever possible," and I would like to add that the ideas, values, and beliefs of fans are also objects to these corporations that manage them.[33] However, while changing minds is one of the main occupations of media companies, they also know that effort is expensive, laborious, and not without pitfalls, so their efforts are often modest. Audience responses to on-screen diversity, LGBTQ+ representation, and interracial relationships have always been matters they have managed, but they have come up with a new tool for the post–civil rights era to help them: baiting, or promising progressive representations, but stopping short of significant change. It is possible that their confrontations with fan fiction editors like Linda Deneroff, Cynthia Levine, and Karen Osman led to the development of this strategy. Baiting keeps liberal fans hopeful enough to keep praising and happy enough to keep coming back for more. It also keeps conservative fans just angry enough to keep complaining and stubborn enough to keep consuming what they preferred beforehand. Stanfill continues, "I argue that power does not only repress; it also produces. This means that making something more possible, more normative, or more common sense is also a form of constraint—one that encourages that outcome."[34] In 2014, when it became known that Daisy Ridley and John Boyega would be the female and male leads in *The Force Awakens*, it seemed possible that the acceptance of interracial relationships was an outcome that Disney wanted to encourage. The company's intentions would become clearer on December 18, 2015.

The Force Awakens opens with Poe Dameron, a Resistance pilot played by Oscar Isaac, accepting part of a map to find Luke Skywalker, who went into hiding at some point after the events of *Return of the Jedi*. First Order stormtroopers, led by Kylo Ren (Adam Driver), arrive soon after, round up the Jakku villagers, and take Dameron hostage. John Boyega's character, known as FN-2187, is among these soldiers, but something keeps him from participating in the massacre. This crisis of conscience leads him to defect, spring Poe Dameron from his captivity, and steal a TIE fighter. With a new name, Finn, coined by Poe, he ends up returning to the desert planet, where he encounters Rey, a character whom the film offers as a clear counterpoint to Finn. He is a loner, captive to an institution; she is a loner, trapped by solitude. He was a child abductee who never knew his family; she was an orphan who did not know her full name. He experienced an intervention telling him to respect the lives of civilians; she had the insight to see the value in the runaway droid BB-8. As in *A New Hope*, the droid carries valuable data and keeps the characters on the go. Finn and Rey escape Jakku together, encounter Chewbacca and Han Solo, and employ the help of this former skeptic of the Force. Finn commits to the Resistance, flirts with Poe, and the data gets to the good guys. But Kylo Ren kidnaps Rey, the First Order unleashes its Starkiller weapon, and the heroes must destroy it.

Screenwriters Lawrence Kasdan, J. J. Abrams, and Michael Arndt left Rey's paternity an unresolved mystery. She could have been related to Obi-Wan Kenobi. She could have been the daughter of Luke Skywalker, or the daughter of Han and Leia, which would have provided a relationship with Kylo Ren, who we learn is Han and Leia's son and who seemed to know who she was. If she were Han's daughter, then his fatherly coaching of Finn in matters of romance would have a deeper resonance. As usual in the *Star Wars* galaxy, paternity is of more interest than maternity. The leading candidates for her parents are the male characters.

Leia had whiteness on three axes (moral, color, and racial), but Rey only possesses racial whiteness and (at this point in *The Force Awakens*) moral whiteness. This difference sets up Rey as a character who forms her own identity, rather than accepting the one presumed for her. By no means is she a Black feminist, but her development does resemble aspects of Patricia Hill Collins's four tenets of Black feminist epistemology. First, her knowledge is built "upon lived experience not upon an objectified position."[35] *The Force Awakens* begins with Rey as an underdog in a scavenger economy, rather than entitled royalty kidnapped by the Empire. Listening to Rey speak, she uses "dialog rather than adversarial debate," as Collins's epistemology describes.[36] Still, in the most notable scene about her "awakening," she experiences bewildering hallucinations upon touching Luke Skywalker's lightsaber. Even though many elements of these visions reprise moments longtime viewers recognized, their meaning was unclear to both Rey and Maz (a Force-sensitive humanoid to whom Han Solo brought Rey, played by the Black actor Lupita Nyong'o). In their conversation together, the two women do not dissect the matter in a masculinist, competitive way; instead, they both spoke from their perspectives. Third, as seen in her encounters, she acts with the "presence of empathy and compassion."[37] Whether protecting a stray droid in *The Force Awakens*, accepting a Wookiee's advice in *The Last Jedi*, or healing a serpent in *The Rise of Skywalker*, Rey uses her knowledge ethically, to help others, even those different from herself. Lastly, Rey feels personal accountability in her relationships and as an agent within the struggle between good and evil. Rather than behaving like truth can be objective, separate from the observer, and then put on a bookshelf, Rey's knowledge is built on the four tenets above.[38] Again, Rey is not a Black woman, but her actions resonate with intellectual frameworks often absent in mainstream feminism.

While Collins emphasizes safe spaces "where Black women speak freely," safety is an important theme for Rey, and it is often found in her relationships.[39] Except when seeking payment for her labors from Unkar Plutt or being kidnapped by Kylo Ren, her relationships in *The Force Awakens* were mostly of her own choosing, on her own terms. The most prominent of these safe relationships was with Finn, which tempered her independence, physical prowess, and agency with vulnerability. There are easily a dozen moments in *The Force Awakens* where Finn and Rey communicate deep concern for each other. One of the most notable occurs when Rey, who has just escaped Kylo Ren's torture chamber, runs across Finn, Han, and Chewbacca in the halls of the First

Order base. "We came back for you," Finn responds, and the two embrace. Many movies feature couples running from explosions, and a few show female protagonists being as equally capable as males, but almost none give the heroine time to thank her male counterpart. Blogger Holly Quinn notes how this behavior deviates from the parochial white feminist ideal: "When she learned that Finn went to such lengths to rescue her, as self-reliant as she was, she wasn't insulted. She was moved, deeply, that he wanted to save her. That—a moment of weakness by some standards—is something that will resonate with a lot of women who exist on the outside of the scope of feminism's more privileged ideals. (Myself included.)"[40]

It mattered that Rey was vulnerable with a Black man, because that showed her expansiveness, plus his worthiness. This endeared a swath of fans who had never witnessed this kind of relationship in the *Star Wars* galaxy. They were seeing it in other speculative (mostly sci-fi, but some fantasy and horror) movies and television shows. In the years leading up to *The Force Awakens*, nearly twenty prominent movies and television shows featured an interspecies relationship, science fiction's modus operandi for representing interracial relationships, including *Misfits* (2009–2013), *The Vampire Diaries* (2009–2017), and *Teen Wolf* (2011–2017). Some of the most notable on the big screen included *District 9* (2009), *Star Trek* (2009), *Avatar* (2009), *Let Me In* (2010), and *Guardians of the Galaxy* (2014). During those same years, half-human hybrids figured prominently in at least a dozen shows and movies: on television, *Merlin* (2008–2012), *Once upon a Time* (2011–2018), and *Falling Skies* (2011–2015); in the movies, again *Star Trek* and *Guardians of the Galaxy*. Human interracial relationships featured in six television series, including *Falling Skies*, *Terra Nova* (2011), *Beauty and the Beast* (2012–2016), and *The 100* (2014–2020). At the same time, there was a decrease in symbolic interracial intimacy, whether innuendo, experimentation, or transformation. It seemed no longer necessary to symbolize interracial relationships in the mass media. Science fiction was in a cluster of works self-consciously pushing norms, as in the late 1960s. Shows just as thoughtful and challenging as *Star Trek* and *Planet of the Apes* abound. These productions primed fans receptive to interracialism to see it in the galaxy far, far away as well.

But the explicit interracial intimacy cluster seemed to fade away around the end of the decade, following three influences. First, even if people didn't fully believe the nation reached a state of postraciality, they may have believed that Barack Obama's 2008 presidential victory had excused them from engaging with the subject of racial mixture from then on. Second, in the years after 2001, interracial intimacy was used in such unimaginative ways in major movies. By centering the conflict over who was born pure wizard in the *Harry Potter* movies (2001–2011), J. K. Rowling unabashedly echoed the eugenics movement of a century earlier without applying a critical lens to that racist belief, introducing kids to slurs like "mudblood" and "muggle." Meanwhile, the fourth installment, *Harry Potter and the Goblet of Fire* (2005), dashed the prospect of a relationship between Harry and Cho Chang, whose name sounds like playground slurs, the only prominent Asian in the series. The actor, Katie Leung, faced racism from fans for her work as a character who served as a placeholder until the white protagonist could commit romantically to another white character.[41]

The *Twilight* films (2008–2012) relied on a color-coding scheme resembling the threefold one in *Star Wars*: literal coloring, racial categorization, and morality that ran from black to white. However, I would add another dimension: sophistication. These became especially apparent when considering the protagonist Bella's suitors. Edward was colored white, racially white, and had an aversion to taking human life. As a vampire, he was the most cultured. Jacob had darker skin and hair and was racially American Indian. As a werewolf, he was more driven by impulses and appetites, including a hunger for human flesh. While the main question in *Star Wars* was whether humanity would survive weapons of mass destruction, in *Twilight*, it was which brand of masculinity Bella would choose. Fans congealed into two camps: Team Edward, which hoped she would choose the white, metrosexual vampire; and Team Jacob, which hoped she would choose the tawny, rugged werewolf.

In *Avatar*, Sam Worthington played Jake Sully, an adventurer who delved into Indigenous culture and, echoing many white savior stories, became more proficient at it than those born into it. Using technology created to promote cross-cultural exchange with the Na'vi, Sully's consciousness morphed into a new, nonhuman body. Director James Cameron's copping from familiar stories helped make the film a success, much like Lucas's did thirty years prior. *Avatar* repackaged the Pocahontas–John Smith narrative in an age when many knew that the source material was problematic.

Third, the emergence of the Marvel Cinematic Universe, which adapted story lines from Marvel comics for the big screen, eschewed interracial relationships entirely. Nonwhite actors like Don Cheadle,

Anthony Mackie, Tessa Thompson, Idris Elba, and Michael Peña played prominent roles, but they were all sidekicks to white male leaders. None of them had their own love interest, so their loyalty to the lead was their one true love. War Machine followed Iron Man, the Falcon served as booster to Captain America, Valkyrie and Heimdall supported Thor, and Luis the ex-con followed Ant-Man. The leaders, meanwhile, maintained a minority sidekick among their platonic relationships, plus a cis, hetero romance. Tony Stark loved Pepper Potts, Steve Rogers missed Peggy Carter, Thor pined for Jane Foster, and Scott Lang won over Hope van Dyne. From *Iron Man* (2008) to *Avengers: Endgame* (2019), the net result is a negligible amount of interracialism.

The Ships Awaken

The first ship to gain attraction after *The Force Awakens* debuted was Kylux, imagining a romance between the principal villain, Kylo Ren, and his counterpart in the military wing of the First Order, General Armitage Hux (played by the white Irish actor Domhnall Gleeson). On-screen, they are rivals, but fans imagined that romantic tension existed between them. Simply postulating is called a "crack ship," but interest in the possibility grew. Their reactions to each other indicated a backstory between them, their contradictory dispositions provided the potential for rich interactions, and their shared mistreatment by Supreme Leader Snoke opened a space for empathy toward them. Some fans constructed a relationship between Kylo Ren and Hux, even though *The Force Awakens* did not suggest that one existed between the characters. But this is part of the fun of shipping: fleshing out romances the canon is miserly toward, imagining that characters follow your own perspectives, and sizing up the odds that the official narratives will follow your vision. In any case, Kylux was a ship fans knew was highly unlikely to materialize in the coming movies; neither Disney nor Lucasfilm had offered any endorsement of the pairing. Kylux shippers supported it for the quartet of rewards all shippers gained from their hobby: community building, deeper engagement with the characters, affirmation of your perspectives, and potential gloating if your vision (or "headcanon") becomes official.

Overshadowing Kylux, though, was Stormpilot, a ship pairing John Boyega's Finn, the AWOL stormtrooper, with Oscar Isaac's Poe Dameron, the ace Resistance pilot. It grew from a great deal of evidence in the movie: Isaac and Boyega demonstrated great compatibility on-screen. The former's character gave the latter his new name, Finn, a significant step in his transformation into a free person. Finn ends up wearing Poe's leather jacket and, later, Poe praises him for how it looks. Observant moviegoers also noticed Isaac's lower lip bite during that exchange, which indicated sexual attraction the pilot had for the former stormtrooper. At 2014's San Diego Comic-Con, Isaac teased the possibility of Poe being gay, especially when he was deflecting questions that would reveal secrets about the plot.[42] On a December 17, 2015, segment on *The Ellen DeGeneres Show* (2003–2022), the two actors engaged in similar teasing, and Isaac explained, "I think it's very subtle romance that's happening. You have to watch it a few times to see the little hints. But there was—at least I was playing romance. In the cockpit, there was a very deep romance happening."[43] Boyega agreed, expressing interest in pursuing the Finn–Poe relationship. This ship did appear to have Disney/Lucasfilm support, making it more likely to come to fruition than Kylux.

We learn that Finn was abducted as a child to become a stormtrooper in the First Order. His is the only unmasked face we see, so it is inconclusive whether racial Blackness was a prerequisite for selection. We learn he had personal relationships with other stormtroopers, who now consider him a "traitor." We also learn that he never felt a bond as he had with Rey. Poe Dameron, on the other hand, lacks this volume of backstory by the end of the movie. We know that he is an excellent pilot who holds favor with General Leia Organa, but his background is a mystery. Unburdened with historical trauma, his fair appearance seemingly marks Poe as white, concealing Oscar Isaac's Latino background. However, the actor wished to make a connection between Poe's backstory and his own, arguing that the pilot was from Yavin, the planet featured in the final scenes of *A New Hope*. The filming location for those portions was in Guatemala, his home country.[44]

Finn and Poe's was an interracial relationship, resembling interracial romances in both the real world and other movies. When motion pictures through the 1960s paired white men with minorities, the relationships bestowed on the white man superiority over the other. Beginning in the 1970s, having learned that African American ticket buying could buoy the whole industry, mainstream movies paired white and Black male stars in more equal relationships, attracting diverse audiences. Nods toward integration joined traditional objectives in mainstream interracial buddy films like *Silver Streak* (1976), *Rocky III* (1982), and

Lethal Weapon (1987), which aimed to do the following: clear the nation's conscience about racial matters; argue that on-screen equality indicated real-life equality; suggest that American capitalism engenders tolerance; and confirm that all men can share in heterosexual male power. Toward those ends, the counterparts in interracial buddy films often interact like lovers in opposites-attract stories: their lives become intertwined, and their relationship becomes one of "comradeship, loyalty, and mutual vulnerability."[45] Finn and Poe do experience these feelings in *The Force Awakens*. However, unlike Melvin Burke Donalson's examples in *Masculinity in the Interracial Buddy Film*, they do not become "the story's center or a focused plot point in the film."[46] However, this was only the first part of a trilogy, so this humble start could flourish in the second and third movies.

At least a dozen internet outlets reported on the possibility of a relationship between the two characters, drawing from the excitement fans shared on Tumblr and Twitter. Not everyone participating in this slash ship was queer, but the attention did indicate mainstream acceptance of these alternative narratives. This gave some queer fans encouragement that the stories they imagined had become less marginal. It also brought attention to a fan activity that gave voices to many women. On the other hand, such an outsize degree of attention had come without journalists developing the skills to cover queer perspectives in fandom. As Angel Wilson wrote in *The Geekiary*, "The main issue with mainstream media's coverage of slash shipping is that, since we're so obscure and don't often leave our isolated communities, they don't quite know how to talk about it. Even worse, this can be an indicator that mainstream press just doesn't know how to talk about queer romance in general, even in regard to non-fandom inspired pairings."[47]

Such communities especially disliked the tendency of reporters to condescend, gawk, and delegitimize queer perspectives with slang like "bromance," a term commonly applied to a cluster of movies in the first decade of the twenty-first century that normalized homosocial love. This began with Peter Jackson's *Lord of the Rings* trilogy (2001–2004), which showcased the hobbit Samwise Gamgee's loyalty for Frodo Baggins as being just as essential to the saga as the warrior Aragorn's prowess. Often, bromance movies, which reflected Donalson's points, inhabited the comedy genre, where laughs could lighten the love men had for each other. *Shaun of the Dead* (2004) tempered the men's affection with both horror and comedy. *Superbad* (2007) couched it in adolescent negotiations of independence. Released after the subgenre had peaked,

I Love You, Man (2009) contrasted Paul Rudd's mild manners with Jason Segal's liberty. These movies placed male-on-male love subordinate to hetero love, shepherding immature characters on a path toward functional adulthood with a woman (of the same race, at that). Released the same year as the Disney purchase of Lucasfilm, *Django Unchained* (2012) gained notoriety for its distortion of history, its sexualization of the Black male body, and its spectacular revenge violence. But looking back, the relationship between Jamie Foxx's Django and Christoph Waltz's Dr. King Schultz shared elements with that of Finn and Poe: Schultz and Poe gave Django and Finn their freedom, dressed them, and set their respective Black men on their paths. In both pairings, the white guys are secondary, but their relationships are egalitarian.

Excitement for a relationship between Finn and Poe grew within the ranks of LGBTQ+ fans, mainstream writers, and nonqueer fans enjoying the on-screen chemistry. LGBTQ+ relationships had appeared in recent *Star Wars* comics, but not yet on the big screen. Although viewers could imagine same-sex relationships in Marvel, Pixar, and Disney films, *Star Wars* could be the first property to incorporate it on the big screen. Since these were characters introduced during an age of increased acceptance of gay relationships and without decades-long reputations to deconstruct, Stormpilot (or Finnpoe) seemed like more of a possibility than ever before. Shippers created art and fiction, most of which was wholesome and romantic. After *The Force Awakens*, they read for hints about the relationship's fruition in reports from Lucasfilm about its focus groups, in updates about the writing process for the next movie, and in interviews given by the stars. Stormpilot was a ship that enjoyed widespread support; even with its queer focus, it did not become the target of a retaliation campaign. But could support for a relationship between a Black man and a white-presenting Latino have thrived because many shippers were willing to support anything but a Black man and a white woman?[48]

By March 2016, many of the top stories on FanFiction.net and Wattpad.com based on *The Force Awakens* paired Rey and Kylo Ren, showing that this ship had surpassed Finnpoe. Four of the top ten most-viewed *Star Wars* stories on Archive of Our Own, the nonprofit open-source repository for fan fiction and other fan works contributed by users founded in 2008, also paired Rey and Kylo Ren. It became the most popular heterosexual ship of the sequel era by far.[49] The "opposites attract" convention in romantic storytelling was a principal reason fans put these two together. The characters had different dispositions and political leanings. Rey was the hero, sworn to protect life, and Kylo Ren was the villain who had murdered people, but fans thought they could make a good couple, probably through her redemption of him. However, more than Count Dracula's targeting Mina in *Dracula* (1931), which involved turning her into an undead bloodsucker; more than *Some Like It Hot* (1959), which featured a male lead (Joe) regretting a long-running deception; more than Claire's infatuation with Bender in *The Breakfast Club* (1985), which was an adolescent crush unlikely to outlast the school year; and even more than Elizabeth Bennet's gradual appreciation of Mr. Darcy's qualities, which were revealed by her visit to Pemberley in *Pride and Prejudice* (1995), Kylo Ren was a murderer who psychically and physically molested three people in the movie, including Rey herself. This goes beyond opposites attract, toward absolving a predator, especially when he is a man of authority.

Reylo shippers point to the tension between the characters as a reason to imagine a romance between them, even though this "tension" is often his abuse and her escaping that abuse. They are misreading his predatory actions as innocuous and her abhorrence of his actions as coy. This is like telling girls mean boys like them.[50] They also argue "that Rey and Kylo are simply the most fascinating people on screen."[51] Surely, they are the principal protagonist and antagonist, but saying they should be a couple because they align with the moral poles of the story, and that everyone in the middle is unworthy, is reductive. Likewise, assuming they are the most interesting is a matter of opinion that lines up with presumptions that the white characters are the main characters. As comedian–actor Aziz Ansari has suggested, "When you look at posters for movies or TV shows, see if it makes sense to switch the title to 'What's Gonna Happen to This White Guy?' (*Forrest Gump*, *The Martian*, *Black Mass*) or if there's a woman in the poster, too, 'Are These White People Gonna Have Sex With Each Other?' (*Casablanca*, *When Harry Met Sally*, *The Notebook*)."[52] All of these rationales made shipping Reylo sound nonracial, but they conceal a deeper racism. *The Force Awakens* as a *Star Wars* story does not need Rey and Kylo Ren to become a couple. In fact, movies and television shows overwhelmingly avoid pairing women with their rapists. Dracula can hypnotize a woman, Joe can dress as a woman, Bender can condescend to a woman, and Mr. Darcy can be aloof, and all can end up with the woman. But physical abuse is a dealbreaker. The motivation for supporting Reylo must have been rooted in something even deeper than mere romance: the protection of white racial purity, which works hand in hand with conventional futurity. Through the sequel trilogy, Reylo supporters showed that their distaste over the villain's behavior paled in comparison to three likely outcomes of a Rey–Kylo romance: the galaxy would return to a state of functional capitalism, where corporations produce and sell fantastic goods (including weapons) without squabbling; the prodigal son would return to lawfulness, likely to lead the Jedi Knights ("the guardians of peace and justice in the old Republic," in the words of Obi-Wan in *A New Hope*); and most importantly, Rey and Kylo Ren would create a heteronormative family with children who would be the next generation of Force users. Reflecting the fear of replacement that vexed white people from the 1990s onward, the racial whiteness of the couple and their children was a priority for these fans. After all, it takes a lot of critical thinking about capitalism, law, race, and sex to break from these three outcomes. In *Star Wars* fan activities, as in real-world, US politics, why would white fans bother?

In November 2014, fans on Tumblr (exclusively small players) began posting about Finnrey. For example, a "prayer circle" about the movie voiced hopes for "an interracial love story in *Star Wars* because I think that would be cool."[53] A high level of emotional investment, expressed in terms of communal faith, was evident over a year before the movie's release. Finnrey fan art also began in November, including Phil Noto's unofficial poster, which showcased Finn as a former stormtrooper and Rey as a scavenger, with Kylo Ren's lightsaber separating them. Fan artists showed they could produce images with a quick turnaround based on whatever the teaser trailer offered them.[54] Tumblrs dedicated to supporting Finnrey began appearing in October 2015 with the final trailer, posting images of Finn and Rey individually or Boyega and Ridley together doing press for the film. Fan art for Finnrey conveyed the qualities of relationships the creators valued. Fans reblogged works because they also found those qualities attractive. For Finnrey, this was joy, gentleness, camaraderie, and affection, whereas Reylo art often communicated turmoil and conflict. Take, for example, the user lorna-ka's "Because They're Adorable," which imbued an exchange Finn and Rey had about taking each other's hand with the chaste vulnerability of new, mutual attraction.[55] The user renisanz's widely reblogged portrait of Finn and Rey showed them forehead to forehead, about to kiss before her departure to recruit Luke Skywalker.[56] Overall, Tumblrs dedicated to Finnrey expressed what they held as priorities in relationships and their appreciation for the new movie. Even more, they promoted the qualities they valued in society.[57]

Finn and Rey's introduction resembled every other film where the male and female leads meet, run around, escape, and express their fondness for each other. Except for the few movies that upend the boy meets girl story, there is no movie in which two characters of the same race go through what they go through and do not become a couple. Their affection for each other was a major component of the movie, making it easy to substantiate from the source material. The chemistry between Boyega and Ridley added to the ship's plausibility. The actors called each other "peanuts," looked quite photogenic, and obviously enjoyed each other's company. Social media produced chatter about them. Essayists on websites like *Den of Geek*, *io9*, *SYFY Wire*, *Screen Rant*, and *Nerdist* drummed up conversation about them. If the new *Star Trek* movies, the Marvel Cinematic Universe, and *The Good Place* (2016–2020) could showcase interracial relationships, *Star Wars* certainly could too. Hand in hand with assembling a more diverse cast, Lucasfilm was doing things differently without George Lucas, yet maintaining the *Star Wars* formula. The sequels could address themes of the original trilogy—for example, that Kylo Ren does not understand the meaning of the story of Darth Vader. The sequels could address themes from the prequels—for example, that forbidding romantic love causes suffering. More so, the sequels could acknowledge that marriages among couples of different races or ethnicities had increased from about 8 percent in 2000 to 10 percent in 2010.[58]

The anti-miscegenation laws of the early twentieth century resulted in the regulation of nonwhite sexual and marital practices, compelling African Americans, Asians, and Indians to white standards, even though segregation kept them far from the realms of white people. Respectability, uprightness, and moderation became "proof of their capacity to be equal."[59] Through respectability politics, minorities participated in this standard, sometimes referring to the laws' reach when warning against interracial marriage. By the 1990s, popular culture joined social policy and multiracial activists to establish "the legitimization of multiracial families, the primacy of (white) maternal love for multiracial children, and suburbanization as the racially normalized condition of family development."[60] These three became major components of the movement to place a multiracial identifier on the US Census. As Habiba Ibrahim argues, "The multiracial movement's ostensible structure of time—a version of temporality that accounted for the legitimacy of interracial couples and subsequent multiracial progeny—is that of the heteronormative family."[61] By corralling Finn and Rey into respectable sexual practices and family values, Finnrey shippers reveal that traditional family values can be the foundation of the hopes placed in their relationship. Following Spock's idealistic parents in *Star Trek*, Athena and Helo in *Battlestar Galactica*, and Neo's unseen interracial parents in the *Matrix* movies, could Finn and Rey become a couple, and then a family? Would they produce mixed offspring who would save the galaxy, right the wrongs of past generations, and bring balance to the Force? If so, their temporality would follow "the straight and narrow paths toward the future laid out for the reproductive family, the law-abiding citizen, the believer in markets."[62] Since these are the same tendencies of any monogamous relationship, what is the difference between Finnrey and Reylo? As the new trilogy unfolded, fans would answer this question, in both their commentary about the movies and how they regarded one another.

One pair of fans celebrating Finn and Rey were picked up by the big players, broadcasting their interracial relationship across various outlets. Victor Sine and Julianne Payne, an engaged interracial couple, were first spotted the last weekend in March 2016. *Entertainment Weekly* reposted tweeted snapshots of them at the FanX Salt Lake comic convention with the caption "The force is strong with this couple."[63] Then *BuzzFeed* followed up with the couple, describing a photo shoot they did with a local photographer, possibly for their engagement photos. As Victor explained, they "fell in love with the franchise," watching the movies in a marathon before *The Force Awakens*. "We also immediately decided that we'd cosplay Finn and Rey."[64] Later interviewed for StarWars.com, they explained how much they identified with Finn and Rey. Victor described Julianne as "feisty" and "protective" of her daughter, Addie: "Over time, we have built a beautiful and trusting relationship; one that we also hope to see grow between Finn, Rey, and BB-8. At first, Rey was the only caretaker to BB-8, but then Finn came into the picture and took on that role as well."[65] Along with drawing parallels between the *Star Wars* characters' relationship and their own, he also connected their hopes for the characters and his hopes for their own lives. As the official *Star Wars* website described, "Seeing Finn and Rey on screen together meant the world to them."[66] This feature article indicated endorsement from Lucasfilm. Their photoshoot was featured by *Cosmopolitan*, *ABC News*, *Kotaku*, *BuzzFeed*, *Good Morning America*, *PetaPixel*, *Daily Mail*, *Yahoo!*, *Fashionably Geek*, *DigitalRev*, and *Laughing Squid*. They later got married, giving a happy ending that conformed to society's hetero norms, validating their relationship, and

Figure 6.3. One of the photos from Victor Sine and Julianne Payne's cosplay photo shoot that went viral in March 2016. Credit: R. Lance Montgomery.

contributing to the belief that more interracial marriage is a sign of racial progress. Imagining Rey and Finn producing children invokes a heteronormative futurity that risks fetishizing an imagined, mixed future with no memory of how it got there. Dreaming away our distaste for "public and personal logics" instead of "attending to what exactly produced them" will lead to the loss of "potentials" that may point us to real solutions to inequality.[67]

In 2015, Tumblr was an active forum for shipping. According to Holly Quinn's observations, Reylo fans undertook three strategies that revealed anti-Black sentiments. First, they created fan art that converted Kylo Ren's torture of Rey into something like a romance novel cover, with Adam Driver as the gallant prince and Daisy Ridley as the pliant damsel. Or they transformed his carrying her away on his spacecraft, unconscious, into a newlywed bridal carry. Second, if the potential for romance existed between a white character and a Black one, like Finnrey, they would find a white alternative that would involve selective rejection of the canon text like *The Force Awakens* script, the movie's novelization, or Lucasfilm-approved comics. Then they would claim that their rewrite of canon made more sense. Reylo fans discredited Finn however they could. Taking her hand was a violation, even though she took his hand a moment later. As an AWOL stormtrooper, he was cowardly and deceptive. They claimed that Rey "friendzoned" Finn, even though they had called such terminology sexist.[68] Rather than violent, entitled, and demeaning, as he had been on-screen, Kylo Ren was depicted as vulnerable, gentle, and gallant. The term *Reylo* expanded from its general definition to include white women fans who attacked fans different from themselves, fans with differing opinions, and even the stars. Later, in August 2017, Reylos would discipline Boyega for dancing at the Notting Hill Carnival, an annual celebration of Caribbean culture, suggesting that his character, Finn, was not worthy of Rey because of it.[69]

As with *The Phantom Menace* backlash and Gamergate, rabid fans attacked critical thinking, especially when anti-racist fans spoke up. Fans of John Boyega's character, especially Black women, withdrew from fan activities on sites like Tumblr. As Holly Quinn describes, "If you didn't leave, and I didn't, it would get nastier and nastier. It would get personal (we were fair game; talking about observed racist patterns was deemed a personal attack on all Reylos). There were smear campaigns. If you defended yourself, they'd sneer that they couldn't wait for you to delete your blog."[70]

The stars became targets too. Daisy Ridley quit social media altogether in August 2016. In March, just a few months prior, she had a misstep, accidentally revealing a user's name in an Instagram post about body-shaming. Her fans barraged that user with messages, and Ridley apologized. In June, she shared her experiences with endometriosis on Instagram, encouraging other women to seek help. In August, she expressed sadness after seeing a memorial for victims of gun violence at the Teen Choice Awards and received a surprising amount of backlash. Some of the comments were pointed at fellow commenters, but others attacked Ridley personally: "Says the woman who kills people with guns in movies. Such hypocrisy in Hollywood. Just shut up, Ridley, and make another Star Wars movie."[71] She had approached social media to be in touch with fans, share her feelings, and make statements on issues, but found the personal attacks too much. Later, she shared, "I don't really think bad vibes should have the sun shone on them." She added, "Like, I don't want to read your thing!"[72]

Tumblr user starwarsfandomh8speopleofcolor followed in December 2016, shortly before the debut of *Rogue One*, the first *Star Wars* spin-off. The Tumblr's third post drew attention to a trend developing on the Archive of Our Own fan fiction clearinghouse: a ship between the white male villain (Director Orson Krennic) and the white female hero (Jyn Erso), who clearly had a predatory relationship in the trailers, was already as popular as the ship between her and a Latino hero (Cassian Andor), who clearly had a mutual relationship.[73]

The hate fueling attacks on John Boyega, Daisy Ridley, and Kelly Marie Tran (see chapter 7) was already there. It is the same hate that fueled attacks on Ahmed Best, excessive CGI, and the abundance of nonhumans in the prequel trilogy (see chapter 5). Later, primed to believe the claims of Gamergate and targeted to support Donald Trump's presidential campaign, this is the same demographic that wanted to Make *Star Wars* Great Again, returning to nondigital effects, revering the original trilogy canon, and preferring its homogeneous casting. Their hate culminated in his election in 2016. The "bad apples" argument abounds in explanations of what happened, but the problem was much bigger than the stereotype of Trump supporters. His candidacy was cast as a "working-class" rebellion against Republican elites. The truth: Trump voters' median household income in May 2016 was $72,000, $10,000 higher than Hillary Clinton and Bernie Sanders supporters.[74] Similarly, journalists wrote that Trump won because of working-class white men. The truth: "After looking at the data from the election last night and talking with a number of social psychologists and political scientists," Jay Van Bavel, professor of psychology and neural science at New York University, concluded, "I think the key driver in this election was white identity."[75] Across age, gender, educational level, and income, all kinds of white voters preferred Trump to Clinton. The real problem was racist white people, and the 2016 election revealed just how many there were.

I firmly reject the "bad apples" argument that points to a hypervocal minority, primarily because these supposed bad apples rear their heads at every move. They must be a movement; they cannot be ignored. Second, these supposed bad apples are so bad as to make death threats against actors in a movie. Third, these supposed bad apples reflect long-standing currents in our society—misogyny, racism, xenophobia, gun violence, narrow conceptions of family—just expressed in ways the social media makes available. The problem is deeper than a difference of opinion (Coke or Pepsi, Pearl Jam or Nirvana, iPhone or Galaxy). It extends beyond toxic fandom to include toxicity in society. This is the same hate that has been with us since the beginning.

CHAPTER 7

Social Media, Fans, and Interracial Relationships (2015–2020)

Introduction

In September 2015, the reality show *Project Greenlight* (2001–2015) returned to HBO for its fourth season. Produced by the actors Matt Damon and Ben Affleck along with film producers Sean Bailey and Chris Moore (who were also white), its premise was to gather and choose up-and-coming filmmakers, offering the winner the opportunity to film a fully funded feature film with a budget of $3 million plus broadcasting on HBO. The screenplay, which had already been chosen, featured as lead characters a Black female sex worker and a white leading man. In the season opener, Affleck, Damon, and other producers began narrowing the candidates from twenty to one. The producer Effie Brown (*Dear White People*, 2014), a Black American woman, advocated for a directing team comprising a Vietnamese man and a white woman, who she believed would treat the characters the best. As the conversation addressed matters of inclusion and representation, Damon interrupted Brown and said, "You do it in the casting of the film, not in the casting of the show." In other words, in front of the camera with the actors, not behind it with the executives, thus absolving the *Project Greenlight* team of weighing in on the issue. Damon invoked merit, a framing essential to derailing discussions of difference and inequality in the post–civil rights era. The thing is, Damon had recently said that merit alone was not the deciding factor in choosing a winner.

Astounded, Brown gasped in response to his statement and said, "Whew, wow, OK. I'm not mad, but hang on."[1] As a Black woman, she had to retreat and present herself as nonthreatening, even though she was a proven colleague. This is a signature experience of underrepresented people in professional settings. The expectation that we adjust to the workplace culture clashes with the responsibility we feel to challenge inequality unnoticed by others, even when our job description compels us to do so. "It is Brown who must tell her colleagues that she is not angry," reaffirm "the love in her heart," and avoid making her white colleagues feel uncomfortable for the ways they are enacting their whiteness.[2] *Project Greenlight* brought in Brown to help with the show's record on diversity, but hers was an uphill battle against the industry status quo. Presenting a competition played out in front of cameras, *Project Greenlight* was like a game. However, it operated within the Hollywood establishment, affected people's careers, and produced a film that entered the marketplace. Finding just one talented finalist who could treat race and gender with sensitivity revealed the industry biases espoused even by professed liberals like Matt Damon.[3]

Having surveyed the two hundred top theatrical releases from 2015 and 1,206 television shows from the 2014–2015 season, the fourth annual Hollywood Diversity Report from the Ralph J. Bunche Center for African American Studies at UCLA concluded that minorities had made gains in five employment arenas: film leads, broadcast scripted leads, broadcast reality and other leads, digital scripted leads, and broadcast scripted show creators. However, they lagged in four categories: film directors, film writers, cable scripted leads, and digital scripted show creators. Minorities also "remain underrepresented in Academy Award and Emmy recipients, and woefully underrepresented on the rosters of the three dominant talent agencies," resulting in a status quo in the dealmaking side of the industry.[4] At the same time, minorities drove ticket sales. Increasingly diverse demographics in the United States led to increased revenue for movies and shows with diverse casts. The most successful movies that year had the most diverse casts. These movies also profited globally, gaining the highest median global box office receipts and the highest median return on investment. In 2015, minorities accounted for most of the ticket sales for five of the top ten films in terms of global box office revenue. In 2015, *The Force Awakens* had the third-highest rate of return (7.44 percent) and the seventh-highest audience minority share of all major motion pictures.[5] Minorities powered the film's success, largely because of the presence of John Boyega and Lupita Nyong'o, hopes for a more inclusive galaxy far, far away, and minorities' acceptance of the new characters' relationships.

Both the debate presented in *Project Greenlight* and the choice facing Lucasfilm between pleasing the old retrograde money or the new diverse money pointed to the importance of decision-makers in bringing underrepresented stories to the big screen. This is the group that makes thoughtful inclusion happen, whether in the boardrooms, in front of the cameras, or within the narratives the audiences see.

Between May 2015 and September 2017, however, leadership on Lucasfilm projects was often in flux. The director and writer Josh Trank quit the untitled Boba Fett television project in May 2015. Later, he revealed, "I quit because I knew I was going to be fired if I didn't quit," alluding to a lack of faith from Lucasfilm and cold feet over his *Fantastic Four* (2015), which neither fans nor critics received well.[6] In August 2015, Colin Trevorrow was announced as the director of the finale of the sequel trilogy, largely because of his success with *Jurassic World* (2015) that summer. He began working on a screenplay with his writing partner, Derek Connolly. In June 2016, Tony Gilroy was brought on to fix the first *Star Wars* Anthology Series movie, *Rogue One*, which had gone adrift under the direction of Gareth Edwards, who had success with the 2014 *Godzilla* remake. Gilroy, who had written four *Bourne* movies (2002–2012) and directed *Michael Clayton* (2007), brought a proven track record to the project. In June 2017, Phil Lord and Christopher Miller were fired from the second *Star Wars* Anthology movie, *Solo*. They had established a humorous style with *The Lego Movie* (2014) and *21 Jump Street* (2012), which they were likely trying to inject into the movie, leading Kathleen Kennedy to announce, "It's become clear that we had different creative visions on this film, and we've decided to part ways."[7] But later it was revealed that they lacked the resilience, efficiency, or confidence needed to helm the project. Veteran director Ron Howard (*Apollo 13*, 1995; *A Beautiful Mind*, 2001; *Rush*, 2013) was hired to finish the movie—released in 2018 under the title *Solo: A Star Wars Story*—which became the least successful *Star Wars* movie ever.[8]

Trevorrow's own movie *The Book of Henry* also came out during the same month Lord and Miller were excused, performing badly with critics and box offices. After that disappointment, he was fired from the third sequel film in September. He had already gone through two rounds of writing, which Lucasfilm had liked at first. But then Disney announced, "Lucasfilm and Colin Trevorrow have mutually chosen to part ways on *Star Wars: Episode IX*."[9] Later, Trevorrow revealed how dismissive Lucasfilm was of his and Derek Connolly's iterations of the script. Lucasfilm approached a few directors and ended up hiring *The Force Awakens* director and cowriter J. J. Abrams to direct and write the installment, which was slated to debut twenty-seven months later. Moviegoers take it for granted that a hired director will stay with the project through completion. If they do not make headlines, then clashes over vision must have been negligible. In the cases where producers hire a director, rather than an independent director seeking producers, keeping that director indicates that they made a good choice in the first place. During this twenty-eight-month period, Lucasfilm lost directors on three *Star Wars* film projects. On the other film, Gareth Edwards received credit, but Tony Gilroy was brought in to complete it.[10]

The Last Jedi

As announced in 2014, the director for the second film in the sequel trilogy would be Rian Johnson, who had success with the teen noir mystery *Brick* (2005) and the time-travel thriller *Looper* (2012). With J. J. Abrams's consent, Johnson scrapped the *Episode VIII* draft that Abrams had written before his own filming of *The Force Awakens* had started. Sharing notes, drafts, and dailies, they worked together to craft the transition between the two movies. Johnson worked independently, with little input, while *The Force Awakens* was in production. As he described it, "No, [Abrams] was really gracious, in just stepping back and giving us a blank slate to work with. The starting point was *The Force Awakens* script, which is quite a big, expansive, wonderful starting point. In that way, we are drawing directly from his work. But from that point forward it was a blank canvas."[11] Lucasfilm approved this shift, even though it obliterated Abrams's plan. Johnson depicted himself as a collaborator, Abrams as personally disinterested, and Lucasfilm as laissez-faire during the same years that the Marvel Cinematic Universe was showing the (monetary, critical, and merchandising) benefits of having a master plan. Most important of all, Johnson chose not to pursue the questions *The Force Awakens* posed: Who was Rey? Who were her parents? Where did the First Order come from? Would Supreme Leader Snoke be a fearsome opponent? Was Finn Force sensitive? These evasions not only confounded expectations, but also left a big pile of Chekhov's guns.[12]

The Last Jedi was a critical and box office success. Many reviewers writing for the big players noticed that the movie was about toxic masculinity, whether the insubordination of Poe Dameron, the verbal abuse of Snoke, the matricidal fits of Kylo Ren, or the narcissistic resignation of Luke Skywalker. Some delighted at the takedown: Poe Dameron learns a lesson after his insubordination to female commanders, Supreme Leader Snoke shames Kylo Ren in front of others, and Kylo Ren attempts to make Rey dependent on him. Luke Skywalker runs away after defeat, refusing to help the Resistance. But after visits by Rey, Chewbacca, R2-D2, and a spirit Yoda, who reminds him to use his mistakes as a teaching tool, he reestablishes his connection with the Force. The original trilogy provided an analogy against militarism, and the prequel trilogy might have held a mirror to corruption, but *The Last Jedi* showcased the shortcomings of white chauvinism. Noting the parallels between gender relations in our society and in the galaxy far, far away, reviewers wondered if "*Star Wars: The Last Jedi* was intended to be a comment, or a cautionary tale as it were, about toxic masculinity and women fighting to subdue it."[13] *Wired*'s review made direct connections between contemporary politics, toxic fans, and the movie's messages: "In themes and plot, *The Last Jedi* asserts again and again that monolithic dominance isn't good for anyone. The movie isn't here to Make the Galaxy Great Again. It's [here] to tell the stories of the people who want to actually fix it."[14] Talking with documentary filmmaker and psychologist Annalise Ophelian, *The Guardian* claimed, "This film gives us women working side by side, women in technical positions, and of course women learning the ways of the Force."[15] Marketing of the movie had emphasized the female and diverse roles, and opening night statistics showed a 10 percent increase in female attendees over the debut of *The Force Awakens*.[16]

Smaller players also noticed the movie's critique of toxic masculinity. The *Los Angeles Review of Books* wrote, "Thus, by connecting female representation to values that challenge and transform toxic masculinity, *The Last Jedi* attempts to supplant the franchise's traditions of hero worship and redemptive violence with compassion, individual agency, and—startlingly, in a few brief moments—strategies of nonviolence."[17] Celebrating the movie's willingness to smash "patriarchal white supremacy," the blog *Bitter Gertrude* described Kylo Ren as "an unstable young white man who had every privilege in life, yet feels like the world has wronged him. Unbeknownst to his family, he finds and communicates with a faraway mentor who radicalizes him with a horrific, authoritarian ideology."[18] The blogger notes that Luke sacrifices himself in a way similar to female characters like Charlotte in the 1952 children's book *Charlotte's Web* and Eleven in *Stranger Things* (2016–present).

Distaste for Luke's death was a big sticking point. At moments, *The Last Jedi* hinted, "This is not going to go the way you think," and, "Let the past die. Kill it if you have to," warnings that the film would question the tropes of the galaxy far, far away. Luke's reunification with the Force should not have been a surprise. Instead of embracing his long-lost lightsaber and joining the Resistance, he is hurt, wounded, and fragile. He has disconnected himself from the Force, yet he dresses in robes, preserves himself, and protects the ancient Jedi texts. These books symbolize how Luke behaves like truth can be objective, separate from the observer, and then put on a bookshelf. Again, reflecting the ideas of Patricia Hill Collins, Rey's knowledge is built on a "preexisting knowledge system" established by the four tenets discussed in chapter 6.[19] Consistently, Rey acts for the common good, often more readily than Luke Skywalker does, especially in *The Last Jedi*. The recluse has rationalized his own retreat from the galaxy's affairs by divorcing knowledge from practice. The movie disposed of Luke Skywalker, who was the old-timers' knight, proxy, and everyman, and compelled them to witness the adventures of the new kind of paladin.

Some critics, mainly men, gave the movie half-star reviews on platforms like Rotten Tomatoes, decrying its political agenda. "I'm all for taking female characters to center stage," wrote one commenter, "but they did it at the expense of the male characters. The men were weak, cowardly, and impulsive. The women were strong, independent leaders. . . . Again I'm all for having strong female leads, but not like this."[20] Rotten Tomatoes and Metacritic reported a critical average in the low 90s and mid-80s, but audience scores in the 50s and 40s, respectively. IMDb's audience score was in the high 60s, higher than the other two, but much lower than the critics' average. This indicated a distaste for what some viewers perceived as compulsory feminism.[21]

One men's rights fan used pirated and downloaded footage of the movie and created a defeminized fan edit. Removing all appearances of women being aggressive, brave, or authoritative, the "Chauvinist Cut" reduced the movie to just forty-six minutes. As one item from the creator's release notes describes, "Asian chick speaks less, doesn't bully Finn, Finn doesn't try to escape, she is never formally introduced. She is just there and occasionally smiles at Finn or screams 'Finn!' She has no sister. Serves her right for all the heinous stuff she did." The end result is "awful."[22] On the other hand, editors have made clips with every word spoken by women or people of color in *Star Wars* and other franchises. The chauvinist editor imitated the methods of marginal groups making statements about the lack of representation.[23]

In publicity for the film, Finn was made smaller, or excluded altogether. In the realm of action figures, he had fewer versions in Hasbro's Black Series line than he did for *The Force Awakens*. Leading up to *The Last Jedi*, fans watchful of representations began to ask #whereisfinn. Noticing that Finn, one of the big three characters, was appearing less, some also asked #whereisrose, sensing that the Resistance fighter Rose Tico (played by the Vietnamese American actor Kelly Marie Tran) would be even less central and more marginal.[24] Johnson built a connection between Rey and Kylo Ren but chose not to build the relationship with Finn. Some viewers noted how often Finn appeared for comic relief in *The Last Jedi*, getting tased (twice!) or walking around in his hospital bedding. In the comics, he was often depicted as humorous, rather than heroic. The comedy did not befit the major hero. (In the original trilogy, that stuff happened to C-3PO, not Luke, Han, or Leia!) Rose and Poe spoke down to him, making light of his suffering as a person. Meanwhile, in *The Last Jedi*, Kylo Ren was given much more sympathy. This happened through close-ups, a more serious tone, and the healing of his wounds—even though he collected those through his villainy in *The Force Awakens*, not heroism like Finn did.[25]

Most of all, Rian Johnson's film sidelined Finn by putting him in a secondary plot (almost in the same way Darth Vader is no longer a sexual threat to Leia when Obi-Wan arrives on the Death Star). Leaving the Resistance fleet to protect Rey is a voluntary mission that he takes on. However, while attempting to protect Rey from the First Order's pursuit of their fleeing vessels does refer to their relationship, it is a subplot akin to a video game side quest that doesn't affect overall gameplay. In contrast, I offer the secondary plot in *Empire Strikes Back*, in which Han, Leia, C-3PO, and Chewbacca separate from Luke and even the Rebel Alliance fleet. They fly straight into an asteroid belt to avoid the Imperials, and then to Cloud City, straight into a trap set to capture the main character, Luke. Han and Leia kiss, solidifying their love story; Han is frozen in carbonite, necessitating a sequel; and Luke runs to save them, leading to his famous confrontation with Darth Vader. In *The Last Jedi*, Finn and Rose go to another city, Canto Bight, to find a hacker who can help the Resistance. This subplot sheds some light on the in-universe society at large but does not develop the characters or bring them together. Essentially, they go on their side mission, Rose says some inspirational stuff, and then they return. It seems unclear just what significance the side quest had for the two characters.

But this conclusion overlooks both Rose Tico's resonance with real-world Asian women's experiences, and the ways Rian Johnson stopped short of developing that connection. According to her dialogue, Rose and her sister, Paige, came from Hayes Minor, a mining colony: "The First Order stripped our ore to finance their military, then shelled us to test their weapons." Although Kelly Marie Tran is of Vietnamese descent, Rose's brief backstory excludes the military engagement usually associated with that country. Instead, the Tico family's experience on Hayes Minor recalls the Marshall Islands, which was the site of US nuclear testing; or Okinawa, which the United States occupies and has used to store nuclear weapons; or Guam, another site of weapons testing that has been called the "tip of the spear" poised against China and North Korea.[26]

To cast a Vietnamese American actor in this role draws attention to the militarism in her world, as in ours. I also argue that her naming weapons dealing as the "one business in the galaxy that'll get you this rich" draws attention to how this is true in the real world too. Flashing iconic spaceships during this exchange hints that our hunger for fictional war reflects our real-world militarism. Second, like the incorporation of Boyega's African background and the nod to Isaac's from Latin America, Rose Tico's accentuates Tran's experience. These are minority actors with histories, and so are their characters. Rose would have to emphasize some memories but set aside others to build coalitions, just as Americans from different Asian nationalities did to build an Asian American identity. But it is unclear whether Hayes was full of people we call "Asian," or was just a multicultural melting pot. Rose does not talk about how militarism had left her vulnerable, a common side effect on women. Nor, given the rarity of what we call Asian bodies in the galaxy far, far away, does *The Last Jedi* offer any new insights into what it means to be a woman physically different from many.

Near the end of *The Last Jedi*, Rose kisses Finn. Given that Finn and Rose were sent on a side mission like minority kids being sent on a beer run; given that Finn was removed from Rey like Darth Vader was removed from Princess Leia; given that Rian Johnson chose to build up the Reylo ship; given that the basket of deplorables hated the possibility of an interracial relationship between Finn and Rey, the coupling of Finn and Rose comes across as a separate and unequal relationship. The mixture of nonwhites can be seen as something that leaves white coupling untainted. On the other hand, minority–minority mixture holds a special place for those who propose that it is a sign of evolved race relations. Lastly, coupling Finn with a minority woman suggests that Finn is not good enough for Rey, even though they've established a loving relationship. And it suggests a way to divert Finn as a potential mate for the white female lead.

Leading up to *The Last Jedi*'s debut, Kelly Marie Tran, the first Asian actor with a big-screen *Star Wars* role, had maintained an active Instagram account, giving a glimpse of her experience, supporting her costars, and promoting the movie. *BuzzFeed News* praised her down-to-earth vulnerability: "TBH, this is the only way to behave when you become famous."[27] But on social media, racist and sexist fans attacked her personally, using racial slurs and comparing her to Jar Jar Binks. At Wookieepedia.com, the preeminent *Star Wars* wiki, users vandalized her entry: "Ching Chong Wing Tong is a dumbass fucking character Disney made and is a stupid, retarded, and autistic love interest for Finn. She better die in the coma because she is a dumbass bitch."[28] Fandom, which owns the page, has removed the vandalism, locked down the page in its previous state, and banned the user from using any Wookieepedia site. On Twitter, insults included comparing her physical appearance to Grace Park, who starred in the recent *Battlestar Galactica* (2003–2010).[29] These were not just marginal trolls, but prominent, verified users like Paul Ray Ramsey, who is publicly known enough to have verified status from Twitter. On June 6, 2018, Tran deleted all her Instagram posts, but left her profile visible, with the following bio: "Afraid, but doing it anyway."[30] The abuse she faced was distinctive because of her race and her gender. She admitted to starting to hate herself, even though she had heard the lies before and had been aware of the challenges "as a person of color in a white-dominated world." She later called leaving social media her "best decision ever," maintaining that she did what was "best for me."[31]

Morten Bay, a PhD candidate at the University of Southern California, examined the tweets mentioning Rian Johnson between December 2017 and July 2018 to uncover "evidence that political influence" was occurring "through manipulation of social media discussions."[32] Among his findings:

> Among the 967 tweets analyzed, 206 expressed a negative sentiment towards the film and its director, which is 21.9 percent or a little more than one in five fans. This number includes all negative tweets analyzed, i.e., also those who came from the 44 accounts identified as bots, sock puppet accounts and trolls. It also includes 61 users who showed clear political agendas in their tweets against the film. Thus, the number of fans whose tweets are purely motivated by a negative stance towards the film is 101 or 10.5 percent.

Overall, 50.9 percent of those tweeting negatively was likely politically motivated or not even human.[33]

Bay admitted that the number of bots was too few to say Russians had stoked the conversation. He described the attacks on the movie's supposed left-wing politics as deliberate and sometimes coordinated, frequently showing no interest in the actual movie, but meant to introduce vitriolic discourse into a supposedly apolitical arena of our lives. Concerned with harassment, Bay intended to "explain potential motivations, not assert a broad conspiracy."[34]

In another study addressing harassment following *The Last Jedi*, Bethany Lacina drew from thousands of tweets published around the film, concluding that "(1) offensive language and hate speech have a modest but clear presence, (2) abusive posts are not due to automated accounts (bots), and (3) posters use more profanity and slurs to talk about women and minorities and to talk to female fans."[35] Abusive fans are regular people who participate in activities like seeing the movies, cosplaying, collecting, and shipping Reylo, along with purveying racism and sexism. As Becca Harrison argued, "It is therefore possible to think that the Reylo ship is valid and meaningful to its community and that it likely needs to address issues of racism at the same time."[36] Lacina noted that popular culture had become an arena of polarization: "Most people who tweet about Star Wars are congenial and skeptical about 'trolls.' But as with other cultural icons—whether it's an all-female 'Ghostbusters' or NFL players kneeling during the national anthem—a significant few respond with anger and hate when gender and race expectations change."[37] In other words, when called on to acknowledge women and minorities, sexists and racists reveal their true selves. I disagree with Lacina's discussion of "expectations." As with reactions to *The Phantom Menace*, visible diversity did not cause the reaction; their preexisting racism and sexism did. The expectation has remained constant: don't be racist and sexist.

Whose *Star Wars* Stories?

As part of Lucasfilm's effort to revitalize its YouTube channel with new, original series, *Our Star Wars Stories* debuted in October 2018. Former host of *Toy Hunter* (2012–2014) Jordan Hembrough traveled the country to talk with a variety of fans about the positive impact that being a *Star Wars* fan has had on their lives. Most notably, seven of the eighteen videos feature racial minorities, three feature nonhetero fans, seven focus on women, and one focuses on a noncis fan. The third episode was the first with a minority, Christina Cato, an African American woman who delved into droid building, honed skills she had never imagined, and began an outreach effort to other woman and girl builders. Through the series, Lucasfilm was clearly casting an inclusive net and featuring a diverse set of fans. In many *Our Star Wars Stories* episodes, minority fans assimilate into already defined norms of fan behavior.

But the series also includes stories beyond those. Amiyrah Martin shares how she incorporates *Star Wars* into everyday play with her family. Justice Schiappa credits the process of designing one's avatar in the *Star Wars* video game *Knights of the Old Republic* as an exercise in self-making. Amy Chrzanowski talks about seeing herself in both Carrie Fisher's Princess Leia and Kelly Marie Tran's Rose Tico. These examples join the four overlooked areas of Black fanship I presented in chapter 3. They also reflect trends of more recent decades: Martin's episode emphasizes a new kind of domesticity, Schiappa's shows a wider variety of gender identities that have entered public discussions, and Chrzanowski's sheds light on transracial, Asian adoption that increased in the 1980s.

Figure 7.1. Christina Cato, a Black woman fan, discusses her experience as a droid builder with *Our Star Wars Stories* host Jordan Hembrough. Credit: StarWars.com.

The producers at Lucasfilm removed the option to leave comments on the *Our Star Wars Stories* YouTube videos. But each does have a count of views, likes, and dislikes. On the one hand, this removes racists from the conversation, showcasing Lucasfilm's inclusive message. But on the other hand, such a high level of curation emphasizes how Lucasfilm is the gatekeeper par excellence of the *Star Wars* brand. The series shows that, together with fans from underrepresented groups, Lucasfilm producers can showcase the potential for inclusivity that *Star Wars* possesses. However, the show depicts a level of inclusion that minority fans do not receive day to day from fellow fans, from the moviemakers, or from fandom in general.[38]

Black fan bloggers continued to have challenges during the sequel trilogy years. African American woman blogger Holly Quinn described this pattern of harassment. Without getting to know her, antagonists would ply the label "anti" to her, assuming she was leading forces against their position (in this case, shipping Reylo). They demanded that she delete her blog. Even after some time had passed, when a *Star Wars* creative quoted her, they swarmed him, calling him an anti as well. The podcast *Fansplaining* invited Holly and some other fans of color to discuss associations between Blackness and deviant sexuality in fan fictions that explored the Finn and Poe ship. Some writers who had deployed that imagery defended it as not necessarily anti-Black, blaming those who pointed out the deviance as the agents of Finnpoe's decline in popularity. (In reality, a variety of factors could cause a ship to become less popular.) As Holly observed, little changed after this conversation, showing a consistent lack of empathy toward Black characters and fans.[39]

Some shippers told Holly that they fantasized about a relationship between Rey and Kylo Ren to cope with their real-world lives. She would tell them that Black fans rely on fan fiction to cope with racism. Shipping Finnrey was often a response to the racism interracial couples have faced historically: "Every time, I was told it wasn't the same. 'Coping,' in the lexicon of fandom, meant dealing with abuse. Racism, in the eyes of fandom, didn't, apparently, fall under abuse. Its impact certainly wasn't something we should bring into fandom."[40] Antagonists claimed that fandom was pure, clean, and innocent, and discussions of social issues—as the work of disingenuous social justice warriors—ruined that. As Holly described, they saw racism as only a headline or an accusation: "It wasn't something people lived with. They were allowed to feel pain. We were not."[41]

Fighting racism became central in the fan work of African American women like the blogger Stitch. Reflecting on the tactics of white female big players in attacking John Boyega, Stitch said, "The Star Wars fandom remains one of the most racist fandoms that I've ever had the displeasure of being in."[42] Willing to engage with fans she finds objectionable, Stitch directly challenged white authors for their negligence. For example, *SYFY Wire*'s Kayleigh Donaldson argued, "It would be unfair and too general to say that Star Wars has a fandom problem. What it has is a white male fandom problem." Stitch disagreed immediately, addressing Donaldson directly on Twitter: "I'd argue that Star Wars has a problem with whiteness, where white fans (of all genders) are so devoted to the status quo that this sort of thing happens. (Plenty of the racist gatekeepers are white women who harass people of color and I think it's important not to forget that)."[43] Several white women—Reylo fans with a lot of influence—were driving a specific kind of anti-Blackness that consisted of three steps. First, considering Kylo Ren the sequel trilogy's true hero. This went beyond simply liking him as a personal favorite; many favored Darth Vader in the original trilogy, yet still acknowledged that Luke Skywalker was the hero. Second, believing that depriving him of a redemption arc was a crime. Redemption arcs are common, but they work best when planted before a story's last act. Darth Vader's put him on that path at the end of *The Empire Strikes Back*, whereas Kylo Ren was as evil and unapologetic as ever at the end of *The Last Jedi*. Third, diminishing Finn and John Boyega whenever and however possible. So, even if Reylo seemed apolitical on the surface, that kind of activity has weaponized the ship along racial lines. Stitch also noted that commentators like Kayleigh Donaldson, Lindsey Romain, and Sarah Sahim have thousands of followers; as influencers, they allow attacks on those who disagree: "And the only people talking about it have zero power in fandom. We're not *The Nerdist* editors or hot shot freelance writers with massive audiences at our platforms of choice. We don't have *The Mary Sue* willing to let us show our asses on the regular in snide 'shipping isn't morality' pieces that don't acknowledge that shipping is informed by our morality. We have small followings and limited access to nerd media essay platforms."[44] Popular white influencers easily targeted less influential Black social media users by calling on their many followers. Black women fans ended up on the defensive just for bringing up matters of race, but efforts to defend oneself from accusations of being a reverse racist are likely to devolve into yes-you-are, no-I'm-not matches. This calling of the hounds often silenced minority fans, likely causing them to retreat to more private fan activities.[45]

The Rise of Skywalker

In the weeks leading up to the release of *The Rise of Skywalker*, J. J. Abrams hammered a nail into the coffin of the Finnpoe ship, describing their relationship as "a far deeper one than a romantic one," praising their bravery and solicitude. This is the kind of statement shippers dread, basically settling the matter of whether a relationship will come to fruition on the big screen. In the same interview, though, he reiterated his goal of wanting a *Star Wars* cast that "looked more the way the world looks than not." This had been evident since *The Force Awakens* cast was revealed in April 2014. Similarly, the original cast of Abrams's show *Lost* (2004–2010), which told the story of the survivors' plane crash on a mysterious Pacific island, included the kinds of people seen on a transpacific flight: an Asian couple, an interracial couple, a single Black father, a Hispanic man, and a Muslim man. As a consolation to those holding out for a romantic relationship between the former stormtrooper and the Resistance pilot, Abrams added, "And in the case of the LGBTQ community, it was important to me that people who go to see this movie feel that they're being represented in the film."[46] This sounded like the promise of an extended presence. In 2017, the live-action version of *Beauty and the Beast* featured a momentary dance between two men. *Avengers: Endgame* (2019) followed with a cameo by codirector Joe Russo playing an openly gay character. It seemed that *Star Wars* would follow with the franchise's first on-screen gay characters.

The Rise of Skywalker debuted on December 19, 2019. Anticipation was high, as this was the conclusion of a forty-two-year-long saga. Fans, viewers, and critics expected the resolution of all outstanding matters. How would the Resistance stop the First Order? How could the Republic rebuild after being struck by a weapon of mass destruction? How would the principal characters relate to one another? Whether Reylo, Finnrey, or even Finnrose, those rooting for these ships wanted fulfilling resolutions of those romantic story lines. The film's plot compelled the characters to fulfill a series of scavenger hunts for mystical objects, with the First Order constantly on their tails. It resurrected Emperor Palpatine, who had seemingly died in *Return of the Jedi*. Near the end of the climactic battle, Palpatine hurls Kylo Ren down a chasm, and Rey deflects his Force lightning onslaught, even though it brings her to the edge of death. Kylo Ren climbs out of the chasm and saves Rey's life through Force healing. When she regains consciousness, they kiss—because who doesn't kiss their former assailant after a near-death experience?—and Kylo Ren dies.

The small players were the first to respond to the movie, often on Twitter, which allowed instantaneous posting of opinions, in some cases before the premiere date.[47] They left me with several impressions. First, Finnrey fans felt *The Rise of Skywalker* ended the saga and resolved the relationships in ways different from its setup. They used statements from John Boyega and *The Rise of Skywalker* cowriter Chris Terrio to validate their support of the Finnrey ship.[48] As one fan in Brazil argued in Portuguese, "triologia virou merda" (the trilogy became shit) when it abandoned the romance between Finn and Rey.[49] Some felt disappointment in the movie because of the Rey–Kylo Ren kiss.[50] Second, they described Finnrey as the kind of romance they would seek in real life: "Anyways, where is my #finnrey ending, I know a good healthy relationship when I see one."[51] Sometimes they did this by eschewing the foundations of the Rey–Kylo relationship: "loving someone who has repeatedly tried to kill you, stalked you using the force, and thrown temper tantrums when things don't go his way among other terrible things sounds like a textbook toxic relationship to me. Should have been #finnrey."[52] Third, supporters of Finnrey felt that the ending pandered to narrow conceptions of the saga that favored whiteness and gave more romantic potential to white characters: "Also bc if he was white they would've made Finnrey a canon romance and not sidelined Finn and made it the poor baby Kylo story."[53] Some rectified the situation by formulating their own "headcanon" to explain it away.[54] Some created alternate endings in artwork.[55] Others created new "edits" to reiterate their love for Finnrey.[56]

Fourth, they pointed out their disappointment at Lucasfilm for buckling to pressure. For example: "I believe a 10-second Reylo moment was planned all along as much as I believe bringing back Palpatine was from the start. But this set up of a romantic arc between Finn and Rey in 2 movies was ignored because a bunch of Reddit shippers didn't like it?"[57] Or "Give us #Finnrey you cowards. Love looks like that, this friendship and affection, goddamn~."[58] Judging from avatars and usernames, Finnrey supporters were very diverse, coming from a wider variety of races and genders than Reylo supporters. On the other hand, some gave no indication of their *Star Wars* fanship by their profile names, avatars, or bios. They openly rejected Reylo, but they expressed little hostility toward Reylo shippers, even when Reylo shippers did so toward other ships. Some called for tolerance of other ships.[59]

Many professional reviewers at outlets were also underwhelmed with the movie, focusing on the level of fan service. The review in the *Los Angeles Times* suggested, "The more accurate way to describe it, I think, is as an epic failure of nerve. This 'Rise' feels more like a retreat, a return to a zone of emotional and thematic safety from a filmmaker with a gift for packaging nostalgia as subversion."[60] *Uproxx* decried the appeasement of fans on social media: "There were times it felt like *The Rise of Skywalker* was put together by reading angry reddit boards, just throwing in anything a fan might possibly want to see. It really is baffling."[61] Similarly, *SlashFilm* disapproved of the efforts to make a crowd-pleaser: "As the story draws to its big, loud climax, and one fan-service moment after another arises, you begin to get the sense that Abrams is just checking off boxes and fulfilling a quota."[62]

Writing for *The Mary Sue*, Princess Weekes asserted that the abandonment of the Finnrey story line was also an abandonment of John Boyega's Finn: "If there is one thing I think is consistent across all the Star Wars sequel movies is that John Boyega's Finn didn't get his due as a character. I know from this title, it seems like my gripe is mostly about shipping, but for me, the pushing aside of Finn and Rey isn't just about their 'relationship' it's about Finn's place in the trio."[63] In our heteronormative, monogamous, and romance-hungry society, whether a character ends up in a romance reflects how worthy they are. Getting the girl is a prize for the most brave, attractive, and talented, and storytelling often reserves those traits for white males.

The consensus among both small players and big players was that Rey and Kylo Ren's kiss was not a fulfilling conclusion to their relationship. These opinions came from shippers with ostensibly various political leanings. However, rather than a brokering of peace between the two ships, each went their own way, as moviegoers do when they leave the multiplex and find their cars. Finnrey fans continued expressing their feelings for Boyega and Ridley's characters, bonding with their allies, and keeping their heads low. Reylo fans continued retrofitting the source material to their desires, shifting the conversations, and enjoying the strength they felt in their numbers.[64]

Along with the activity around #finnrey and #reylo on Twitter and major reviews of *The Rise of Skywalker*, video reviews on YouTube also revealed what both big players and small players were saying about the movie. As I mentioned in chapter 6, these videos also tutor fans in matters of storytelling, even if they present them in humorous ways. I narrowed down my analysis to videos that would emphasize storytelling craft over those that could be sexist, racist, or inflammatory just for the sake of it. I avoided videos that antagonized the liberal-inclusive values that Lucasfilm itself presented. After all, this is where most *Star Wars* fans reside, ideologically.[65]

Notably, big players and small players, male and female, presumably white and minority, echoed one another in criticizing the movie. While the big players in print repeated the matter of fan service, YouTube video makers also critiqued the kiss between Rey and Kylo Ren. Jenny Nicholson recounted, "[In] one scene ... he gets redeemed and then wordless fight and then wordless resurrection of Rey, awkward eye contact, wordless kiss, and then wordlessly flopping over dead. It just feels so awkward, it got uncomfortable chuckles in every screening I went to. . . . I mean, 'I love you' is awkward on a first date, so I'm just gonna go ahead and say that pouring your life force into somebody, kissing them, and then falling over dead and vanishing from this plane of existence is also awkward on a first date." Nicholson did not feel they had developed "some kind of relationship foundation" to have them kiss.[66] Although George Lucas's writing in the prequel trilogy was stiff, it did establish that Anakin and Padmé had romantic feelings, which they professed to each other in *Attack of the Clones*. From there, viewers had to take the characters' words at face value. *Revenge of the Sith* followed, playing out the repercussions of these two characters secretly marrying. Romance, intimacy, and kinship remained mysteries in the sequel trilogy, just as they had in the two previous trilogies, and *The Rise of Skywalker* expected us to accept a third act romance between two people who had spent two and a half movies molesting, maiming, and slaying each other.

Moth's Audio and Videos, a small player, was incredulous over the sudden redemption of Kylo Ren, who had spent the trilogy committing murder, genocide, torture, and slavery, concluding, "It doesn't sound like he's good after all." He jested that if kissing Rey were meant to be a great reward for a male character, the kiss the movie produced was "a huge bullet" that Finn dodged: "Disney, the cowards that they are, listened to these fans, and have admitted to giving them what they wanted with regard to fan service like Reylo, not what they thought would make a good story."[67]

The animated spoof produced by *How It Should Have Ended* poked fun at Rey's newfound ability to grab things out of nowhere, plus ghost Jedi Knights' ability to wield physical objects to propose that she arm prominent dead Jedi with lightsabers. After they slay the resurrected Palpatine, Julius Caesar style, they notice Rey and Kylo Ren kissing. "Did that feel out of nowhere for anybody else?" Mace Windu asks.[68] *Honest Trailers* compared fans' reactions to *The Last Jedi* to Gamergate, proposing that Disney "panicked and tried to match the pieces back together in this hollowed-out shell of a trilogy that's missing any consistency in its plot themes or characters, unless you fill in the blanks on Twitter, read all the novels, and happen to be running some Fortnite squads with the boys during the crossover event." In other words, it took too much fan knowledge to understand the movie. Emphasizing a shot of the Rey–Kylo Ren kiss, *Honest Trailers* argued that the film "managed to do the impossible: unite fans who loved *The Last Jedi* and fans who hated *The Last Jedi* by pleasing none of them."[69] YouTubers repeatedly focused on the sidelining of Finn. They looked back on the trilogy, noting that he was the greatest, most original asset the films had. The YouTuber Thor Skywalker polled his viewers, finding that they believed Finn had the most wasted potential of all sequel characters. Looking back on the trilogy, many believed his sidelining began in *The Last Jedi*. Some noted that his sidelining began immediately after *The Force Awakens*. Many noticed that *The Rise of Skywalker* had him yell "Rey!" a lot.[70]

Okiro, a Black YouTuber whose principal fandom is *Star Wars*, argued that Finn was a strong presence in *The Rise of Skywalker*; reducing him to yelling "Rey" overlooked his maturation through the trilogy. Posting in July 2020, Okiro suggested that major portions of Finn's story were cut from *The Rise of Skywalker*. More of Finn's backstory was to be revealed, his romance with Rey was to progress, and his Force awareness was to serve the plot, restoring what might have been his trajectory at the end of *The Force Awakens*.[71] Indeed, Boyega had been optimistic leading into *The Rise of Skywalker*. The plans to put a lightsaber into Finn's hands had been discussed, the storyboards were drawn, and the scenes were shot. But, as cowriter Chris Terrio (*Argo*, 2012) described, they had to patch the movie as they were shooting it:

> I've never rewritten a film as much as this one.... It's like the tide. There's a new script every morning. But we just keep going at it and going at it, loosely thinking that it's not good enough. It's never good

enough. Luckily, the production team is so good that they can shift and adjust. We're course-correcting as we go—we're trying things, and some things don't work and some things aren't ambitious enough. Some things are overly ambitious. Some things are too dense. Some things are too simple. Some things are too nostalgic. Some things are too out-of-left field. We're finding our balance.[72]

The demands for changes came from higher up the ladder, often at the behest of Disney executives. More elements were removed during reshooting and editing, and you could see the disappointment on cast members' faces as they had to discuss the final product.[73]

An interracial and gay relationship did appear in *The Rise of Skywalker*, in the last minutes, after the final battle, when all the Resistance forces returned to their hidden base. The white woman in the relationship had appeared in the prior film as well, but her name was never uttered on-screen. Her partner, played by Black British actor Vinette Robinson, was a new addition in *The Rise of Skywalker* who never spoke, was not spoken to, and was not ever mentioned by name. Just as small players and big players critiqued the movie's Rey–Kylo Ren kiss, they decried this one, but for different reasons: it was a "blink-and-you'll-miss-it moment" that barely counted as representation. They recognized that Lucasfilm had baited them and rejected the notion that the studio deserved congratulations for the first same-sex kiss in a *Star Wars* movie. The kiss indicated little more than Disney/Lucasfilm's willingness to produce such superficial images to manage the fans.[74]

What Did Finn Want to Say?

On December 31, 2019, John Boyega joked that, with Kylo Ren gone, Finn and Rey would have sex: "It's not about who she kisses but who eventually lays the pipe."[75] Reactions to this revealed a double standard: It is acceptable to talk about intimacy between Han and Leia, or Rey and Kylo Ren, or even joke about Luke and Leia, unearthing the fact that sex is right below the surface in the galaxy far, far away. But pairing Finn and Rey elicited a special reaction from some fans: in particular, the urge to remove Boyega and Finn (and their imagined amalgam) as sexual threats. Rather than shrinking away or retracting his jokes, Boyega stuck to them. His critics tried to blur matters between Finn and Rey and Boyega and Ridley, but he spelled out the distinction between fantasized romances and real-world relationships: "You obviously don't know the difference between a fictional world and reality." Then he posted a collage of interactions between Rey and Kylo Ren, including his torturing her and her defeating him in lightsaber combat, with the caption "Star Wars romance."[76] The graphic pointed out the moments between the two characters that contradict the notion that they would be romantic at all, but it also pointed out that romantic relationships in *Star Wars* movies are problematic in general.

Critiques of Boyega gained an academic veneer with Katie McCort's article on Medium.com, "When Systemic Hatred of Women Online Goes Unnoticed, What Does It Say about Us?,"[77] which equated Finnrey fans (and Boyega) with misogynist violence. Like rank-and-file Reylo

Figure 7.2. December 31, 2019, tweet by John Boyega, including a collage critiquing Lucasfilm's depiction of romance in the sequel trilogy. Credit: John Boyega.

fans, she uses sexism narrowly, as a shield against scrutiny of Reylo fans' motivations. McCort mistook the number of Finnrey mentions for inactivity or indifference. Indeed, Reylo was a more popular ship, but indifference was not the reason for Finnrey's lesser visibility. Instead, the expressions of explicit and implicit bias against interracial relationships, the hostility against discussions of race, and the retreat from the hostile environment on social media precipitated Finnrey fans' seeming inactivity. McCort rejected mentions that did not use shorthand (Finnrey or Reylo, meaning the relationship). However, she did count data that used Finnrey or Reylo as a noun (meaning the enthusiast). In fact, "Reylo" is mentioned only once and is never used for a larger argument. McCort cast Finnreys' substantive critiques of Reylos as attacks on their persons. She also showed her distaste for the New Year's Eve conversation, using it to characterize Boyega, his fans, and fans of Finnrey as hateful, rather than acknowledge that targets of racism may feel anger.[78]

Venting is part of the labor minority fans do to seek empathy, but McCort equated disagreement with harassment. Often, it is done in an outspoken way, in the vernacular of the group, rather than letting it fester quietly. But McCort defined antis as a group "known for demonizing, demoralizing, and/or dehumanizing any individual in a shipping fandom who they deemed to be promoting 'problematic' content through the fiction they consumed."[79] This assumes all dissent is hostile, but also makes taking offense more injurious than producing offense. Her essay makes civil Finnrey fans responsible for everything all Finnrey fans do. At the same time, this maneuver evades acknowledging the deplorable segments of Reylo fanship. It puts a lot of effort into denying that Reylo fans could be racist, and then suggests that Reylos and all women are one and the same. This maneuver aims to draw attention away from racist white women's dirty hands. She referred to individuals who disagreed but had not directed their statements toward anyone as harassers. In addition, McCort revealed their usernames, exposing them to possible retaliation.

As Becca Harrison later questioned in a rebuttal to McCort's arguments, "Why don't we see *any* of the original Reylo posts? By focusing on the replies and using 'women' vs 'antis,' McCort's work covertly erases race from the narrative while simultaneously amplifying the feelings of white women who are allegedly endangered by the anger of women of colour. Never mind if that anger is justified."[80] By saying "when the left leans right," by arguing that both the alt-right and the anti-racists constitute their own "bullying hive mind," McCort sets up a false equivalence, like Donald Trump's "very fine people on both sides" comment after the unrest initiated by white supremacists in Charlottesville, Virginia, in August 2017. But there is a difference between liberal progressives and the alt-right, as Harrison spells out. Finnrey fans do not have the infrastructure to strike back like retrograde Reylos do. Second, they are likely to retreat from the battle and keep doing what they love. Third, like many liberals, most Finnreys are open-minded pacifists. They are not systematic, like McCort tried to argue. Her essay reflects parochial white feminism, false equivalence, and anti-Blackness.

On January 14, 2020, Derek Connolly and Colin Trevorrow's draft script for *Episode IX* leaked via Robert Meyer Burnett and his YouTube channel, The Burnettwork. Nine days later, on Reddit, twenty pieces of art created exclusively for Trevorrow's story appeared, and he confirmed their authenticity. In the wake of tepid reception for *The Rise of Skywalker*, fans reacted enthusiastically to the glimpse into what could have been. Written in 2016, *Duel of the Fates* stuck with Kylo Ren rather than reinvigorating an old villain, Palpatine, as *The Rise of Skywalker* did. Force sensitivity became a possibility for regular characters, not just members of famous *Star Wars* families. By building on what *The Last Jedi* had to offer, rather than emphasizing fan service, *Duel of the Fates* might not have strained viewers' suspension of disbelief as much as *The Rise of Skywalker* wound up doing.[81]

Trevorrow's story took a more overt approach to the politics of the galaxy far, far away. While the sequel trilogy took a vague good-versus-evil, us-versus-them approach, *Duel of the Fates* ascribed practices to the First Order that the Resistance opposed in the name of democracy. The First Order is blocking communications, limiting Princess Leia's ability to recruit for the Resistance. In a heroic scene at a First Order power plant, Rey's actions inspire migrant workers to aid the resistance. Trevorrow's script also incorporated imagery of First Order stormtroopers separating children from families. All three of these were hot-button topics those years via the role of the internet in censorship/misinformation, migrant and immigrant workers, and detention of Latin American children at the US border.[82]

In January 2020, Amazon began selling a *Star Wars* T-shirt featuring Boyega's Finn and Ridley's Rey with large letters asking, "What Did Finn Want to Say?"—referring to a matter left unresolved by *The Rise of Skywalker*.[83] Twice in the movie, Finn says to Rey he has something to tell her, but he never gets to. This kind of dangling thread is a screenwriting no-no that fans and writers noticed, with frustration. This

T-shirt must have gone into production and received the license from Lucasfilm shortly after the release of the film. The product is a money grab, illustrating how entertainment producers rely on fandom for revenue, and how licensors and manufacturers can capitalize on criticism. It reflects one of the many criticisms of the film voiced by viewers, fans, and critics. All three of these factions exhibited familiarity with screenwriting conventions, making the unresolved question of Finn's intentions considerable enough to inspire a licensed answer.

Abrams had a diplomatic response to dissatisfaction with the movie: "We knew starting this that any decision we made—a design decision, a musical decision, a narrative decision—would please someone and infuriate someone else. And they're *all* right."[84] Abrams condensed the working relationship with the director of *The Last Jedi*: "We had conversations with Rian at the beginning. It's been nothing but collaborative. The perspective that, at least personally, I got from stepping away from it and seeing what Rian did, strangely gave us opportunities that would never have been there, because of course he made choices no one else would have made."[85] Abrams praised the arc Johnson had created for Luke Skywalker and let that stand. However, he did retcon Johnson's retcon, making Rey's parents famous after all (Rey's father was the son of the Emperor Palpatine, making her Darth Sidious's granddaughter). He and cowriter Chris Terrio "felt they had to up the ante— taking her despair at being 'no one' and revealing that there may be an even more unsettling answer than that."[86]

Abrams claimed Finn wanted to tell Rey he was Force sensitive, and Terrio emphasized how the Force was guiding Finn's action and making him feel Rey's defeat at Palpatine's hands. Both ideas were true: Finn was Force sensitive, and he loved Rey. Regardless, wishing for a relationship between characters is one thing, but putting it on-screen is another. Fans can ship, processing their unrequited feelings as much as they need to, but change results from producers who commit to materializing that story. Disney and Lucasfilm prevented that from happening in the *Star Wars* sequel trilogy.[87]

Conclusion

What Is the Story of *Star Wars* and Diversity?

With the Skywalker saga complete, it is possible to look back and ask, "What is the story of *Star Wars*?" a question that produces various answers, depending on which aspect of the cultural phenomenon you focus on. On a literal level, it is the story of heroic individuals realizing their potential by challenging the forces of militarism. Every *Star Wars* movie, show, comic, and novel is built on this theme. Adorning that message are character types, situations, and sayings we recognize as on-brand for *Star Wars*. The answer becomes harder to pinpoint if we ask about interracialism, diversity, and inclusion, the broader areas this book addresses. Then, the story of *Star Wars* is the servitude of nonhumans to humans; the cooperation of droids and humanoids with the human lead characters; and the violence between humans and their subordinates. These three types of racial interactions characterize both US history and popular culture, so their prevalence is no surprise.

The nine movies of the Skywalker saga have no explicit interracial intimacy. On a symbolic level, it appears seven times: Darth Vader molests Princess Leia in *A New Hope*; Lando Calrissian kisses Princess Leia in *The Empire Strikes Back*; Jabba enslaves Princess Leia in *Return of the Jedi*; midi-chlorians impregnate Shmi in *The Phantom Menace*; Sand People abuse Shmi in *Attack of the Clones*; Poe and Finn flirt, and Rey kisses Finn in *The Force Awakens* (it's platonic, but the whole movie is their romance); and Rose kisses Finn in *The Last Jedi*. The prequel trilogy challenged viewers with reproductive technologies, familial relations, and conceptions of diversity that symbolized interracial relations in ways viewers never had to consider in the galaxy far, far away. In a time when interracial marriage was high, multiple checking on census forms was a norm, and in popular culture, mixture became more visible, less fantastic, and easy to portray in realistic genres, *The Force Awakens* launched the sequel trilogy with an interracial relationship. *Star Wars*, like many other science fiction franchises, did not try to explain human racial diversity; it never took the polygenesis approach, suggesting different races spawned independently along an explicit hierarchy. Finn and Rey were two compatible humans who met, had an adventure together, and enjoyed mutual affection for each other.

Similarly, the nine movies have no explicitly mixed characters. Its symbolically mixed characters consist of two cyborgs: General Grievous and Darth Vader, the most pivotal character in the whole saga. Proceeding historically from 1977 to 1983, Darth Vader went from mystery with an African American voice to cyborg, to restored, spectral, white man. Following the saga from *Episode I* to *Episode VI*, Darth Vader went from white boy made by midi-chlorians and a human mother, to cyborg, to restored white man. Most viewers would consider Darth Vader racially white but, even among those, many have acknowledged the impact of James Earl Jones's distinctive, African American voice.

Star Wars, Diversity, and the Actors

The principal actors of the original trilogy found that their fortunes turned as the favor for those movies turned. Mark Hamill appeared less on-screen but became a leading voice talent, most notably in *Batman: The Animated Series* (1992–1995). Carrie Fisher played notable supporting roles in movies, but also became a respected script doctor, and then novelist and memoirist. Harrison Ford became a prominent leading man through the 1980s and 1990s, gaining recognition as Indiana Jones in *Raiders of the Lost Ark* (1981), Rick Deckard in *Blade Runner* (1982), and Jack Ryan in *Patriot Games* (1992). He gained Oscar, BAFTA, and Golden Globe nominations for his performance in *Witness* (1985) and Golden Globe nominations for his performances in *The Mosquito Coast* (1986), *The Fugitive* (1993), and *Sabrina* (1995). Some actors in the prequel trilogy, including Ewan McGregor, Natalie Portman, Liam Neeson, and Samuel L. Jackson, had made their names before *The Phantom Menace*, and have continued their careers without appearing in subsequent *Star Wars* movies. Some, like David Mayhew, Anthony Daniels, and David Prowse, thrived on the fan circuit. But others, like Jake Lloyd and Hayden Christensen, suffered from their association with the prequels.

As a point of comparison, though, we have ten characters whose names are uttered and who are played by Asian American and Pacific Islanders in all the *Star Wars* shows and movies, half of which were in the saga films. Around the same number of characters whose names are uttered were played by Latinx actors, with half of those in the saga films. While nearly two dozen Black actors have played extras, thirteen have played named roles, with just five in the saga.[1] Of those, five were Black men: James Earl Jones has credited David Prowse with doing "all the hard work of wearing the hot suit," yet he communicated "the character's mental and emotional state," complicating the racial makeup of the character to this day.[2] Billy Dee Williams felt like "an alternative to the usual WASP hero" as Lando Calrissian.[3] Ahmed Best as Jar Jar Binks in the prequel trilogy went from colorblind optimism to despair because of the abuse he faced. Besides a uniquely colored lightsaber, Samuel L. Jackson wanted a dignified death for Mace Windu, not one that recalled disposable Black characters of the past.[4] Playing Finn in the sequel trilogy, John Boyega found himself the target of excessive scrutiny in both his on-screen and personal lives. The actors span thirty-five years, and they are very different individuals with different personalities. However, having been in the spotlight with prominent on-screen roles, they have discussed the following commonalities: first, their experiences working in *Star Wars* reflect the experiences of minority actors throughout the industry; second, they felt they were working in a system antagonistic to their perspectives; and third, their race determined their experiences. Lando, Mace Windu, and Finn are each known as the Black character in their respective trilogies.

Lastly, the movies' story lines bar their characters from intimacy with anyone of a different racial group. Obi-Wan Kenobi arrives on the Death Star, distracting the Sith Lord from menacing Princess Leia. Although gainfully employed and responsible to many, Lando is cast as less trustworthy than Han Solo. Jar Jar Binks operates as the adoptive child of the principal characters, unworthy of affection from even his own people. Mace Windu is one of many Jedi who honors his vow of chastity, unlike Anakin Skywalker. Even though Finn is a character from our supposedly more accepting era, the movies thwart his relationships with Rey, Poe, and Rose Tico. Diverse casting and reliance on representation isn't necessarily producing progressive story lines. As Brandi Wilkins Catanese concludes in her analysis of *The Pelican Brief* (1993) and *Devil in a Blue Dress* (1995), "Despite liberal aphorisms to the contrary, love in Hollywood films is not (color)blind."[5] In other words, as long as their presence is exceptional rather than transgressive, colorblindness itself will compel moviemakers to stifle the interracial potential between Black male and white female characters. In the post–civil rights era, this has been true for Black actors across genres, whether Sidney Poitier, Billy Dee Williams, Denzel Washington, or John Boyega. The goal is not to increase the number of visible interracial relationships, but rather to bring about a world with more equality. Imagining Finn with Rey, or Finn with Poe, or Finn with Rose at least primes us for dismantling the barriers that have oppressed us—white supremacy, sexism, exploitation, and cultural orthodoxy. That is the difference between those three Finn ships and Reylo.

In his Accelerate TV master class, held six months after *The Last Jedi*, John Boyega described the process of auditioning for *The Force Awakens*. After the British sci-fi film *Attack the Block* (2011), he had been going for as many big titles as he could, often not getting auditions when his white actor friends did. His agent, Femi Oguns, managed to get Boyega in the door, presenting him with a do-or-die situation: "It was either I book *Star Wars*, or I'm gonna go to Jamaica and sell pineapples." His first audition went badly, but J. J. Abrams kept him in the running. The next eight months consisted of fitness training, studying previous *Star Wars* cast members, and visiting the set. Eventually, word got around that he was in the running for *The Force Awakens*, which led to the producers of *Terminator Genisys* (2015) and *Justice League* (2017) showing more interest in him. To pursue any of these three roles, he would have to refuse the other two. Even though the process with Lucasfilm was in limbo, he thought, "Imagine we miss out of *Star Wars*, man, because we just wanted to book something?"[6]

Boyega gave his best at his last audition, in front of all the bigwigs, leading to Abrams calling him in for a conversation. At a restaurant in London's Mayfair district, he asked the actor, who was feeling insecure about his recent performance, "Are you ready to become a leader, because this will mean something more than just a role. People will be like, 'This is inspirational.' Are you ready to do that?" After elucidating the significance of the Black actor's casting, Abrams spelled it out: "John, you're the star of *Star Wars*."[7] John's character was to be as central to the sequel trilogy as Luke, Han, and Leia were to the original, or Anakin, Obi-Wan, or Padmé were to the prequels. In addition to this verbal agreement, both the *Episode VII* shot list and the director's outline of the trilogy indicated that Boyega's performance would be remembered as a central part of the saga. Abrams also reminded him of the "significant lifetime commitment to this thing," that John would never be able to escape having been a part of the galaxy far, far away.[8] Becoming emotional in front of the audience of young Black actors, many of whom were Nigerian like himself, at the 2018 master class engagement, Boyega recalled how much he suffered, how much of his life he put into the process, and how achieving his dream was not what anyone expected from someone with his background. Seeing his agent after receiving the good news, he told him, "Femi, we did it. We made history, we did it."[9] Because of the significance of his casting, the centrality of his role, and the plans Abrams had for Finn, it looked like he would be neither a "red shirt" like Dodge in *Planet of the Apes* (1968), who dies quickly; nor Al Powell, who aids John McLean in *Die Hard* (1988); nor any of a dozen minority sidekicks in the Marvel Cinematic Universe. Instead, he would be a "big damn hero" like Laurence Fishburne's Morpheus (*The Matrix*, 1999), Will Smith's Agent J (*Men in Black*, 1997), or Samuel L. Jackson's Jules Winnfield (*Pulp Fiction*, 1994).[10]

Things turned out differently, resulting in the sidelining of Finn. Evidence of this appeared shortly before *The Force Awakens* premiere, in the form of a leaked shot list for the movie, which must have existed in December 2014. In that document, which laid out the scenes J. J. Abrams was working on at the time, Finn's Force plot receives more development through a stronger connection with Anakin and Luke Skywalker's lightsaber that ends up in his hands. He does not want to run and hide from the fight, as he does on the planet Takodona in the final movie. Also, he is not given the lowly job of custodial worker on the Starkiller base. Later, Boyega found *The Last Jedi* script, which introduced him to Finn's deprioritization, hard to accept: "What I would say to Disney is do not bring out a black character, market them to be much more important in the franchise than they are and then have them pushed to the side. It's not good."[11] He believed Kelly Marie Tran and Oscar Isaac also received similar treatment. Although minority actors have gained visibility in recent decades, the entertainment industry continues its habits of associating intelligence, bravery, and beauty with white characters. By habit, it sustains white supremacist thinking this way. Sadly, as shown by the kerfuffle around *Project Greenlight*, it is the "casting of the show," even before it is the "casting of the movie." So far, the most effective way to stop reproducing this is by having someone in the room to dissent, double-check, and expand the conversation.[12]

As Boyega reflected, the racism in the moviemaking process can bring out frustration, isolation, and anger, but the experience also made him more vocal about racial matters:

> I'm the only cast member who had their own unique experience of that franchise based on their race. Let's just leave it like that. It makes you angry with a process like that. It makes you much more militant; it changes you. Because you realise, "I got given this opportunity but I'm in an industry that wasn't even ready for me." Nobody else in the cast had people saying they were going to boycott the movie because [they were in it]. Nobody else had the uproar and death threats sent to their Instagram DMs and social media, saying, "Black this and black that and you shouldn't be a Stormtrooper." Nobody else had that experience. But yet people are surprised that I'm this way. That's my frustration.[13]

As the Black actor entering the *Star Wars* spotlight in the 2010s, Boyega had to deal with technologies and media that Best and Williams did not. But beyond the specificities of the times, beyond whatever disappointment he might have had about his role, and beyond whatever feelings he might have about the powers that be, Boyega spoke up about what happened to him, and how isolating the experiences were. In the end, he joined Jones, Williams, Jackson, and Best in being the lone Black actor on the (*Star Wars*) block. That they had to do this over and over in every decade since the 1970s shows how little things have changed.

Star Wars, Diversity, and the Fans

Although civil rights legislation had passed just over a decade before, schools had begun to desegregate, and the government was promoting affirmative action, *Star Wars* did not demand that fans accept a radically inclusive world in 1977. At the same time, the film was popular across all racial groups. This has led to a dilemma in *Star Wars* fanship from the beginning: all were welcome to watch, enjoy, and participate in fan activities, but for much of the *Star Wars* phenomenon, white fans have enjoyed an invisible jetpack, which made it easier for them to enjoy the films. As journalist Geena Hardy wrote regarding *The Force Awakens*, "For all the potential a science fiction fantasy franchise like Star Wars has in its visual universe, the franchise's limits lie with the people who act as its gatekeepers and fall back on the rotating doors of nostalgic callbacks or reinterpretations of old material. Most of these gatekeepers, to be absolutely clear, are white men and women of the aforementioned generations who found places in *Star Wars*'s strongest houses: Film and television."[14] In fact, the white cast, the white narratives, the white tropes, and the white coloring in the original trilogy energized the invisible jetpack. White fans have had a possessive investment in that whiteness. They treasure those canonical elements because of their whiteness and resist new ways of interpreting *Star Wars*. At best, they tolerate minority fans, but only insofar as they resemble the tokens from the original trilogy. This is part of what makes *Star Wars* a post–civil rights era phenomenon: minorities are not excluded de jure, just de facto.

African American responses to the first *Star Wars* movie have shown how minorities might respond to the saga, namely with skepticism. As a response to historical exclusion, some minority viewers have resisted taking Darth Vader's racial whiteness for granted. My friend thought of him as Black, and I think of him as white and mixed. Many of us have stories that feature racism along with childhood role-playing. With the rise of the internet, minority fans can find solidarity with others who share similar experiences with racism. But even with increased visibility, minority fans have slipped into safe spaces free of microaggressions, antipathy, and conservatism. So, as with minority actors participating in the movies, minority fans have felt limited acceptance and persistent tokenism. These problems are endemic to society, not just geek culture.

This book focuses on shipping as a fan activity because it shows what stories fans imagine, share, incorporate, seek—and ultimately invest in emotionally. One can imagine anything, including Lando and Leia; Padmé's dark-haired first love from the Legislative Youth Program; or Finn and Rey. But these ships are rare, revealing what stories fans ignore, stifle, reject, and oppose. They might do this in terms of "not canon," "not right," or "preachy," but the message remains: racial endogamy is the norm. To root for Finnrey was to hope against hope. On the one hand, America was more accepting. Television shows sometimes presented interracial romances, and maybe Abrams would return to them. On the other hand, Americans were full of implicit bias and fear of replacement. As a result, endogamy remained the norm.[15] Big-screen entertainment had not been as adventurous as its small-screen counterparts, and negative reactions to *The Last Jedi* scared Lucasfilm.

Star Wars, Diversity, and the Producers

By contrast, *Star Trek*, created by Gene Roddenberry, centered diversity, making it the main concern of the show. We can see this in his universe's dialectics, casting, and story lines. Holding *Star Wars* and *Star Trek* next to each other shows how each is a product of the conscious efforts of some individuals. Ultimately, whether there would be diversity, inclusion, and even interracial intimacy in *Star Wars* movies lies with its creators. For the producers, directors, and writers of *Star Wars*, the story of diversity can be split between the Lucas years (1973–2012) and the Disney years (2012–present). They made the choices of how the galaxy works, who plays what role, and how race is lived in their science fiction world. George Lucas intentionally kiboshed Glynn Turman and wrote only one significant Black role in both the original trilogy and the prequel trilogy. He "didn't want to make *Guess Who's Coming to Dinner*," and the animus of the times corroborated this hesitancy.[16]

Truth is, there are more continuities between the two eras than shifts. The sequel trilogy, conceived by a later generation of writers, producers, and directors who could have done it differently, also avoided an interracial relationship because of the more deplorable segment of our society. In December 2020, author Alan Dean Foster, who had written the novelization of the 1977 original and returned to write the novelization of *The Force Awakens*, spoke on the YouTube channel Midnight's Edge about his process. As an adaptor of screenplays, he mainly fixes some things in the story and some things in the science. Working from the screenplay, Foster said, "There was obviously the beginnings of a relationship between John Boyega's character and Daisy Ridley's character."[17] But the executives at Disney had him remove these hints, even if they remained potent as ever on the screen. Unaware of Disney and Rian Johnson's efforts to replace Finn with Kylo Ren, Foster also believed that *Episode VIII* would further develop the romance. This is the most direct evidence I have encountered showing Disney and Lucasfilm's efforts to center whiteness and censor interracial intimacy.

J. J. Abrams explained how fundamental it was to have a plan: "You just never really know, but having a plan I have learned—in some cases the hard way—is the most critical thing, because otherwise you don't know what you're setting up. You don't know what to emphasize. Because if you don't know the inevitable of the story, you're just as good as your last sequence or effect or joke or whatever, but you want to be leading to something inevitable."[18] Taken alongside John Boyega's accounts of both the promises the director made to him when he was cast and the extensive changes made to *The Rise of Skywalker*, Abrams's admission that there was no plan confirms that the main characters' arcs would have been much different if Lucasfilm committed to a strategy for the sequel trilogy from the get-go. Instead, Lucasfilm gave their directors great leeway, which led to replacing inexperienced newcomers with veterans to fix *Rogue One*, *Solo*, and *The Rise of Skywalker*. Rian Johnson followed his own judgment for *The Last Jedi*, producing a movie that disregarded Abrams's three-episode outline and challenged fans in multiple ways. Although no confession exists, fans, critics, and journalists have concluded that Disney and Lucasfilm capitulated to racist and sexist responses to the middle of the trilogy.[19]

These shake-ups led to abandonment of more adventurous facets within the new movies. Neither the willpower nor the momentum nor the imagination remained for the interracial relationship that *The Force Awakens* established. In the dilemma between seeking new, diverse money or old, white money, Disney and Lucasfilm cowered from the toxic racist fans, giving them something monoracial, reflecting the 1980s, instead of something diverse, reflecting the 2010s. Repeatedly, revenues and critical acclaim have proven Hollywood's timidity over interracial relationships wrong—consider the success of films like *Guess Who's Coming to Dinner* (1967) and *Get Out* (2017). Of the sequel movies, *The Force Awakens* had the highest gross and the most favorable critical acclaim.[20]

Interracialism is bound to appear, whether on a symbolic or explicit level, because it cannot be hidden. Its suppression will draw attention to itself. Just as whiteness defines itself by nonwhiteness (i.e., Blackness), purity defines itself by hybridity. Even in the post–civil rights era, producers stymie the presence of explicit interracial intimacy, but they end up drawing attention to it anyway because of the reasons I laid out in chapter 1. Increased diversity in casting would create further disparities between minority actors' appearances in predominantly white settings and the romantic options available for their characters. Science fiction tropes of hybridity would remain prominent, but without the racial stigma once associated with them. Observant viewers would continue to spot these two currents, utilizing the new fora available to them to discuss the issue, influencing others, and tugging control of movies' interracial messages further away from the producers.

Baiting stands as the major studios' solution to appease fans and viewers wanting more diverse representations, especially in the realm of Disney. Its live-action princess movies, its Marvel Cinematic Universe, and its Lucasfilm movies have all engaged in promising minority, interracial, and gay representation. This keeps the politically liberal fans engaged with their products without jeopardizing a loss of revenue or engagement from more conservative fans. Delivering one-second kisses, background dancers, or pronoun revelations also keeps Hollywood's risk factor about the same level as that of the 1950s, when two interracial kisses appeared in *Island in the Sun* (1957). Society has changed, but the entertainment industry's decisions have not. With the *Star Wars* sequel movies, baiting and switching is apparent in the underutilization of John Boyega's Finn. This became most apparent in his potential interracial romances with three characters: Oscar Isaac's Poe, Kelly Marie Tran's Rose, and Daisy Ridley's Rey. Putting Rey with Adam Driver's Kylo Ren showed a dedication on the part of Lucasfilm, by design or default, to white racial purity, against interracial relationships.

Fans supporting on-screen interracial relationships in the galaxy far, far away had no recourse against the politics of the sequel trilogy. The fan outlets they controlled were fewer, and less lucrative, than those of conservative white men who, for example, earned thousands of dollars for their brand of YouTube videos. Stories by Holly Quinn, Stitch, and Charles Pulliam-Moore (a Black critic who had previously confessed, "*Star Wars* fans are why I've never really been able to love the franchise") show how harassment works to silence fans with progressive values.[21] Just as Amiyrah Martin's family found private, domestic ways to enjoy *Star Wars*, others participated in fan activities that reflected their values and gained less attention. For example, a GoFundMe user going by "Rose Tico" raised $8,100 to support the Cybersmile Foundation, an organization that works against cyberbullying, harassment, and digital abuse.[22]

Fan activities by those who hope for interracial and LGBTQ+ relationships remain on the margins compared to fan activities in the mainstream. They are the speculative fiction of speculative fiction itself. If, along with shipping, fan fiction is "a way of the culture repairing the damage done in a system where contemporary myths are owned by corporations instead of owned by the folk," shipping interracial relationships hopes to expand the definition of who the folk are to begin with.[23] This is a realm vexed with disappointment. But as José Esteban Muñoz wrote, "The eventual disappointment of hope is not a reason to forsake it as a critical thought process, in the same way that even though we can know in advance that felicity of language ultimately falters, it is nonetheless essential."[24] Even if the preparation, the conditions, or the execution of speaking is incorrect, and even if things turn out differently than one hopes, having spoken one's utopia is still significant.[25]

As I began writing this book, I often wished I had chosen *Star Trek* instead of *Star Wars*. Gene Roddenberry's realm has mixed characters, stories of their adjustment to the mainstream, and a core mission of cultural pluralism. But the galaxy far, far away has gripped me since I was a boy looking for friendship, adventure, and spectacle. As my myth of choice, it comes to mind now that I am a scholar making sense of racial mixture, our historical moment, and the conversations we engage in. Concurrently, I have developed a skill that I employ in my writing and my teaching that I identified in the introduction as "mixed race analysis." Reading this book should result in the tools to consider familiar things like *Star Wars* from that fruitful perspective. Chapter 1 provided history of racial mixture in film history, and science fiction in particular. Chapters 2 and 3 gave a lesson in how prominent characters can operate as something other than how they appear racially, especially when considering the point of view of different viewers. Chapter 4 warned of the uses of characters praised as feminist as bulwarks against racial mixing. Using the innovations in family making George Lucas introduced in the 1999–2005 movies as a starting point, chapter 5 offered instruction on how deeper themes can work in conjunction with viewers' racial prejudice to shape a trilogy's legacy. Finally, the last two chapters offered ways to evaluate recent conversations about popular culture, politics, and race through the fan activity of shipping. Ultimately, whether interracial relationships appear in major motion pictures depends on the producers, and hopefully the later chapters will alert readers to the bait-and-switch game they play, in which they promise to reflect the real world's diversity but deliver messages that differ only nominally from those portrayed since the movie industry's earliest days.

In this book, I have used mixed race not only to reveal interracialism, but also to spotlight how *Star Wars* mirrors our society's beliefs, provides allegories for difficult topics, and showcases how we treat one another. I use the metaphor of "mirroring" to describe how science fiction works address their current moments. *Star Wars* movies are reflections of George Lucas and the other creators, and us, in a particular historical time. In terms of diversity, gender, and inclusion, they can disappoint. So many elements echoed previous films that it seemed very familiar. It is squarely a product of the post–civil rights era. It is liberal, but not anti-racist. It has a creed, but not convictions. In short, the story of *Star Wars* is the story of race since the legislative gains of the 1960s. The conceptual limitations of the galaxy far, far away, the shortcomings of its producers, and the toxicity of fanship are the limitations, shortcomings, and toxicity of our society.

Notes

Preface

1. The *Star Wars* saga consists of nine films, released in the following order: *Episode IV: A New Hope* (1977), originally titled *Star Wars* when it first premiered in theaters and later retitled. I refer to this movie throughout the book as *Star Wars*. This was followed by *Episode V: The Empire Strikes Back* (1980) and *Episode VI: Return of the Jedi* (1983), completing the original trilogy. The prequel trilogy includes *Episode I: The Phantom Menace* (1999), *Episode II: Attack of the Clones* (2002), and *Episode III: Revenge of the Sith* (2005). The sequel trilogy comprises *Episode VII: The Force Awakens* (2015), *Episode VIII: The Last Jedi* (2017), and *Episode IX: The Rise of Skywalker* (2019). Two Anthology Series films were released during the sequel trilogy years: *Rogue One* (2016) and *Solo* (2018). For the sake of simplicity, generally, I will not be using episode numbers when discussing any of the films.
2. "Catholic Priest Who Burned Cross on Couple's Yard in 1977 Comes Forward," *ABC News*, August 23, 2017, https://abcnews.go.com/US/catholic-priest-burned-cross-couples-yard-1977-forward/story?id=49385654.
3. Henry Jenkins, "Acafandom and Beyond: Week Two, Part One (Henry Jenkins, Erica Rand, and Karen Hellekson)," *Pop Junctions*, June 20, 2011, http://henryjenkins.org/blog/2011/06/acafandom_and_beyond_week_two.html; Kristen Thompson, "What Are Aca/Fans?," *David Bordwell's Website on Cinema*, October 24, 2006, http://www.davidbordwell.net/blog/2006/10/24/what-are-acafans.
4. Henry Jenkins, "Fandom Studies as I See It," *Journal of Fandom Studies* 2, no. 2 (2014): 90.
5. "Left of Black with André Carrington," posted February 22, 2017, YouTube, 00:19:57, https://youtu.be/XXMqlHE2PQU.
6. Erin A. Cech, "When we praise passion, we reward privilege. That's the nutshell of a thoughtful convo w/ @ruthetam this week on @NPRLifeKit....," Twitter, February 5, 2022, https://x.com/CechErin/status/1489911066939

252743; Ruth Tam and Sylvie Douglis, "It's OK to Not Be Passionate about Your Job," *NPR*, February 1, 2022, https://www.npr.org/2022/01/31/1076978534/the-trouble-with-passion-when-it-comes-to-your-career. Note that the social media site X, formerly known as Twitter, is referred to as Twitter throughout the book for purposes of clarity.
7. Erin A. Cech, "Loving Your Job Is a Capitalist Trap," *The Atlantic*, November 12, 2021, https://www.theatlantic.com/culture/archive/2021/11/danger-really-loving-your-job/620690.
8. Joseph Campbell, *The Power of Myth* (New York: Anchor Books, 1991), 113.

Introduction

1. Mel Stanfill, "The Unbearable Whiteness of Fandom and Fan Studies," in *A Companion to Media Fandom and Fan Studies*, ed. Paul Booth (Hoboken, NJ: John Wiley and Sons, 2018), 305.
2. Rebecca Wanzo points out John Fiske's 1992 evasion in her own 2015 essay. In discerning the difference between *fanship* and *fandom*, I follow Stephen Reysen and Nyla R. Branscombe's suggestion that the former refers to "identification with the fan interest," while the latter refers to "identification with other fans." Writing a project that covers race relations, representations, and inclusion—none of which can be taken for granted—throughout the *Star Wars* phenomenon, I associate fanship with the feeling, and fandom with the people. See John Fiske, "The Cultural Production of Fandom," in *The Adoring Audience: Fan Culture and Popular Media*, ed. Lisa A. Lewis (London: Routledge, 1992), 30–49; Reysen and Branscombe, "Fanship and Fandom: Comparisons between Sport Fans and Non-sport Fans," *Journal of Sport Behavior* 33 (January 2010): 176; Rebecca Wanzo, "African American Acafandom and Other Strangers: New Genealogies of Fan Studies," *Transformative Works and Cultures* 20 (2015): https://doi.org/10.3983/twc.2015.0699.
3. Alexis Lothian, *Old Futures: Speculative Fiction and Queer Possibility* (New York: New York University Press, 2018), 4.
4. José Esteban Muñoz, *Cruising Utopia: The Then and There of Queer Futurity* (New York: New York University Press, 2009), 172.
5. Lothian, *Old Futures*, 3; Muñoz, *Cruising Utopia*, 4.
6. Stuart Hall, "Encoding and Decoding in the Television Discourse," in *Essential Essays, Volume 1*, ed. David Morley (Durham, NC: Duke University Press, 2019), 257–276.
7. bell hooks, "The Oppositional Gaze: Black Female Spectators," in *Black Looks: Race and Representation* (Boston: South End Press, 1992), 126.
8. Toni Morrison, *Playing in the Dark: Whiteness and the Literary Imagination* (Cambridge, MA: Harvard University Press, 1992), 6.
9. Matthew Pratt Guterl, *Seeing Race in Modern America* (Chapel Hill: University of North Carolina Press, 2013), 3.

10. Gretchen Livingston and Anna Brown, "Trends and Patterns in Intermarriage," Pew Research Center, May 18, 2017, https://www.pewresearch.org/social-trends/2017/05/18/1-trends-and-patterns-in-intermarriage; Brittany Rico, Rose M. Kreider, and Lydia Anderson, "Examining Change in the Percent of Married-Couple Households That Are Interracial and Interethnic: 2000 to 2012–2016," United States Census Bureau, April 26, 2018, https://www.census.gov/library/working-papers/2018/demo/SEHSD-WP2018-11.html; Brittany Rico, Rose M. Kreider, and Lydia Anderson, "Race, Ethnicity and Marriage in the United States," United States Census Bureau, July 9, 2018, https://www.census.gov/library/stories/2018/07/interracial-marriages.html; Sabrina Tavernise, Tariro Mzezewa, and Giulia Heyward, "Behind the Surprising Jump in Multiracial Americans, Several Theories," *New York Times*, August 13, 2021, https://www.nytimes.com/2021/08/13/us/census-multiracial-identity.html.
11. Michael C. Dawson and Lawrence D. Bobo, "One Year Later and the Myth of a Post-racial Society," *Du Bois Review: Social Science Research on Race* 6, no. 2 (December 2009): 247–249; Brian Resnick and Sarah Frostenson, "Exit Polls: A Broad Range of White People Voted Trump for President," *Vox*, November 9, 2016, https://www.vox.com/policy-and-politics/2016/11/9/13574032/exit-polls-white-people-voted-trump-for-president; Vanessa Williams and Scott Clement, "Why Support for Interracial Marriage Is Much More Common Than Interracial Marriage Itself," *Washington Post*, May 25, 2017, https://www.washingtonpost.com/news/post-nation/wp/2017/05/25/why-support-of-interracial-marriage-is-much-more-common-than-interracial-marriage-itself.
12. Claretta Bellamy, "Support for Black Lives Matter Movement Is Declining, According to New Poll," *NBC News*, November 16, 2021, https://www.nbcnews.com/news/nbcblk/support-black-lives-matter-movement-declining-according-new-poll-rcna5746; Ruth Igielnik, Scott Keeter, and Hannah Hartig, "Behind Biden's 2020 Victory," Pew Research Center, June 30, 2021, https://www.pewresearch.org/politics/2021/06/30/behind-bidens-2020-victory; Tim Marcin, "Nearly 20 Percent of Americans Think Interracial Marriage Is 'Morally Wrong,' Poll Finds," *Newsweek*, March 14, 2018, https://www.newsweek.com/20-percent-america-thinks-interracial-marriage-morally-wrong-poll-finds-845608.
13. Daniel Bernardi, *"Star Trek" and History: Race-ing toward a White Future* (New Brunswick, NJ: Rutgers University Press, 1998); andré m. carrington, *Speculative Blackness: The Future of Race in Science Fiction* (Minneapolis: University of Minnesota Press, 2016); Adilifu Nama, *Black Space: Imagining Race in Science Fiction Film* (Austin: University of Texas Press, 2008); Rukmini Pande, *Squee from the Margins: Fandom and Race* (Iowa City: University of Iowa Press, 2018).
14. Dion Boucicault, *The Octoroon* (Upper Saddle River, NJ: Literature House, 1970); Josiah C. Nott and George R. Gliddon, *Types of Mankind or, Ethnological Researches: Based upon the Ancient Monuments, Paintings, Sculptures, and Crania of Races* [. . .] (Philadelphia: J. B. Lippincott,

1854); Reginald Horsman, *Race and Manifest Destiny: The Origins of American Racial Anglo-Saxonism* (Cambridge, MA: Harvard University Press, 2009); Eric Lott, *Love and Theft: Blackface Minstrelsy and the American Working Class*, 20th anniv. ed. (New York: Oxford University Press, 2013); Samuel Morton, "Hybridity in Animals, Considered in Reference to the Question of the Unity of the Human Species," *American Journal of Science and Arts* 3 (1847): 39–50, 203–212; Peggy Pascoe, *What Comes Naturally: Miscegenation Law and the Making of Race in America* (Oxford: Oxford University Press, 2010); Louis Ruchames, "Race, Marriage, and Abolition in Massachusetts," *Journal of Negro History* 40, no. 3 (1955): 250–273; Werner Sollors, *Neither Black nor White yet Both: Thematic Explorations of Interracial Literature* (New York: Oxford University Press, 1997).

15. Earl Lewis and Heidi Ardizzone, *Love on Trial: An American Scandal in Black and White* (New York: W. W. Norton, 2001); Stow Persons, *Ethnic Studies at Chicago, 1905–45* (Urbana: University of Illinois Press, 1987); Edward Byron Reuter, *The Mulatto in the United States: Including a Study of the Role of Mixed-Blood Races throughout the World* (Boston: Badger, 1918); Everett V. Stonequist, "The Problem of the Marginal Man," *American Journal of Sociology* 41, no. 4 (1935): 1–12; Vernon J. Williams, *Rethinking Race: Franz Boas and His Contemporaries* (Lexington: University Press of Kentucky, 1996); Joel Williamson, *New People: Miscegenation and Mulattoes in the United States* (Baton Rouge: Louisiana State University Press, 1995).

16. G. Reginald Daniel, "Beyond Black and White: The New Multiracial Consciousness," in *Racially Mixed People in America*, ed. Maria P. P. Root (Newbury Park, CA: Sage Publications, 1992), 333–341; Maria P. P. Root, "A Bill of Rights for Racially Mixed People," in *The Multiracial Experience: Racial Borders as the New Frontier*, ed. Root (Thousand Oaks, CA: Sage Publications, 1996), 3–14.

17. G. Reginald Daniel, Laura Kina, Wei Ming Dariotis, and Camilla Fojas, "Emerging Paradigms in Critical Mixed Race Studies," *Journal of Critical Mixed Race Studies* 1, no. 1 (2014): 7.

18. Minelle Mahtani, *Mixed Race Amnesia: Resisting the Romanticization of Multiraciality* (Vancouver: UBC Press, 2014), 8.

19. "Star Wars: The Year's Best Movie," *Time*, May 30, 1977.

20. "Star Wars."

21. Theodore W. Allen, *The Invention of the White Race*, 2nd ed. (London: Verso, 2012); A. Leon Higginbotham and Barbara K. Kopytoff, "Racial Purity and Interracial Sex in the Law of Colonial and Antebellum Virginia," *Georgetown Law Journal* 77, no. 6 (1989): 1967–2029; A. B. Wilkinson, *Blurring the Lines of Race and Freedom: Mulattoes and Mixed Bloods in English Colonial America* (Chapel Hill: University of North Carolina Press, 2020).

22. Orlando Patterson, *Slavery and Social Death: A Comparative Study* (Cambridge, MA: Harvard University Press, 1982), 13.

23. Pierre F. Tiako, *Machine Learning: Concepts, Methodologies, Tools, and Applications* (Hershey, PA: IGI Global, 2012), 803.
24. Joe R. Feagin, *The White Racial Frame: Centuries of Racial Framing and Counter-Framing*, 3rd ed. (New York: Routledge, 2020), 25.
25. Feagin, 5.
26. Feagin, 23.
27. Adrienne Rich, "Disloyal to Civilization: Feminism, Racism, Gynephobia (1978)," in *On Lies, Secrets, and Silence: Selected Prose, 1966–1978* (New York: W. W. Norton, 1979), 299.
28. Boucicault, *The Octoroon*; William Wells Brown, *Clotel, or, The President's Daughter: A Narrative of Slave Life in the United States* (Boston: Bedford / St. Martin's, 2011); Sollors, *Neither Black nor White yet Both*.
29. Forrest Wickman, "Star Wars Is a Postmodern Masterpiece," *Slate*, December 13, 2015, http://www.slate.com/articles/arts/cover_story/2015/12/star_wars_is_a_pastiche_how_george_lucas_combined_flash_gordon_westerns.html.
30. Martin Luther King Jr., *Where Do We Go from Here: Chaos or Community?* (1967; repr., Boston: Beacon Press, 2010), 10.
31. Eduardo Bonilla-Silva, *White Supremacy and Racism in the Post–Civil Rights Era* (Boulder, CO: Lynne Rienner Publishers, 2001), 48.
32. Isaac Asimov, "Runaround," in *I, Robot* (New York: Bantam Books, 2008), 37.
33. Donna Haraway, "A Manifesto for Cyborgs: Science, Technology, and Socialist Feminism in the 1980s," in *The Haraway Reader* (New York: Routledge, 2004), 65.

Chapter 1. The History of On-Screen Science Fiction Interracial Intimacy (1902–1987)

1. Kayti Burt, "A Tribute to the First Ever Science Fiction Film: A Trip to the Moon," *Den of Geek*, November 23, 2019, https://www.denofgeek.com/movies/a-tribute-to-the-first-ever-science-fiction-film-a-trip-to-the-moon; Alissa Wilkinson, "How Georges Méliès' Films Are Still Influencing Cinema, More Than 100 Years Later," *Vox*, May 3, 2018, https://www.vox.com/culture/2018/5/3/17311222/georges-melies-google-doodle-trip-moon-conquest-pole-effects.
2. John Rieder, *Colonialism and the Emergence of Science Fiction* (Middletown, CT: Wesleyan University Press, 2008); Robert J. C. Young, *Colonial Desire: Hybridity in Theory, Culture, and Race* (London: Routledge, 1995).
3. This discussion of trends draws from the collection of science fiction movies and television shows produced by an advanced search at IMDb.com. These searches were executed in February 2021, covering 1977 through 2019, the years of the nine *Star Wars* saga movies. They all rate at least 6.0 out of 10.0, indicating good favor with fans and a modicum of quality. They also each have at least twelve thousand ratings, capturing some gems,

but also excluding works too obscure. To narrow down these 530 titles, I picked through the lists of examples on TVTropes.org pages for three phenomena prevalent in nonrealistic fictional genres. The first, "Half-Human Hybrid," describes the creation of offspring by humans and "any intelligent species in existence." The second, "Interspecies Romance," describes "romance, sexual or otherwise, between two different species." The third, "Robosexual," describes "romantic or sexual relations" between a human and a sentient machine. Discussions with fellow acafans of mixed race and science fiction brought the list to 125, which I coded for the following terms: symbolic interracial intimacy, ambiguous bodies, explicit interracial intimacy, and mixed offspring. See "Half-Human Hybrid," *TV Tropes*, August 24, 2021, https://tvtropes.org/pmwiki/pmwiki.php/Main/HalfHumanHybrid; "Interspecies Romance," *TV Tropes*, July 23, 2021, https://tvtropes.org/pmwiki/pmwiki.php/Main/InterspeciesRomance; "Robosexual," *TV Tropes*, October 14, 2021, https://tvtropes.org/pmwiki/pmwiki.php/Main/Robosexual.

4. Susan Courtney, *Hollywood Fantasies of Miscegenation: Spectacular Narratives of Gender and Race, 1903–1967* (Princeton, NJ: Princeton University Press, 2005), 9.
5. Richard Brody, "The Worst Thing about 'Birth of a Nation' Is How Good It Is," *New Yorker*, February 1, 2013, https://www.newyorker.com/culture/richard-brody/the-worst-thing-about-birth-of-a-nation-is-how-good-it-is.
6. "Cable Act of 1922," Immigration History, accessed October 26, 2021, https://immigrationhistory.org/item/cable-act.
7. Gregory D. Black, *Hollywood Censored: Morality Codes, Catholics, and the Movies* (Cambridge: Cambridge University Press, 1994), 41–45, 50–52; Gerald R. Butters, *Banned in Kansas: Motion Picture Censorship, 1915–1966* (Columbia: University of Missouri Press, 2007), 148–149, 187–189; Courtney, *Hollywood Fantasies of Miscegenation*, 5, 14–16, 103–117, 112–190, 193; Thomas Patrick Doherty, *Hollywood's Censor: Joseph I. Breen and the Production Code Administration* (New York: Columbia University Press, 2007), 2, 6–8, 11, 107; Mick LaSalle, *Complicated Women: Sex and Power in Pre-Code Hollywood* (New York: St. Martin's Press, 2000), 20, 62–65, 77.
8. Rachel F. Moran, *Interracial Intimacy: The Regulation of Race and Romance* (Chicago: University of Chicago Press, 2001), 64.
9. Anthony B. Chan, *Perpetually Cool: The Many Lives of Anna May Wong (1905–1961)* (Lanham, MD: Scarecrow Press, 2003), 259–260.
10. Jim Paul, "The Medieval Mind of George Lucas," *Salon*, May 18, 1999, https://www.salon.com/1999/05/18/lucas.
11. J. W. Rinzler, *The Making of Star Wars: The Definitive Story behind the Original Film* (New York: Ballantine Books, 2007), 247.
12. Stuart Hall, "The Local and the Global: Globalization and Ethnicity," in *Dangerous Liaisons: Gender, Nation, and Postcolonial Perspectives*, ed. Anne McClintock, Aamir Mufti, and Ella Shohat (Minneapolis: University of Minnesota Press, 1997), 174.

13. Adilifu Nama, *Black Space: Imagining Race in Science Fiction Film* (Austin: University of Texas Press, 2008), 30.
14. Kevin J. Wetmore, *The Empire Triumphant: Race, Religion and Rebellion in the "Star Wars" Films* (Jefferson, NC: McFarland, 2005), 129.
15. LeiLani Nishime, "The Mulatto Cyborg: Imagining a Multiracial Future," *Cinema Journal* 44, no. 2 (2005): 36.
16. Nishime, 36.
17. Hernán Vera and Andrew M. Gordon, *Screen Saviors: Hollywood Fictions of Whiteness* (Lanham, MD: Rowman and Littlefield, 2003), 34.
18. Brian Jay Jones, *George Lucas: A Life* (New York: Back Bay Books, 2016), 25, 130, 131, 140, 171, 174, 182; Dale Pollock, *Skywalking: The Life and Films of George Lucas* (New York: Harmony Books, 1983), 142; Rinzler, *Making of "Star Wars,"* 4–5, 19, 21, 47, 93, 296, 298.
19. Lydia Saad, "Gallup Vault: Americans Slow to Back Interracial Marriage," *Gallup*, June 21, 2017, https://news.gallup.com/vault/212717/gallup-vault-americans-slow-back-interracial-marriage.aspx.
20. Peter Biskind, *Easy Riders, Raging Bulls: How the Sex-Drugs-and-Rock 'n' Roll Generation Saved Hollywood* (New York: Simon and Schuster, 1998), 16.
21. Biskind; Mark Harris, *Pictures at a Revolution: Five Movies and the Birth of the New Hollywood* (New York: Penguin, 2008).
22. Donald Bogle, *Toms, Coons, Mulattoes, Mammies, and Bucks: An Interpretive History of Blacks in American Films*, 5th ed. (New York: Bloomsbury Academic, 2016); Ed Guerrero, *Framing Blackness: The African American Image in Film* (Philadelphia: Temple University Press, 1993); Nama, *Black Space*; Mark A. Reid, *Redefining Black Film* (Berkeley: University of California Press, 1993); Komozi Woodard, "Rethinking the Black Power Movement," New York Public Library, accessed October 28, 2021, https://wayback.archive-it.org/11788/20200108191632/http://exhibitions.nypl.org/africanaage/essay-black-power.html; Nancy Wang Yuen, *Reel Inequality: Hollywood Actors and Racism* (New Brunswick, NJ: Rutgers University Press, 2017).
23. Gene Roddenberry, "The *Star Trek* Philosophy," *Inside "Star Trek,"* Columbia Records, 1976.
24. Daniel Bernardi, *"Star Trek" and History: Race-ing toward a White Future* (New Brunswick, NJ: Rutgers University Press, 1998), 29–31.
25. Ruth Berman, "Vulcan Pendant," *Inside "Star Trek,"* July 1968.
26. Edward Gross and Mark A. Altman, *The Fifty-Year Mission: The Complete, Uncensored, Unauthorized Oral History of "Star Trek"—the First 25 Years* (New York: Thomas Dunne Books, 2016), 35.
27. Gene Demby, "Leonard Nimoy's Advice to a Biracial Girl in 1968," *NPR*, February 27, 2015, https://www.npr.org/sections/codeswitch/2015/02/27/389589676/leonard-nimoys-advice-to-a-biracial-girl-in-1968; Leonard Nimoy, "Spock: Teenage Outcast," *FaVE*, May 1968.
28. Demby, "Leonard Nimoy's Advice to a Biracial Girl in 1968"; Nimoy, "Spock."

29. Office of the Press Secretary, "Statement by the President on the Passing of Leonard Nimoy," White House, February 27, 2015, https://obamawhitehouse.archives.gov/realitycheck/the-press-office/2015/02/27/statement-president-passing-leonard-nimoy; Jason Sperber, "Spock as Interplanetary Mixed-Race Muse," *Nerds of Color*, September 13, 2013, https://thenerdsofcolor.org/2013/09/13/spock-as-muse.
30. andré m. carrington, *Speculative Blackness: The Future of Race in Science Fiction* (Minneapolis: University of Minnesota Press, 2016); Nichelle Nichols, *Beyond Uhura: "Star Trek" and Other Memories* (London: Boxtree, 1996); George Takei, *To the Stars: The Autobiography of George Takei, Star Trek's Mr. Sulu* (New York: Pocket Books, 1994).
31. Pollock, *Skywalking*, 151.
32. Jones, *George Lucas*, 47, 199–201; Pollock, *Skywalking*, 150–152; Rinzler, *Making of "Star Wars,"* 67–69.
33. Will Lerner, "Harrison Who? Here's the Actor Who Almost Played Han Solo," *Yahoo! Entertainment*, December 20, 2017, https://www.yahoo.com/entertainment/harrison-heres-actor-almost-played-han-solo-180046786.html.
34. Hugh Armitage, "Star Wars Came Very Close to Casting a Black Han Solo," *Digital Spy*, May 7, 2017, https://www.digitalspy.com/movies/a832429/star-wars-black-han-solo-glynn-turman.
35. Lerner, "Harrison Who?"
36. Armitage, "Star Wars Came Very Close to Casting a Black Han Solo."
37. Jones, *George Lucas*, 201; Pollock, *Skywalking*, 151.
38. Jones, *George Lucas*, 200; Pollock, *Skywalking*, 144, 212; Rinzler, *Making of "Star Wars,"* 107.
39. Thomas Bacon, "The Original Story of Luke Skywalker's Sister (before It Was Retconned to Be Leia)," *Screen Rant*, February 2, 2019, https://screenrant.com/star-wars-luke-skywalker-sister-leia-retcon; Eric Robinette, "Did Harrison Ford Really Hate Being Han Solo in Star Wars?," *Cheat Sheet*, January 16, 2020, https://www.cheatsheet.com/entertainment/did-harrison-ford-really-hate-being-han-solo-in-star-wars.html.
40. Nishime, "Mulatto Cyborg," 47.

Chapter 2. What Are You, Darth Vader? (1977–1980)

1. Rosina Lippi-Green, *English with an Accent: Language, Ideology, and Discrimination in the United States* (London: Routledge, 1997); Thomas Purnell, William Idsardi, and John Baugh, "Perceptual and Phonetic Experiments on American English Dialect Identification," *Journal of Language and Social Psychology* 18, no. 1 (March 1999): 10–30; Christine M. Sapienza, "Aerodynamic and Acoustic Characteristics of the Adult African American Voice," *Journal of Voice* 11, no. 4 (1997): 410–416; Laura Staum, personal communication with author via Zoom, November 16, 2021.
2. Martín is responding to a scene from Kevin Smith's 1997 film *Chasing Amy*, which uses a Black character (Hooper X) to lampoon Afrocentric

thought, namely the notion that Darth Vader is African American. See "Shades of Evil: The Construction of White Patriarchal Villainy in the *Star Wars* Saga," in *Men in Color: Racialized Masculinities in U.S. Literature and Cinema*, ed. Josep M. Armengol (Newcastle upon Tyne: Cambridge Scholars Publishing, 2010), 145–146.

3. Kwame Anthony Appiah, "What Does It Mean to 'Look Like Me'?," *New York Times*, September 21, 2019, https://www.nytimes.com/2019/09/21/opinion/sunday/minorities-representation-culture.html.
4. Mark Dery, "Black to the Future: Interviews with Samuel R. Delany, Greg Tate, and Tricia Rose," *South Atlantic Quarterly* 92, no. 4 (Fall 1993): 736.
5. Dorothy Gilliam, "The Black Heavies," *Washington Post*, September 11, 1977, https://www.washingtonpost.com/archive/lifestyle/1977/09/11/the-black-heavies/aea624b9-768d-4689-830b-e07db7773e05.
6. Jay Castello, "Darth Vader, the Problematic Fanzine Fave of 1977," *Polygon*, February 12, 2023, https://www.polygon.com/23583700/darth-vader-fan-art-1977-zines.
7. Castello.
8. Chris Heath, "The Pursuit of Excellence," *Details*, August 1991; Anna Everett, "Johnny Depp and Keanu Reeves: Hollywood and the Iconoclasts," in *Pretty People: Movie Stars of the 1990s*, ed. Everett (New Brunswick, NJ: Rutgers University Press, 2012), 242.
9. I chose lists of essential villains from ScreenCraft.org and PopSugar.com because they were the most complete examples of this kind of guide. The leading guidebooks on creative writing also emphasize character types, as does the work of Joseph Campbell. With its economic form, screenwriting especially draws from New Criticism's exclusive attention to the text. See Joseph Campbell, *The Hero with a Thousand Faces* (Princeton, NJ: Princeton University Press, 2004); Lajos Egri, *The Art of Dramatic Writing: Its Basis in the Creative Interpretation of Human Motives* (New York: Simon and Schuster, 1960); Syd Field, *Screenplay: The Foundations of Screenwriting* (New York: Delacorte Press, 1982); Robert McKee, *Story: Substance, Structure, Style, and the Principles of Screenwriting* (New York: ReganBooks, 1997); Ken Miyamoto, "15 Types of Villains Screenwriters Need to Know," *ScreenCraft*, August 26, 2015, https://screencraft.org/2015/08/26/15-types-of-villains-screenwriters-need-to-know; and "Your Ultimate Guide to Every Type of Movie Villain," *PopSugar*, October 27, 2015, https://www.popsugar.com/entertainment/Types-Movie-Villains-38854045.
10. Trudier Harris, "The Trickster in African American Literature," National Humanities Center, accessed November 27, 2021, http://nationalhumanitiescenter.org/tserve/freedom/1865-1917/essays/trickster.htm.
11. Harris claims that tricksters are "amoral," giving "no thought to right or wrong." They are interested in their own survival, but their stories of equalizing the playing field serve an aspirational purpose in African American literature.
12. Courtney Terry, "It Ain't Trickin' If You Got It: Pre-colonial African Trickster Deity Traditions Manifest in New Millennium Rap Music," *Phylon*

54, no. 2 (2017): 58–79; John W. Roberts, *From Trickster to Badman: The Black Folk Hero in Slavery and Freedom* (Philadelphia: University of Pennsylvania Press, 1990), 2–56.
13. Mich Nyawalo, "From 'Badman' to 'Gangsta': Double Consciousness and Authenticity, from African-American Folklore to Hip Hop," *Popular Music and Society* 36, no. 4 (2013): 460.
14. Cecil Brown, *Stagolee Shot Billy* (Cambridge, MA: Harvard University Press, 2003), 21–58; Bobby Seale, *Seize the Time: The Story of the Black Panther Party and Huey P. Newton* (Baltimore: Black Classic Press, 1991), 4.
15. Lydia Millet, "Becoming Darth Vader," in *A Galaxy Not So Far Away: Writers and Artists on Twenty-Five Years of "Star Wars,"* ed. Glenn Kenny (New York: Henry Holt, 2002), 133–135.
16. Joel Dinerstein, *The Origins of Cool in Postwar America* (Chicago: University of Chicago Press, 2017), 4–5.
17. "James Earl Jones," IMDb, accessed May 6, 2023, https://www.imdb.com/name/nm0000469; "Jane Alexander," IMDb, accessed May 6, 2023, https://www.imdb.com/name/nm0000737.
18. Over the years, fans have come to associate James Earl Jones most with Darth Vader. For example, an informal poll at TheForce.net asking, "Who contributed the most to the character of Darth Vader?" gives James Earl Jones 70.5 percent of the votes, with George Lucas coming in second. Another informal poll from 2020 asking, "Who is the best at acting as Darth Vader?" excludes James Earl Jones as an option, much to the chagrin of that discussion board's participants. Across video games, shows, movies, and advertisements, the white American actor Matt Sloan has voiced Darth Vader the most times (twenty). Scott Lawrence, an African American actor, follows with seventeen, and then James Earl Jones with eleven. Abraham Benrubi and Clint Bajakian, both white American actors, lag behind with four instances each. "Darth Vader," Behind the Voice Actors, accessed November 28, 2021, https://www.behindthevoiceactors.com/characters/Star-Wars/Darth-Vader; Kevin Burns, dir., *Empire of Dreams: The Story of the Star Wars Trilogy* (Los Angeles: Prometheus Entertainment, 2004); Darth_Falcon, "Who Contributed the Most to the Character of Darth Vader?," *Jedi Council Forums*, August 5, 2006, https://boards.theforce.net/threads/who-contributed-the-most-to-the-character-of-darth-vader.24576204; Darth McPorg, "Who Is the Best at Acting as Darth Vader? (Your Opinion)," Wookieepedia, August 25, 2020, https://starwars.fandom.com/f/p/4400000000000068781; Brian Jay Jones, *George Lucas: A Life* (New York: Back Bay Books, 2016), 238; Dale Pollock, *Skywalking: The Life and Films of George Lucas* (New York: Harmony Books, 1983), 178, 213; Paul Scanlon, "George Lucas: The Wizard of 'Star Wars,'" *Rolling Stone*, August 25, 1977, https://www.rollingstone.com/feature/george-lucas-the-wizard-of-star-wars-2-232011.
19. Allyson Vanessa Hobbs, *A Chosen Exile: A History of Racial Passing in American Life* (Cambridge, MA: Harvard University Press, 2014), 14.

20. "Daughter Discovers Father's Black Lineage," *NPR*, October 2, 2007, https://www.npr.org/2007/10/02/14896871/daughter-discovers-fathers-black-lineage.
21. MSNBC broadcast posted to YouTube on December 14, 2015, as "Melissa Harris Perry Says Star Wars Is Racist," 00:00:55, https://youtu.be/VDFnrNtqAjo.
22. "MSNBC Host Melissa Harris-Perry Claims Star Wars Is Racist," posted December 14, 2015, YouTube, 00:09:38, https://youtu.be/sydjzqokujc; Paul Detrick, "Will *Star Wars: The Force Awakens* Trigger Fans? At Least One," *Reason*, December 19, 2015, https://reason.com/2015/12/19/star-wars-force-awakens-trigger-warning; "Darth Vader Was Black," private YouTube video (no longer available), accessed April 16, 2018, https://youtu.be/4jX3oLuPKrU; Joe Otterson, "MSNBC Host Slams 'Star Wars' for 'Black Guy' Villain Darth Vader (Video)," *The Wrap*, December 14, 2015, https://www.thewrap.com/msnbc-host-slams-star-wars-for-black-guy-villain-darth-vader-video; Jack Shepherd, "Star Wars Is Racist Because Darth Vader Is 'a Black Guy', MSNBC's Melissa Harris Perry Suggests," *Independent*, December 16, 2015, https://www.independent.co.uk/arts-entertainment/films/news/msnbc-s-melissa-harris-perry-implies-star-wars-is-racist-because-darth-vader-is-a-black-guy-a6775406.html; "Melissa Harris Perry: Star Wars Is Racist Because Vader Was a 'Black Guy,'" posted December 15, 2015, YouTube, 00:06:01, https://youtu.be/hlQsKANDqlw.
23. There have been later, genuine instances of whites suggesting Darth Vader was African American. See, for instance, comedian Charles Ross's show *One Man "Star Wars,"* in which he reenacted scenes from the original trilogy, including Luke expressing astonishment when he finally saw Darth Vader without his helmet, saying, "I thought you were Black!" In a 2006 fan film, *The Vader Files*, Steven Frailey rearranged scenes in which Darth Vader appeared, overdubbing them with dialogue by James Earl Jones from many other movies. The end result tells the story of a Black Company Man exhausted by his job. "Vader Sessions," posted June 27, 2006, YouTube, 00:09:26, https://youtu.be/6A0rwG39Jzk.

Chapter 3. Early Fanship, the Invisible Jetpack, and Black Fans (1977–1982)

1. John May, "Darth Vader Lives," *Star Wars Official Poster Monthly*, November 1977.
2. May.
3. Paul Scanlon, "George Lucas: The Wizard of 'Star Wars,'" *Rolling Stone*, August 25, 1977, https://www.rollingstone.com/feature/george-lucas-the-wizard-of-star-wars-2-232011.
4. Craig Miller, December 20, 1977, "Open Letters to Star Wars Zine Publishers (1981)," Fanlore, last modified July 5, 2024, https://fanlore.org/wiki/Open_Letters_to_Star_Wars_Zine_Publishers_(1981)#1977.

5. Rebecca Wanzo, "African American Acafandom and Other Strangers: New Genealogies of Fan Studies," *Transformative Works and Cultures* 20 (September 2015): https://doi.org/10.3983/twc.2015.0699.
6. Peggy McIntosh, "White Privilege: Unpacking the Invisible Knapsack," *Peace and Freedom Magazine*, August 1989.
7. Wanzo, "African American Acafandom and Other Strangers."
8. Phil Archbold, "What It Was Really Like to See Star Wars in 1977," *Looper*, September 18, 2020, https://www.looper.com/249198/what-it-was-really-like-to-see-star-wars-in-1977; Tim Clodfelter, "Stephen Colbert Reminisces about Original 'Star Wars,'" *Winston-Salem Journal*, September 8, 2015, https://journalnow.com/entertainment/arts/stephen-colbert-reminisces-about-original-star-wars/article_e438156e-2f35-5668-b7f4-fe10d6ddf888.html; "'Star Wars': What It Felt Like the First Time," *Today*, April 20, 2005, https://www.today.com/popculture/star-wars-what-it-felt-first-time-wbna7562991.
9. Ryan Lambie, "Star Wars: How an Empty Box Became a Must-Have Item in 1977," *Den of Geek*, December 18, 2019, https://www.denofgeek.com/movies/star-wars-how-an-empty-box-became-a-must-have-item-in-1977.
10. Jeff (M. J. Fisher) Johnston, "A New Fandom: Star Wars," *Spectrum*, n.d.; "Are You a Nurd?," *National Lampoon*, October 1974; Joan Marie Verba, *Boldly Writing: A Trekker Fan and Zine History, 1967–1987*, 2nd ed. (Minnetonka, MN: FTL Publications, 2003), 46, 50.
11. "The Many Origin Stories of 'Nerd,'" Merriam-Webster, accessed December 26, 2021, https://www.merriam-webster.com/words-at-play/word-history-nerd; Mel Stanfill, "Doing Fandom, (Mis)Doing Whiteness: Heteronormativity, Racialization, and the Discursive Construction of Fandom," in "Race and Ethnicity in Fandom," ed. Robin Anne Reid and Sarah Gatson, special issue, *Transformative Works and Cultures* 8, no. 1 (November 2011): https://journal.transformativeworks.org/index.php/twc/article/view/256/243.
12. Paul M. Kienitz, "A Historical Timeline of the Word 'Nerd,'" accessed December 26, 2021, https://paulkienitz.net/nerd-history.html.
13. Keith Hayward, "'Life Stage Dissolution' in Anglo-American Advertising and Popular Culture: Kidults, Lil' Britneys and Middle Youths," *Sociological Review* 61, no. 3 (2013): 525–548.
14. Alondra Nelson, "Introduction: Future Texts," *Social Text* 20, no. 2 (Summer 2002): 9.
15. Ytasha L. Womack, *Afrofuturism: The World of Black Sci-Fi and Fantasy Culture* (Chicago: Chicago Review Press, 2013), 5.
16. Shawn Taylor, "The Dark Side of *Star Wars*," *Nerds of Color*, September 30, 2013, https://thenerdsofcolor.org/2013/09/30/the-dark-side-of-star-wars.
17. Taylor.
18. Mark Jacobson, "Richard Pryor Is the Blackest Comic of Them All," *New West Magazine*, August 30, 1976.
19. Mel Watkins, *On the Real Side: A History of African American Comedy* (New York: Simon and Schuster, 1994), 557–558.

20. Watkins, 559–560.
21. William Friedman Fagelson, "Fighting Films: The Everyday Tactics of World War II Soldiers," *Cinema Journal* 40, no. 3 (2001): 94–112; Lawrence W. Levine, *Highbrow/Lowbrow* (Cambridge, MA: Harvard University Press, 2009), 169–242; Eddie Murphy, "Black Movie Theaters," *Eddie Murphy*, CBS Records, 1982; "Why Some Blacks Prefer 'Whiter' Movie Theaters," *TheGrio*, May 28, 2010, https://thegrio.com/2010/05/28/why-some-blacks-prefer-whiter-movie-theaters.
22. Karen Hellekson, "The Fan Experience," in *A Companion to Media Fandom and Fan Studies*, ed. Paul Booth (Newark, NJ: John Wiley and Sons, 2018), 74.
23. Susan Florini's examination of Black Twitter's #demthrones subculture that grew around *Game of Thrones* (2011–2019) presents characteristics that may have descended from talking in the cinema, namely: (1) how it is enclaved from mainstream fanship; (2) the use of "Black cultural commonplaces and intertextualities with Black popular culture"; and (3) its affinity for a world with a "dearth of Black bodies," much like in *Star Wars*. Susan Florini, "Enclaving and Cultural Resonance in Black *Game of Thrones* Fandom," in "Fans of Color, Fandoms of Color," ed. Abigail De Kosnik and andré carrington, special issue, *Transformative Works and Cultures*, no. 29 (2019): https://doi.org/10.3983/twc.2019.1498.
24. Will Brooker, *Using the Force: Creativity, Community, and "Star Wars" Fans* (New York: Continuum, 2002), 57.
25. Brooker, 29–62.
26. Janet Staiger, *Perverse Spectators: The Practices of Film Reception* (New York: New York University Press, 2000), 51.
27. Harry Allen, "Planet Rock: *Star Wars* and Hip-Hop," in *A Galaxy Not So Far Away: Writers and Artists on Twenty-Five Years of "Star Wars,"* ed. Glenn Kenny (New York: Henry Holt, 2002), 153.
28. Real Thing, "Can You Feel the Force?," *Can You Feel the Force?*, Pye Records, 1979.
29. Instant Funk, "Dark Vader," *Instant Funk*, Salsoul Records, 1979.
30. Instant Funk.
31. Kool Moe Dee, "How Ya Like Me Now," *How Ya Like Me Now*, Jive Records, 1987.
32. Big Daddy Kane and Biz Markie, "Just Rhymin' with Biz," *Just Rhymin' with Biz / Let Go My Eggo*, Cold Chillin' Records, 1995.
33. DJ Jazzy Jeff & the Fresh Prince, "He's the DJ, I'm the Rapper," *He's the DJ, I'm the Rapper*, Jive Records, 1988.
34. Womack, *Afrofuturism*, 21.
35. "The Best Star Wars References in the History of Rap Music," *Wired*, December 15, 2015, https://www.wired.com/2015/12/star-wars-rapper-fans.
36. "Black starship control, walk like I'm Darth Vader / My green limousine, purple Mauri alligators." Kool Keith, "Dark Vader," *Spankmaster*, Overcore Records, 2001.

37. "My Chevy's outside and it's sittin' on Kobe's / And I keep the hood with me like Obi-Wan Kenobi." Ludacris and Gucci Mane, "Party No Mo'," *Battle of the Sexes*, Disturbing Tha Peace Records, 2010.
38. Big Sean, "Celebrity," *Finally Famous (Super Deluxe Edition)*, GOOD Music, 2011; Big Sean, Drake, and Kanye West, "Blessings," *Dark Sky Paradise*, GOOD Music, 2015; Notorious B.I.G., Method Man, and Redman, "Rap Phenomenon," *Born Again*, Bad Boy Records, 1999.
39. Nas, "Star Wars," *Illmatic: 10th Anniversary Platinum Edition*, Columbia Records, 2004.
40. Fugees, "The Beast," *The Score*, Ruffhouse Records, 1996.
41. Talib Kweli, "Get By," *Quality*, Rawkus Records, 2003.
42. A Tribe Called Quest and Busta Rhymes, "Wild Hot," *Rhyme and Reason (Original Motion Picture Soundtrack)*, Priority Records, 1997.
43. Eminem, Slaughterhouse, and Yelawolf, "Shady CXVPHER," *Shady XV*, Shady Records, 2014.
44. Jay Electronica, "Annakin's Prayer," *Scratches and Demo Tape Volume 1*, FWMJ's Rappers I Know, 2008.
45. Notorious B.I.G., Method Man, and Redman, "Rap Phenomenon."
46. Mark Anthony Neal, *Looking for Leroy: Illegible Black Masculinities* (New York: New York University Press, 2013), 6.
47. "Black Star Wars Fans—We Do Exist!," posted May 4, 2015, YouTube, 00:07:32, https://youtu.be/k6sh0Tzmmk8.
48. "Black Star Wars Fans—We Do Exist!"; Stephen J. Sansweet, "Gearing Up for May the 4th, and with Good Reason," StarWars.com, May 1, 2013, https://www.starwars.com/news/gearing-up-for-may-the-4th-and-with-good-reason; Mike Snider, "May the Fourth: What Is Star Wars Day and When Did It Start?," *USA Today*, May 4, 2021, https://www.usatoday.com/story/tech/2021/05/04/star-wars-day-2021-meme-thats-overtaken-online-galaxy/4873284001.
49. "Black Star Wars Fans—We Do Exist!"; Amiyrah Martin, "About Me," *4 Hats and Frugal*, accessed August 8, 2024, https://4hatsandfrugal.com/about-amiyrah-martin.

Chapter 4. Princess Leia, Lando Calrissian, and Fan Imaginations (1977–1983)

1. "Star Wars: The Year's Best Movie," *Time*, May 30, 1977.
2. Vincent Canby, "'Star Wars' a Trip to a Far Galaxy That's Fun and Funny," *New York Times*, May 26, 1977.
3. Roger Ebert, "Star Wars Movie Review and Film Summary (1977)," RogerEbert.com, May 25, 1977, https://www.rogerebert.com/reviews/star-wars-1977.
4. Jack Kroll, "'Star Wars' at 40: The 1977 Review of George Lucas's Original Film," *Newsweek*, May 30, 1977, https://www.newsweek.com/star-wars-george-lucas-40-years-carrie-fisher-anniversary-614373.

Notes to Pages 91–100   **219**

5. Pauline Kael, "Contrasts: George Lucas's 'Star Wars,'" *New Yorker*, September 18, 1977, https://www.newyorker.com/magazine/1977/09/26/star-wars-review-pauline-kael.
6. Ruth Rosen, *The World Split Open: How the Modern Women's Movement Changed America*, rev. ed. (New York: Penguin, 2006).
7. Stephenie Meyer, "Frequently Asked Questions: Breaking Dawn," Stephenie Meyer.com, accessed February 7, 2022, https://stepheniemeyer.com/the-books/breaking-dawn/frequently-asked-questions-breaking-dawn#feminist.
8. Carol Hanisch, "The Personal Is Political: The Women's Liberation Movement Classic with a New Explanatory Introduction," CarolHanisch.org, January 2006, http://www.carolhanisch.org/CHwritings/PIP.html.
9. Hanisch.
10. Dale Pollock, *Skywalking: The Life and Films of George Lucas* (New York: Harmony Books, 1983), 213.
11. Elvis Mitchell, "Works Every Time," in *A Galaxy Not So Far Away: Writers and Artists on Twenty-Five Years of "Star Wars,"* ed. Glenn Kenny (New York: Henry Holt, 2002), 78.
12. "1980 The Empire Strikes Back Interview with Carrie Fisher and Billy Dee Williams," posted January 10, 2013, YouTube, 00:06:58, https://youtu.be/9D6Zq0x23Ng?t=331s.
13. "Billy Dee Williams Interview 1980 (Lando Calrissian) Brian Linehan's City Lights," posted February 5, 2018, YouTube, 00:09:29, https://youtu.be/trBc9IY5Pbc.
14. Lynn Norment, "Ebony Interview with Billy Dee Williams," *Ebony*, January 1981.
15. "Luke and Leia's Deleted Kiss Extended," posted January 19, 2016, YouTube, 00:03:23, accessed February 7, 2022, https://youtu.be/IQMYug2usuk.
16. Mae Abdulbaki, "5 Things You Didn't Know about Luke and Leia's Kiss in *Empire Strikes Back*," *Inverse*, May 17, 2020, https://www.inverse.com/entertainment/star-wars-empire-strikes-back-luke-leia-kiss-history; Thomas Bacon, "The Original Story of Luke Skywalker's Sister (before It Was Retconned to Be Leia)," *Screen Rant*, February 2, 2019, https://screenrant.com/star-wars-luke-skywalker-sister-leia-retcon; Brian Cronin, "Movie Legends Revealed: Were Luke and Leia Intended to Be Twins When They Kissed in 'Empire'?," *CBR*, September 16, 2015, https://www.cbr.com/movie-legends-revealed-were-luke-leia-intended-to-be-twins-when-they-kissed-in-empire.
17. Gunnar Myrdal, *An American Dilemma: The Negro Problem and Modern Democracy* (New York: Harper and Brothers, 1944), 58.
18. Adilifu Nama, *Black Space: Imagining Race in Science Fiction Film* (Austin: University of Texas Press, 2008), 32.
19. Scott Chernoff, "Among the Clouds," *Star Wars Insider*, July 1998.
20. Chernoff.
21. I have reached this conclusion from searches of the online databases Archive of Our Own, Fandom, Fanlore, and Wattpad. See also Gail Abelove,

drawing of Lando Calrissian in *Organia*, ed. Beverly Lorenstein and Judith Gran, July 1982, available online at https://fanlore.org/wiki/File:Organia27.jpg.
22. Judy Klemesrud, "Billy Dee Williams: 'The Black Clark Gable' Branches Out," *New York Times*, September 19, 1976, https://www.nytimes.com/1976/09/19/archives/billy-dee-williams-the-black-clark-gable-branches-out.html.
23. Eventually, Lando got a sex life on-screen with the stand-alone movie, *Solo: A Star Wars Story* (2018), which retroactively fills in the backstory for him, Han Solo, and Chewbacca. Jonathan Kasdan, one of the movie's screenwriters, stated that he had imagined Lando as "pansexual," and he believed that Williams's and Donald Glover's performances had a "fluidity" to them. However, he was speaking of his thought process while writing, not Disney/Lucasfilm's position. Glover later quipped, "How can you not be pansexual in space? There's so many things to have sex with." Glover's statements joined Kasdan's in baiting those sympathetic to LGBTQ+ representation, not in shaping the final product. In *Solo*, it is apparent that Lando has an intimate relationship with L3-37, his navigation droid. But she dies, and the heroes plug her parts into the *Millennium Falcon*'s systems. "Donald Glover on Lando Being 'Pansexual' in 'Solo: A Star Wars Story,'" posted May 22, 2018, YouTube, 00:01:07, https://youtu.be/89LHRi8h6nA; Mike Snider, "Billy Dee Williams Returns as Colt 45 Spokesman," *USA Today*, March 27, 2016, https://www.usatoday.com/story/money/2016/03/27/billy-dee-williams-returns-colt-45-spokesman/82258846; George White, "Avon Calling on Minority Skills: Strategy: For Reasons of Profit, the Company Goes beyond Affirmative Action," *Los Angeles Times*, September 16, 1991, https://www.latimes.com/archives/la-xpm-1991-09-16-fi-1850-story.html.
24. Jane Firmstone, "The Latest Thing on the Burner," *Alderaan*, June 1981.
25. Howard Roffman, July 30, 1981. The text of this and all the other letters cited in this section are available online at "Open Letters to Star Wars Zine Publishers (1981)," Fanlore, last modified July 5, 2024, https://fanlore.org/wiki/Open_Letters_to_Star_Wars_Zine_Publishers_(1981)#The_First_Letters:_July_and_August_1981.
26. It is unclear whether every one of the twelve that my source mentions had violations. Linda Deneroff, August 4, 1981.
27. Deneroff.
28. Deneroff.
29. Deneroff.
30. Maureen Garrett, August 1981.
31. Garrett.
32. Maureen Garrett, September 16, 1981.
33. José Esteban Muñoz, *Cruising Utopia: The Then and There of Queer Futurity* (New York: New York University Press, 2009), 18.
34. Maureen Garrett, October 30, 1981.
35. Henry Jenkins, *Textual Poachers: Television Fans and Participatory Culture* (New York: Routledge, 2013), 221.

36. Brandi Wilkins Catanese, *The Problem of the Color[blind]: Racial Transgression and the Politics of Black Performance* (Ann Arbor: University of Michigan Press, 2011), 85.
37. Brad Ricca, "Princess Leia and the Gold Metal Bikini: The Pop Culture Connections," StarWars.com, September 18, 2014, https://web.archive.org/web/20190419065943/https://www.starwars.com/news/princess-leia-and-the-gold-metal-bikini-the-pop-culture-connections.
38. Noah Berlatsky, "The 'Slave Leia' Controversy Is about More Than Objectification," *The Guardian*, November 5, 2015, https://www.theguardian.com/film/2015/nov/05/slave-leia-controversy-star-wars-objectification; Laura Mulvey, "Visual Pleasure and Narrative Cinema," *Screen* 16, no. 3 (Autumn 1975): 6–18.
39. Edward W. Said, *Orientalism* (New York: Pantheon Books, 1978), 1–6.
40. Paul Michel Baepler, "The Barbary Captivity Narrative in American Culture," *Early American Literature* 39, no. 2 (2004): 222.
41. Baepler, 222; Said, *Orientalism*, 1–6.
42. Ricca, "Princess Leia and the Gold Metal Bikini"; J. W. Rinzler, *The Making of Star Wars: The Definitive Story behind the Original Film* (New York: Ballantine Books, 2007).
43. Neval Avci, "'The Sons of New-England': Barbary Captivity and the Transatlantic Production of Anglo-American Identities," *Journal for Early Modern Cultural Studies* 21, no. 1 (2021): 71.
44. Said, 1–6.
45. Brandon P. Seto, "Paternalism and Peril: Shifting U.S. Racial Perceptions of the Japanese and Chinese Peoples from World War II to the Early Cold War," *Asia Pacific Perspectives* 13, no. 1 (Spring/Summer 2015): 66.
46. Carol Caldwell, "Carrie Fisher: A Few Words on Princess Leia, Fame and Feminism," *Rolling Stone*, July 21, 1983, https://www.rollingstone.com/movies/movie-news/carrie-fisher-a-few-words-on-princess-leia-fame-and-feminism-190633.
47. Mulvey, "Visual Pleasure and Narrative Cinema," 17.
48. J. W. Rinzler, *The Making of Star Wars "Return of the Jedi": The Definitive Story* (New York: Ballantine Books, 2013), 138.
49. "Carrie Fisher Roasts George Lucas at AFI Life Achievement Award," posted February 5, 2009, YouTube, 00:04:19, https://youtu.be/lZ97s396kb0.
50. Carrie Fisher, *Wishful Drinking* (New York: Simon and Schuster, 2008), 87–88.
51. Carrie Fisher, "Daisy Ridley," *Interview*, October 28, 2015, https://www.interviewmagazine.com/film/daisy-ridley.
52. Colin Hanks, "So, the other night, on May the 4th to be exact, I sat down with my 4 year old daughter and showed her Star Wars: A New Hope. It was her first time watching it. . . . ," Instagram, May 9, 2015, https://www.instagram.com/p/2e3rwfIt4N.
53. John Scott Lewinsky, "Belly Dancer Turns Sci-Fi Fantasies into Career," *Wired*, September 9, 2008, https://www.wired.com/2008/09/amiri-leia-s.

54. Hannah Foxx, "Sex and Star Wars: Why Slave Leia Is My Most Popular Role Play," Moonlite Bunny Ranch blog, November 7, 2017, https://www.bunnyranch.com/blog/featured/slave-leia.
55. American racial thinking influenced the original trilogy, and that thinking likely resonated with most of its audience. About 60 percent of the world box office for *Star Wars* came from within the United States, 53 percent for *The Empire Strikes Back*, and 66 percent for *Return of the Jedi*. The trilogy's success was so colossal, surprising, and satisfying that it proved that Hollywood's marketing strategy was sound. The movies also did well in the anglophone world and Japan. But they did not appear in China or India. "Star Wars Franchise Box Office History," *The Numbers*, accessed May 2, 2024, https://www.the-numbers.com/movies/franchise/Star-Wars#tab=summary.
56. Patricia Arquette's Oscars 2015 acceptance speech against sexism in Hollywood acknowledged the forms that affected only white actors like herself. The media was happy to celebrate this dimension of her feminist stance. However, upon further reflection, critics explained how Arquette was repeating an age-old conception of feminism that could see from only a white point of view. See Eliana Dockterman, "Don't Tear Down Patricia Arquette for a Well-Intentioned Speech," *Time*, February 23, 2015, https://time.com/3718634/oscars-2015-patricia-arquette-feminism; and Nyasha Junior, "Patricia Arquette's Remarks Explain Why Some Black Women Don't Call Themselves Feminists," *Washington Post*, February 24, 2015, https://www.washingtonpost.com/posteverything/wp/2015/02/24/patricia-arquettes-remarks-explain-why-some-black-women-dont-call-themselves-feminists.

Chapter 5. Don't Ask the Prequels Where Babies Come From (1999–2005)

1. Ahuva Cohen, "The Mothership Strikes Back," *Women's Studies Quarterly* 44, no. 1/2 (2016): 321.
2. Robert G. Lee, *Orientals: Asian Americans in Popular Culture* (Philadelphia: Temple University Press, 1999), 7.
3. Peter Biskind, *Easy Riders, Raging Bulls: How the Sex-Drugs-and-Rock 'n' Roll Generation Saved Hollywood* (New York: Simon and Schuster, 1998), 422–424; Brian Jay Jones, *George Lucas: A Life* (New York: Back Bay Books, 2016), 103, 178, 254; Dale Pollock, *Skywalking: The Life and Films of George Lucas* (New York: Harmony Books, 1983), 238–240.
4. Ethan Alter, "'The Phantom Menace' at 20: How the First Episode of the 'Star Wars' Saga Created Toxic Fandom," *Yahoo! Entertainment*, May 17, 2019, https://www.yahoo.com/lifestyle/star-wars-the-phantom-menace-20th-anniversary-toxic-fandom-nostalgia-jar-jar-binks-ahmed-best-george-lucas-225601377.html.
5. John Blake, "How Trump's Victory Turns into Another 'Lost Cause,'" *CNN*, December 28, 2016, https://www.cnn.com/2016/12/28/us/lost-cause-trump/index.html; David Blight, "Trump Has Birthed a Dangerous New

'Lost Cause' Myth. We Must Fight It," Yale MacMillan Center, January 13, 2022, https://glc.yale.edu/news/trump-has-birthed-dangerous-new-lost-cause-myth-we-must-fight-it; Thomas Dodman, *What Nostalgia Was: War, Empire, and the Time of a Deadly Emotion* (Chicago: University of Chicago Press, 2018), 1–3; Alan T. Nolan, "Anatomy of the Myth," in *The Myth of the Lost Cause and Civil War History*, ed. Gary W. Gallagher and Alan T. Nolan (Bloomington: Indiana University Press, 2000), 11–34.

6. *Spaced*, series 2, episode 2, "Change," directed by Edgar Wright, written by Simon Pegg and Jessica Hynes, aired March 2, 2001.
7. Lothrop Stoddard, *The Rising Tide of Color against White World-Supremacy* (New York: Scribner, 1920).
8. Steven Liss, "America's Immigrant Challenge," *Time*, Fall 1993.
9. Liss.
10. Michael A. Fletcher, "Interracial Marriages Eroding Barriers," *Washington Post*, December 28, 1998.
11. Scott Mendelson, "20 Years Ago, 'Star Wars: Special Edition' Made 'Star Wars' Special Again," *Forbes*, February 1, 2017, https://www.forbes.com/sites/scottmendelson/2017/02/01/20-years-ago-star-wars-special-edition-made-star-wars-special-again/?sh=560910882a61.
12. The characters Angel and Spike are redeemed by their love for a pure, white woman. The same will be true in the prequel trilogy, with Anakin (who is human and midi-chlorian) and Padmé. During the sequel trilogy years, some fans longed for the redemption of Kylo Ren, grandson of the symbolically mixed Anakin, through an imagined romance with Rey, another pure, white woman.
13. Joe Morgenstern, "Our Inner Child Meets Young Darth Vader," *Wall Street Journal*, May 19, 1999, https://www.wsj.com/articles/SB927082592439077365.
14. Eric Harrison, "A Galaxy Far, Far Off Racial Mark?," *Los Angeles Times*, May 26, 1999, https://www.latimes.com/archives/la-xpm-1999-may-26-ca-40965-story.html. In the late 1990s, international box office revenues closed the gap with domestic. With an eye on these growing markets, Hollywood developed worldwide marketing strategies. Coming four years before the first simultaneous worldwide release (*The Matrix Revolutions*), *The Phantom Menace*'s Asian stereotypes reflect Lucas's thoughtlessness more than an attempt at global appeal. Still, at 54 percent, the prequel trilogy's international box office revenue reflected global trends, likely influencing Disney executives during the following decade. See Phil Hoad, "The Rise of the International Box Office," *The Guardian*, August 11, 2011, https://www.theguardian.com/film/filmblog/2011/aug/11/hollywood-international-box-office; "Star Wars Franchise Box Office History," *The Numbers*, accessed May 2, 2024, https://www.the-numbers.com/movies/franchise/Star-Wars#tab=summary.
15. "Racial Stereotypes? That Lucas Movie Menace Really Is a Phantom," *Los Angeles Times*, May 29, 1999, https://www.latimes.com/archives/la-xpm-1999-may-29-ca-42109-story.html; Michael Okwu, "Jar Jar Jarring,"

CNN, June 14, 1999, http://edition.cnn.com/SHOWBIZ/Movies/9906/09/jar.jar/.
16. Okwu.
17. Gregory Kane, "Seeing Racism in Jar Jar Is Seeing Phantom Menace," *Baltimore Sun*, June 4, 1999, https://www.baltimoresun.com/news/bs-xpm-1999-06-05-9906050180-story.html.
18. Okwu, "Jar Jar Jarring."
19. Ron Magid, "Master of His Universe: Interview with George Lucas," *American Cinematographer*, September 1999.
20. Magid.
21. Magid.
22. Magid.
23. Martin Luther King Jr., *Where Do We Go from Here: Chaos or Community?* (1967; repr., Boston: Beacon Press, 2010), 10.
24. Okwu, "Jar Jar Jarring."
25. Will Brooker, "Readings of Racism: Interpretation, Stereotyping and *The Phantom Menace*," *Continuum* 15, no. 1 (2001): 15–32.
26. Will Brooker, *Using the Force: Creativity, Community, and "Star Wars" Fans* (New York: Continuum, 2002).
27. David Cassel, "'Star Wars' Lovers Call for Jar Jar's Head," *Salon*, May 28, 1999, https://www.salon.com/1999/05/28/jar_jar.
28. Cassel.
29. KILL Jar Jar Binks NOW, last updated April 24, 2003, https://www.angelfire.com/nv/jarjarbinksmustdie/frames.html.
30. Michael Nordine, "Jar Jar Binks Actor Ahmed Best Opens Up about Racism-Fueled Backlash," *IndieWire*, January 5, 2019, https://www.indiewire.com/2019/01/jar-jar-binks-actor-ahmed-best-racism-suicide-contemplation-1202032520.
31. Ahmed Best, "20 years next year I faced a media backlash that still affects my career today. This was the place I almost ended my life. It's still hard to talk about. . . . ," Twitter, July 3, 2018, https://web.archive.org/web/20220917201212/https:/twitter.com/ahmedbest/status/1014222723764162561; Nordine, "Jar Jar Binks Actor Ahmed Best Opens Up"; "That Moment I Opened Up About Suicide," posted January 4, 2019, YouTube, 00:11:03, https://youtu.be/qfNiSkd3HfI.
32. Peter Travers, "Star Wars: Episode I—The Phantom Menace," *Rolling Stone*, May 19, 1999, https://www.rollingstone.com/movies/movie-reviews/star-wars-episode-i-the-phantom-menace-101886.
33. J. Hoberman, "All Droid Up," *Village Voice*, May 18, 1999, https://www.villagevoice.com/1999/05/18/all-droid-up.
34. Todd McCarthy, "Star Wars: Episode I—The Phantom Menace," Variety, May 17, 1999, https://variety.com/1999/film/reviews/star-wars-episode-i-the-phantom-menace-1117499730.
35. "Top 10 Reasons Why the Star Wars Prequels Are Hated," posted May 31, 2017, YouTube, 00:10:42, https://youtu.be/YvosjX9Zt1U. This video's countdown included bad acting, weak romance scenes, bad writing,

forcing in cameos from the original trilogy, too much politics, midichlorians, Anakin's whining, too much CGI, convoluted plots, and Jar Jar Binks.

36. "The Top 5 Things the Star Wars Prequels Did Horribly, Horribly WRONG—IHE," posted May 31, 2015, YouTube, 00:07:29, https://youtu.be/rtQo MuvGKd0. This video's countdown included too much CGI, ruining Yoda, ruining the Force, crowded scenery, and bad writing.

37. "Triumph Attends the Premiere of 'Star Wars: Attack of the Clones'—Late Night with Conan O'Brien," posted May 3, 2019, YouTube, 00:11:43, https://youtu.be/YKT7bx-fmtk.

38. Mel Stanfill, "Doing Fandom, (Mis)Doing Whiteness: Heteronormativity, Racialization, and the Discursive Construction of Fandom," in "Race and Ethnicity in Fandom," ed. Robin Anne Reid and Sarah Gatson, special issue, *Transformative Works and Cultures* 8, no. 1 (November 2011): https://journal.transformativeworks.org/index.php/twc/article/view/256/243.

39. Germain Lussier, "That Time When Triumph the Insult Comic Dog Mocked Me for Loving *Star Wars*," *Gizmodo*, November 11, 2015, https://gizmodo.com/that-time-when-triumph-the-insult-comic-dog-mocked-me-f-1741820888.

40. Cohen, "Mothership Strikes Back," 322.

41. "Executive Leadership," Ariel Investments, accessed March 25, 2022, https://www.arielinvestments.com/our-team; Bethany McLean, "Why Sheryl Sandberg, Bill Bradley, and Oprah Love Mellody Hobson," *Vanity Fair*, March 30, 2015, https://www.vanityfair.com/news/2015/03/mellody-hobson-ariel-investments-fighting-stereotype; "George Lucas: OWN (Oprah Winfrey Network) Interview—RED TAILS," posted April 19, 2014, YouTube, 00:10:14, https://youtu.be/PigBCbjfwy4; "First Look: George Lucas on His Relationship | Oprah's Next Chapter | Oprah Winfrey Network," posted January 19, 2012, YouTube, 00:01:21, https://youtu.be/LbGrmJ0ST_A; Kim Quillen, "Who Is Mellody Hobson? The Next Board Chair of Starbucks Has Deep Connections to High Finance, Philanthropy and 'Star Wars,'" *Seattle Times*, December 9, 2020, https://www.seattletimes.com/business/starbucks/who-is-mellody-hobson-the-next-board-chair-of-starbucks-has-deep-connections-to-high-finance-philanthropy-and-star-wars.

42. Marco R. della Cava, "George Lucas," *USA Today*, January 6, 2012, https://www.pressreader.com/usa/usa-today-international-edition/20120106/281530812882723.

43. Della Cava.

44. John Eligon, "The 'Some of My Best Friends Are Black' Defense," *New York Times*, February 16, 2019, https://www.nytimes.com/2019/02/16/sunday-review/ralph-northam-blackface-friends.html; Christopher Ingraham, "Three Quarters of Whites Don't Have Any Non-white Friends," *Washington Post*, August 25, 2014, https://www.washingtonpost.com/news/wonk/wp/2014/08/25/three-quarters-of-whites-dont-have-any-non

-white-friends; Malaika Jabali, "A Lawmaker Calling Her 'Black Friend' 'Hostile and Unpleasant' Is Peak Weaponized Victimhood," *Essence*, December 29, 2021, https://www.essence.com/news/patricia-morgan-and-the-black-friend.
45. Robin DiAngelo, *White Fragility: Why It's So Hard for White People to Talk about Racism* (Boston: Beacon Press, 2018), 139–141; Michael Harriot, "7 Rules for White People with Black Friends," *The Root*, April 5, 2018, https://www.theroot.com/7-rules-for-white-people-with-black-friends-1825023173; Zach Johnson, "George Lucas Marries Mellody Hobson: See Their Romantic Wedding Picture!," *US Weekly*, June 25, 2013, https://www.usmagazine.com/celebrity-news/news/george-lucas-marries-mellody-hobson-see-their-romantic-wedding-picture-2013256.
46. Chinyere K. Osuji, *Boundaries of Love: Interracial Marriage and the Meaning of Race* (New York: New York University Press, 2019), 22.
47. Osuji, 60.
48. Della Cava.
49. Osuji, *Boundaries of Love*, 61.
50. Maria P. P. Root, "Within, between, and beyond Race," in *Racially Mixed People in America*, ed. Root (Newbury Park, CA: Sage Publications, 1992), 3; Maria P. P. Root, "A Bill of Rights for Racially Mixed People," in *The Multiracial Experience: Racial Borders as the New Frontier*, ed. Root (Thousand Oaks, CA: Sage Publications, 1996), 9.

Chapter 6. Four Ships Sailed. Which Would Land? (2012–2016)

1. Garry Whannel, *Media Sport Stars: Masculinities and Moralities* (London: Routledge, 2002), 206.
2. Andreas M. Kaplan, "Social Media, Definition and History," in *Encyclopedia of Social Network Analysis and Mining*, ed. Reda Alhajj and Jon Rokne (New York: Springer, 2014), 1825–1827.
3. Clive Thompson, "Brave New World of Digital Intimacy," *New York Times*, September 5, 2008, https://www.nytimes.com/2008/09/07/magazine/07awareness-t.html.
4. Frank Newport, "In U.S., 87% Approve of Black–White Marriage, vs. 4% in 1958," *Gallup*, July 25, 2013, https://news.gallup.com/poll/163697/approve-marriage-blacks-whites.aspx.
5. Clare Foran, "'Angry Asian Man' Stands Up against Racism," *Daily Pennsylvanian*, March 18, 2011, https://www.thedp.com/article/2011/03/angry_asian_man_stands_up_against_racism.
6. Lori Kido Lopez, "Fan Activists and the Politics of Race in *The Last Airbender*," *International Journal of Cultural Studies* 15, no. 5 (September 2012): 431–445.
7. Bao Phi, "NOCs (Nerds of Color)," *Minneapolis Star Tribune*, January 20, 2010, https://www.startribune.com/nocs-nerds-of-color/82188702.
8. Ron Eglash, "Race, Sex, and Nerds: From Black Geeks to Asian American Hipsters," *Social Text* 20, no. 2 (2002): 53.

9. Rod T. Faulkner, "Blerd Defined," *The Outtake*, January 16, 2016, https://medium.com/the-outtake/blerd-defined-b20305b22e9f.
10. Adam Bradley, "The Black Nerds Redefining the Culture," *New York Times*, June 28, 2021, https://www.nytimes.com/2021/03/24/t-magazine/black-nerds-culture.html; "Move Over Urkel, There Are New 'Blerds' Around," *NPR*, November 20, 2012, https://www.npr.org/2012/11/20/165539918/move-over-urkel-there-are-new-blerds-around; Mekeisha Madden Toby, "The Rise of the Black Nerd in Pop Culture," *CNN*, March 31, 2012, https://www.cnn.com/2012/03/31/showbiz/rise-of-black-nerds/index.html; Clinton Yates, "Donald Glover, Issa Rae, Baratunde Thurston: The Rise of the Black Nerd?," *Washington Post*, November 26, 2012, https://www.washingtonpost.com/blogs/therootdc/post/donald-glover-issa-rae-baratunde-thurston-the-rise-of-the-black-nerd/2012/11/26/7015b27e-37dd-11e2-a263-f0ebffed2f15_blog.html.
11. William Evans and Omar Holmon, *Black Nerd Problems* (New York: Gallery Books, 2021), 5–6.
12. Evans and Holmon, 7.
13. fansofcolor, "FAQ: Fans of Color," *Fans of Color*, August 12, 2014, https://fansofcolor.tumblr.com/post/94543526690/faq.
14. mcufandomhatespeopleofcolor, "Why the AOS Fandom Hates People of Color," *MCU Fandom Hates People of Color*, October 31, 2014, https://mcufandomhatespeopleofcolor.tumblr.com/post/101430588612/why-the-aos-fandom-hates-people-of-color.
15. Alex Ben Block, "Disney to Buy Lucasfilm for $4.05 Billion; New 'Star Wars' Movie Set for 2015," *Hollywood Reporter*, October 30, 2012, https://www.hollywoodreporter.com/news/general-news/disney-buy-lucasfilm-405-billion-384448.
16. Nathalia Holt, "The Women Who Run the 'Star Wars' Universe," *New York Times*, December 22, 2017, https://www.nytimes.com/2017/12/22/movies/star-wars-last-jedi-women-run-universe.html.
17. Molly Fischer, "The Great Awokening: What Happens to Culture in an Era of Identity Politics?," *The Cut*, January 10, 2018, https://www.thecut.com/2018/01/pop-cultures-great-awokening.html.
18. Dan Golding, *Star Wars after Lucas: A Critical Guide to the Future of the Galaxy* (Minneapolis: University of Minnesota Press, 2019), 90.
19. Aja Romano, "What We Still Haven't Learned from Gamergate," *Vox*, January 7, 2021, https://www.vox.com/culture/2020/1/20/20808875/gamergate-lessons-cultural-impact-changes-harassment-laws.
20. Milo Yiannopoulos, "Feminist Bullies Tearing the Video Game Industry Apart," *Breitbart*, September 1, 2014, https://www.breitbart.com/europe/2014/09/01/lying-greedy-promiscuous-feminist-bullies-are-tearing-the-video-game-industry-apart.
21. Yiannopoulos.
22. Yiannopoulos.
23. YouTube via Jimmy Blake and Nomia Iqbal, "Star Wars: John Boyega Reacts to Black Stormtrooper Racism," *BBC*, December 1, 2014, https://www.bbc.com/news/newsbeat-30274359.

24. YouTube via Nick Mangione, "'Star Wars: The Force Awakens' Teaser Brings Out the Galaxy's Racists," *Observer*, December 1, 2014, https://observer.com/2014/12/star-wars-the-force-awakens-teaser-brings-out-the-best-and-worst-of-the-internet.

25. Twitter via Themandalorianwolf, "Where Is Finn? The Erasure and Sidelining of a Star Wars Protagonist," *The SWSC*, October 7, 2019, https://web.archive.org/web/20210513145023/https://the-swsc.com/2019/10/07/where-is-finn-the-erasure-and-sidelining-of-a-star-wars-protagonist.

26. Twitter via Themandalorianwolf.

27. Instagram via Blake and Iqbal, "Star Wars: John Boyega Reacts to Black Stormtrooper Racism."

28. Chloe Bryan, "Is 'Don't Feed the Trolls' Actually Good Advice? It's Complicated," *Mashable*, October 25, 2018, https://mashable.com/article/should-i-respond-to-trolls; Film Crit Hulk, "Don't Feed the Trolls, and Other Hideous Lies," *The Verge*, July 12, 2018, https://www.theverge.com/2018/7/12/17561768/dont-feed-the-trolls-online-harassment-abuse.

29. Twitter via Jessica Lechenal, "#BoycottStarWarsVII: People Boycott *The Force Awakens* Because It Promotes 'White Genocide,'" *The Mary Sue*, October 19, 2015, https://web.archive.org/web/20220103030640/https:/www.themarysue.com/boycott-star-wars-vii-because-why-again.

30. Carol M. Swain, *The New White Nationalism in America: Its Challenge to Integration* (Cambridge: Cambridge University Press, 2002), 16.

31. "14 Words," Anti-Defamation League, accessed May 5, 2022, https://www.adl.org/education/references/hate-symbols/14-words; "White Genocide," Anti-Defamation League, accessed May 2, 2022, https://www.adl.org/resources/glossary-terms/white-genocide.

32. Gene Demby, "That Cute Cheerios Ad with the Interracial Family Is Back," *NPR*, January 30, 2014, https://www.npr.org/sections/codeswitch/2014/01/30/268930004/that-cute-cheerios-ad-with-the-interracial-family-is-back; Stuart Elliott, "Vitriol Online for Cheerios Ad with Interracial Family," *New York Times*, May 31, 2013, https://www.nytimes.com/2013/06/01/business/media/cheerios-ad-with-interracial-family-brings-out-internet-hate.html; Reginald Oh, "Fear of a Multiracial Planet: *Loving*'s Children and the Genocide of the White Race," *Fordham Law Review* 86, no. 6 (2018): 2761–2772.

33. Mel Stanfill, *Exploiting Fandom: How the Media Industry Seeks to Manipulate Fans* (Iowa City: University of Iowa Press, 2019), 3.

34. Stanfill, 6.

35. Patricia Hill Collins, "Patricia Hill Collins: Intersecting Oppressions," 2006, https://www.sagepub.com/sites/default/files/upm-binaries/13299_Chapter_16_Web_Byte_Patricia_Hill_Collins.pdf.

36. Collins.

37. Collins.

38. Collins.

39. Patricia Hill Collins, *Black Feminist Thought: Knowledge, Consciousness, and the Politics of Empowerment* (New York: Routledge, 2000), 100.

40. diversehighfantasy, "How White Feminism Is Doing Rey Wrong," *Full-Color Fantasy*, December 21, 2015, https://diversehighfantasy.tumblr.com/post/135646146501/how-white-feminism-is-doing-rey-wrong.
41. Stephen Iervolino, "'Harry Potter' Series Veteran Katie Leung Said She Was Told to Deny Racist Attacks from Online Fans," *ABC News*, March 12, 2021, https://abcnews.go.com/GMA/Culture/harry-potter-series-veteran-katie-leung-told-deny/story?id=76412751; Kelly Marie Tran, "Kelly Marie Tran: I Won't Be Marginalized by Online Harassment," *New York Times*, August 21, 2018, https://www.nytimes.com/2018/08/21/movies/kelly-marie-tran.html.
42. "Oscar Isaac on 'Star Wars: The Force Awakens,' His Best and Worst Day on Set, and More," posted December 17, 2015, YouTube, 00:03:56, https://youtu.be/n7N17DN8wRk.
43. "The Cast of 'Star Wars: The Force Awakens' Is Here!," posted December 17, 2015, YouTube, 00:03:17, https://youtu.be/fuAwgmz7jTc.
44. Sigal Ratner-Arias, "Oscar Isaac's 'Star Wars' Character May Be from Yavin 4," *Big Story*, May 7, 2015, https://web.archive.org/web/20151226174025/http://bigstory.ap.org/article/47f8a03a513b4810a5bb829c5d7e906d/oscar-isaacs-star-wars-character-may-be-yavin-4.
45. Robert A. Strikwerda and Larry May, "Male Friendship and Intimacy," in *Rethinking Masculinity: Philosophical Explorations in Light of Feminism*, ed. Larry May, Robert A. Strikwerda, and Patrick D. Hopkins (Lanham, MD: Rowman and Littlefield, 1996), 81–83.
46. Melvin Burke Donalson, *Masculinity in the Interracial Buddy Film* (Jefferson, NC: McFarland, 2006), 10.
47. Angel Wilson, "Everyone Is Talking about Our 'Star Wars' Slash Ship," *The Geekiary*, December 27, 2015, https://thegeekiary.com/everyone-is-talking-about-our-star-wars-slash-ship/28782.
48. Monique Jones, "#Stormpilot: How Finn/Poe Could Become Canon (and Why It's a Good Thing)," *Nerds of Color*, March 24, 2016, https://thenerdsofcolor.org/2016/03/24/stormpilot-how-finnpoe-could-become-canon-and-why-its-a-good-thing.
49. Spencer Kornhaber, "50 Shades of Rey," *The Atlantic*, March 30, 2016, https://www.theatlantic.com/entertainment/archive/2016/03/reylo/471768.
50. Kornhaber.
51. Kornhaber.
52. Aziz Ansari, "Aziz Ansari on Acting, Race and Hollywood," *New York Times*, November 15, 2015, https://www.nytimes.com/2015/11/15/arts/television/aziz-ansari-on-acting-race-and-hollywood.html.
53. bespins, "Prayer Circle for Daisy Ridley to Be Han and Leia's Daughter," *punch it, chewie*, November 29, 2014, https://bespins.tumblr.com/post/103916481187/prayer-circle-for-daisy-ridley-to-be-han-and.
54. philnoto, "Star Wars—Episode VII—Now in Color!," *Your Nice New Outfit*, November 29, 2014, https://philnoto.tumblr.com/post/103864548251/star-wars-episode-vii-now-in-color-i-wanted-to.

55. lorna-ka, "TFA—Because They're Adorable," DeviantArt, January 25, 2016, https://www.deviantart.com/lorna-ka/art/TFA-Because-they-re-adorable-586705105.
56. renisanz, "Finn X Rey," *bonjour*, December 25, 2015, https://renisanz.tumblr.com/post/135876835109/x.
57. ao3feed-jedistorm, "Archive," *Finn/Rey AO3*, January 31, 2016, https://ao3feed-jedistorm.tumblr.com/archive/2016/1; finnrey-is-canon, "Archive," *a boy, a girl and the universe*, December 31, 2015, https://finnrey-is-canon.tumblr.com/archive/2015/12; fyeahfinnrey, "Archive," *you looked at me like no one ever had*, October 31, 2015, https://fyeahfinnrey.tumblr.com/archive/2015/10; reyandfinn, "Archive," *rey is my child*, December 31, 2015, https://reyandfinn.tumblr.com/archive/2015/12; thescavengerandthestormtrooper, "Archive," *finnrey for the winrey*, December 31, 2015, https://thescavengerandthestormtrooper.tumblr.com/archive/2015/12; wecamebackforyou, "Archive," *who she already adores*, January 31, 2016, https://wecamebackforyou.tumblr.com/archive/2016/1.
58. Rose M. Kreider, "A Look at Interracial and Interethnic Married Couple Households in the U.S. in 2010," US Census Bureau, April 26, 2012, https://www.census.gov/newsroom/blogs/random-samplings/2012/04/a-look-at-interracial-and-interethnic-married-couple-households-in-the-u-s-in-2010.html.
59. Rachel F. Moran, *Interracial Intimacy: The Regulation of Race and Romance* (Chicago: University of Chicago Press, 2001), 61.
60. Habiba Ibrahim, *Troubling the Family: The Promise of Personhood and the Rise of Multiracialism* (Minneapolis: University of Minnesota Press, 2012), 44.
61. Ibrahim, 3.
62. Alexis Lothian, *Old Futures: Speculative Fiction and Queer Possibility* (New York: New York University Press, 2018), 3.
63. Allison Slater Tate, "Baby BB-8 Helps Family Channel the Force in Awesome 'Star Wars' Costumes," *Today*, March 30, 2016, https://www.today.com/parents/baby-bb-8-helps-family-channel-force-awesome-star-wars-t83406; Andrea Towers, "Star Wars: Rey, Finn Pose with Baby BB-8 at Salt Lake Comic Con," *Entertainment Weekly*, March 29, 2016, https://ew.com/article/2016/03/29/star-wars-rey-finn-baby-bb-8-salt-lake-comic-con. The FanX Salt Lake photo in question is no longer available on the above webpages, but it can still be viewed as part of the original tweet; see She Beautiful When She Angry, "how fucking perfect is this family I mean," Twitter, March 28, 2016, https://x.com/SeitanSlut/status/714542626721103873.
64. Jenna Guillaume, "This Couple Did a Photo Shoot as Rey and Finn from 'Star Wars' and It's Adorable," *Buzzfeed*, April 7, 2016, https://web.archive.org/web/20160408232450/https://www.buzzfeed.com/jennaguillaume/finnrey-feels#.sm1aenqDx; Justin Page, "Adorable Couple Dress Up as Finn and Rey with Their Sweet Little Girl as Baby-8," *Laughing Squid*, April 18, 2016, https://laughingsquid.com/adorable-couple-dress-up-as-finn-and-rey-with-their-sweet-little-girl-as-baby-8.

Notes to Pages 164–166   231

65. Bryan Young, "From Jakku to Salt Lake Comic Con: Talking with the Internet's Favorite Real-Life Finn and Rey," StarWars.com, April 13, 2016, https://web.archive.org/web/20210123043928/http://www.starwars.com/news/from-jakku-to-salt-lake-comic-con-talking-with-the-internets-favorite-real-life-finn-and-rey.
66. Young.
67. Ibrahim, *Troubling the Family*, xxxi; R. Lance Montgomery, "The Real Finn and Rey," *RLphotoArt Blog*, April 5, 2016, http://www.rlphotoart.com/blog/the-real-finn-and-rey; R. Lance Montgomery, "The Real Finn & Rey Get Married," *RLphotoArt Blog*, July 26, 2016, http://www.rlphotoart.com/blog/the-real-finn-rey-get-married.
68. diversehighfantasy, "Racism in the Star Wars Fandom: The Tumblr Years," *Full-Color Fantasy*, January 15, 2020, https://diversehighfantasy.tumblr.com/post/190278683781/racism-in-the-star-wars-fandom-the-tumblr-years; Holly Quinn, personal communication with author via Twitter's private messaging feature, April 4, 2022; Stitch, "Stitch on Fansplaining's Two-Part Episode about Race and Fandom!," *Stitch's Media Mix*, May 22, 2016, https://stitchmediamix.com/2016/05/22/stitch-on-fansplainings-two-part-episode-about-race-and-fandom. In a conversation via Twitter's private messaging feature, Holly Quinn (aka diversehighfantasy on Tumblr) gave pointers on finding examples of Reylo art: "Tumblr isn't the easiest to navigate going back a few years, but I'll look through my blog. One place where you can find 2 and 3 is the Jedi Council forum, which has battled racism against Finn since 2014. They've removed a lot of posts that broke their strict TOS [terms of service] (for example, around 2018 they included any degrading language toward Finn in its 'no racism' rule, including referring to him as the janitor). That was a big change in moderation, which previously only counted very overt posts that used slurs as racist. Even being strict, there are always users in Finn's forum arguing that he was never more than a side character."
69. Tobi Akingbade, "Criticising John Boyega's Dancing at Notting Hill Carnival Is Ignorant AF," *Metro*, August 31, 2017, https://metro.co.uk/2017/08/31/criticising-john-boyegas-dancing-at-notting-hill-carnival-is-ignorant-af-6892885; Scott Mendelson, "Controversy over John Boyega Dance Video Is Manufactured Outrage," *Forbes*, August 31, 2017, https://www.forbes.com/sites/scottmendelson/2017/08/31/in-fake-star-wars-news-john-boyegas-dancing-offended-just-one-person/?sh=6b15ced3282d.
70. diversehighfantasy, "Racism in the Star Wars Fandom."
71. Kenzie Bryant, "Daisy Ridley Deletes Instagram Account over Post about Gun Violence," *Vanity Fair*, August 3, 2016, https://www.vanityfair.com/style/2016/08/daisy-ridley-quits-instagram.
72. Daisy Ridley later returned to Instagram in April 2022. See David Mack, "'Star Wars' Actor Daisy Ridley Said She Will Never Return to Social Media," *BuzzFeed News*, June 26, 2019, https://www.buzzfeednews.com/article/davidmack/daisy-ridley-social-media.
73. starwarsfandomh8speopleofcolor, "becketted: Well, thank fuck for that at least. It was so ridiculous that before the movie came out the white villain/

232 Notes to Pages 167–171

    white lead crack ship...," *Star Wars Fandom Hates People of Color*, December 17, 2016, https://starwarsfandomh8speopleofcolor.tumblr.com/post/154584490398/becketted-well-thank-fuck-for-that-at-least-it.

74. Nate Silver, "The Mythology of Trump's 'Working Class' Support," *FiveThirtyEight*, May 3, 2016, https://fivethirtyeight.com/features/the-mythology-of-trumps-working-class-support.

75. Brian Resnick and Sarah Frostenson, "Exit Polls: A Broad Range of White People Voted Trump for President," *Vox*, November 9, 2016, https://www.vox.com/policy-and-politics/2016/11/9/13574032/exit-polls-white-people-voted-trump-for-president.

Chapter 7. Social Media, Fans, and Interracial Relationships (2015–2020)

1. *Project Greenlight*, season 4, episode 1, "Do You Want to Direct This Movie?," written by Alex Keledjian, aired September 13, 2015.
2. Brittney Cooper, "Matt Damon's Staggering Meritocracy Lie: What His 'Project Greenlight' Blow-Up with Effie Brown Really Shows," *Salon*, September 16, 2015, https://www.salon.com/2015/09/16/matt_damons_staggering_meritocracy_lie_what_his_project_greenlight_blow_up_with_effie_brown_really_shows.
3. Kristen Warner, "Okay, let's talk Project Greenlight Ep 1. Was waiting for the clip. Someone posted partial point. Let's start here," Twitter, September 14, 2015, https://twitter.com/kristenwarner/status/643457330059735040.
4. In the remaining two metrics (cable scripted show creators and cable reality and other leads), minorities "held their ground." See Darnell Hunt, Ana-Christina Ramón, Michael Tran, Amberia Sargent, and Vanessa Díaz, "2017 Hollywood Diversity Report: Setting the Record Straight," Ralph J. Bunche Center for African American Studies at UCLA, February 21, 2017, 1–2.
5. The report noted, "Relatively diverse films excelled at the box office between 2011 and 2015, regardless of genre." Hunt et al., 65.
6. Matt Patches, "The Post-Disaster Artist," *Polygon*, May 5, 2020, https://www.polygon.com/2020/5/5/21246679/josh-trank-capone-interview-fantastic-four-chronicle; "Star Wars Anthology Director Josh Trank Quits to Pursue 'Creative Opportunities,'" *The Guardian*, May 1, 2015, https://www.theguardian.com/film/2015/may/02/star-wars-anthology-director-josh-trank-quits-to-pursue-creative-opportunities.
7. Borys Kit and Kim Masters, "Ron Howard Steps In to Direct Han Solo Movie (Exclusive)," *Hollywood Reporter*, June 22, 2017, https://www.hollywoodreporter.com/movies/movie-news/star-wars-han-solo-movie-ron-howard-steps-direct-1015674.
8. Ben Child, "Why Does Star Wars Keep Losing Its Directors?," *The Guardian*, September 11, 2017, https://www.theguardian.com/film/2017/sep/11/star-wars-lose-directors-trevorrow-lucasfilm; Aaron Couch, "Tony Gilroy

on 'Rogue One' Reshoots: They Were in 'Terrible Trouble,'" *Hollywood Reporter*, April 5, 2018, https://www.hollywoodreporter.com/movies/movie-news/star-wars-rogue-one-writer-tony-gilroy-opens-up-reshoots-1100060; Kit and Masters, "Ron Howard Steps In to Direct Han Solo Movie"; Zack Sharf, "'Solo' Actor Says Phil Lord and Chris Miller 'Weren't Prepared' for 'Star Wars,' Alden Ehrenreich 'Just Not Good Enough,'" *IndieWire*, March 26, 2018, https://www.indiewire.com/2018/03/solo-actor-phil-lord-chris-miller-werent-prepared-star-wars-alden-ehrenreich-not-good-1201943599.

9. Sam Moore, "Colin Trevorrow Drops Out of Directing 'Star Wars: Episode IX,'" *NME*, September 6, 2017, https://www.nme.com/news/colin-trevorrow-not-directing-star-wars-episode-ix-2134588.

10. Ben Fritz, "Intrigue and Drama on the Han Solo Set," *Wall Street Journal*, May 10, 2018, https://www.wsj.com/articles/intrigue-and-drama-on-the-han-solo-set-1525961998; Moore, "Colin Trevorrow Drops Out of Directing 'Star Wars: Episode IX.'"

11. Conner Schwerdtfeger, "What J. J. Abrams Thinks about *The Last Jedi*, According to Rian Johnson," *CinemaBlend*, December 18, 2017, https://www.cinemablend.com/news/1745629/what-jj-abrams-thinks-about-the-last-jedi-according-to-rian-johnson.

12. Hoai-Tran Bui, "'Star Wars: The Last Jedi': Rian Johnson Reportedly Scrapped J. J. Abrams' Episode 8 Story," *SlashFilm*, March 6, 2018, https://www.slashfilm.com/556708/jj-abrams-episode-8-story-rian-johnson; David Kamp, "*Star Wars: The Last Jedi*, the Definitive Preview," *Vanity Fair*, May 24, 2017, https://www.vanityfair.com/hollywood/2017/05/star-wars-the-last-jedi-cover-portfolio.

13. Hanna Flint, "'Star Wars: The Last Jedi' and Its Unexpected Examination of Toxic Masculinity (Spoilers)," *Yahoo! Entertainment*, December 15, 2017, https://www.yahoo.com/lifestyle/star-wars-last-jedi-unexpected-examination-toxic-masculinity-spoilers-115626888.html.

14. Angela Watercutter, "*Star Wars: The Last Jedi* Will Bother Some People. Good," *Wired*, December 15, 2017, https://www.wired.com/story/star-wars-last-jedi-inclusion.

15. Ophelian claimed the movie contains the "first truly Bechdel Test passing scene" in the history of the franchise. The Bechdel Test is a measure of the independence of women characters; to pass, a work must have two named women who speak to each other about something other than a man. Only a handful of *Star Wars* movies pass, including *The Force Awakens*, *Rogue One*, *The Last Jedi*, and *The Rise of Skywalker*. See Bechdel Test Movie List, accessed June 2, 2022, https://bechdeltest.com; Anna Smith, "A Force for Good: Why the Last Jedi Is the Most Triumphantly Feminist Star Wars Movie Yet," *The Guardian*, December 18, 2017, https://www.theguardian.com/film/2017/dec/18/star-wars-the-last-jedi-women-bechdel-test.

16. Brad Brevet, "'Star Wars: The Last Jedi' Delivers Second Largest Opening Ever," *Box Office Mojo*, December 17, 2017, https://www.boxofficemojo.com/article/ed3848340484.

17. Dan Hassler-Forest, "'The Last Jedi': Saving Star Wars from Itself," *Los Angeles Review of Books*, December 22, 2017, https://lareviewofbooks.org/article/the-last-jedi-saving-the-star-wars-we-love.
18. Melissa Hillman, "'This Is Not Going to Go the Way You Think': The Last Jedi Is Subversive AF, and I Am Here for It," *Bitter Gertrude*, December 20, 2017, https://bittergertrude.com/2017/12/20/this-is-not-going-to-go-the-way-you-think-the-last-jedi-is-subversive-af-and-i-am-here-for-it; German Lopez, "The Radicalization of White Americans," *Vox*, August 18, 2017, https://www.vox.com/identities/2017/8/18/16151924/radicalization-white-supremacists-nazis.
19. Patricia Hill Collins, "Patricia Hill Collins: Intersecting Oppressions," 2006, https://www.sagepub.com/sites/default/files/upm-binaries/13299_Chapter_16_Web_Byte_Patricia_Hill_Collins.pdf.
20. Anne Cohen, "Kylo Ren's Pecs Prove *Star Wars* Is about Women Now," *Refinery29*, December 19, 2017, https://www.refinery29.com/en-us/2017/12/185735/star-wars-last-jedi-cast-women-movie-review; Kevin P. Sullivan, "In case you're wondering about the low audience scores for #TheLast Jedi, here's a sample from a 1/2-star Rotten Tomatoes review," Twitter, December 15, 2017, https://twitter.com/KPSull/status/941751182942523392.
21. "Star Wars: Episode VIII—The Last Jedi (2017)," IMDb, accessed December 15, 2017, https://www.imdb.com/title/tt2527336; "Star Wars: Episode VIII—The Last Jedi Reviews," Metacritic, accessed December 15, 2017, https://www.metacritic.com/movie/star-wars-episode-viii---the-last-jedi; Rotten Tomatoes, "Star Wars: The Last Jedi," accessed December 15, 2017, https://www.rottentomatoes.com/m/star_wars_the_last_jedi; Avi Selk, "Is a Men's Rights Activist Sabotaging 'The Last Jedi's' Review Scores—or Do People Just Hate It?," *Washington Post*, December 21, 2022, https://www.washingtonpost.com/news/comic-riffs/wp/2017/12/21/is-a-mens-rights-activist-sabotaging-the-last-jedi-review-scores-or-do-people-just-hate-it.
22. Jacob Shamsian, "Some Guy Made a Sexist 46-Minute Cut of 'The Last Jedi' by Editing Out the Women—and It's Awful," *Insider*, January 16, 2018, https://www.insider.com/sexist-star-wars-last-jedi-edit-less-no-women-2018-1.
23. Rachelle Hampton, "*The Last Jedi* 'Chauvinist' Cut Is a Mess. But Fan Edits Can Be Used for Good," *Slate*, January 18, 2018, https://slate.com/human-interest/2018/01/last-jedi-de-feminized-fan-edit-shows-the-incoherence-of-misogyny.html; Madison Malone Kircher, "These Popular Movies Are Just Seconds Long When You Only Include the Lines Said by People of Color," *Business Insider*, July 8, 2015, https://www.businessinsider.com/movies-edited-to-include-only-lines-from-people-of-color-2015-7; Chris Wade and Abraham Riesman, "See Every Line Spoken by a Woman Not Named Leia in the Original Star Wars Trilogy," *Vulture*, December 13, 2017, https://www.vulture.com/2015/12/star-wars-all-female-lines-excluding-leia.html.
24. Themandalorianwolf, "Where Is Finn? The Erasure and Sidelining of a Star Wars Protagonist," *The SWSC*, October 7, 2019, https://web.archive.org

/web/20210513145023/https://the-swsc.com/2019/10/07/where-is-finn-the-erasure-and-sidelining-of-a-star-wars-protagonist.
25. "The Rise of Skywalker, Finn, and Character Abandonment," posted January 6, 2020, YouTube, 00:14:22, https://youtu.be/x9peykbPsUY; Stitch, "The Last Jedi: Thoughts," *Stitch's Media Fix*, December 17, 2017, https://stitchmediamix.com/2017/12/17/the-last-jedi-thoughts; Themandalorianwolf, "Where Is Finn?"
26. Alfred Peredo Flores, *Tip of the Spear: Land, Labor, and US Settler Militarism in Guåhan, 1944–1962* (Ithaca, NY: Cornell University Press, 2023); Chris Gelardi, "Guam: Resisting Empire at the 'Tip of the Spear,'" *The Nation*, November 2, 2021, https://www.thenation.com/article/world/guam-resistance-empire; Jon Mitchell, *Poisoning the Pacific: The US Military's Secret Dumping of Plutonium, Chemical Weapons, and Agent Orange* (Lanham, MD: Rowman and Littlefield, 2020); Tom Taylor, *Star Wars Age of Resistance—Rose Tico*, no. 1 (New York: Marvel Comics, 2019).
27. Rachael Krishna, "We Must Protect Kelly Marie Tran and Her Instagram Account at All Costs," *BuzzFeed News*, December 4, 2017, https://www.buzzfeednews.com/article/krishrach/kelly-marie-tran-discovering-what-its-like-to-be-famous-is#.ifmeO1GgMZ.
28. Anna Menta, "Racist Attacks against Kelly Marie Tran Posted to Rose Tico's 'Wookieepedia' Page," *Newsweek*, December 19, 2022, https://www.newsweek.com/racist-rose-tico-wookieepedia-page-753063.
29. Twitter and Fandom via David Moye, "Kelly Marie Tran of 'Last Jedi' Facing Racist, Sexist Comments Online," *HuffPost*, December 27, 2022, https://www.huffpost.com/entry/kelly-marie-tran-racists-last-jedi_n_5a4400fee4b06d1621b6b2bb.
30. Instagram via "Star Wars Actress Kelly Marie Tran Deletes Instagram Posts after Abuse," *BBC*, June 6, 2018, https://www.bbc.com/news/world-asia-44379473.
31. Antoinette Bueno, "Kelly Marie Tran on Why Quitting Social Media Was Her Best Decision Ever (Exclusive)," *Entertainment Tonight*, October 2, 2020, https://www.etonline.com/kelly-marie-tran-on-why-quitting-social-media-was-her-best-decision-ever-exclusive-154102; Kelly Marie Tran, "Kelly Marie Tran: I Won't Be Marginalized by Online Harassment," *New York Times*, August 21, 2018, https://www.nytimes.com/2018/08/21/movies/kelly-marie-tran.html.
32. Morten Bay, "Weaponizing the Haters: *The Last Jedi* and the Strategic Politicization of Pop Culture through Social Media Manipulation," *First Monday* 23, no. 11 (November 2018): https://doi.org/10.5210/fm.v23i11.9388.
33. Bay.
34. Steven Zeitchik, "So Did Russian Bots Try to Bring Down Star Wars? After Furor, Man Who Authored Study Says Not Exactly," *Washington Post*, October 3, 2018, https://www.washingtonpost.com/business/2018/10/03/so-did-russian-bots-try-bring-down-star-wars-after-furor-man-who-authored-study-says-not-exactly.

35. Bethany Lacina, "Star Wars Twitter Analysis," n.d., https://www.bethanylacina.net/docs/lacina_starwarstwitterII.pdf; Bethany Lacina, "Who Hates Star Wars for Its Newfound Diversity? Here Are the Numbers," *Washington Post*, September 6, 2018, https://www.washingtonpost.com/news/monkey-cage/wp/2018/09/06/who-hates-star-wars-for-its-newfound-diversity-here-are-the-numbers.
36. Rebecca Harrison, "It's a Trap: Reylos, Racism, and the Whiteness of Data in the Harassment of Women Online," *Medium*, January 17, 2020, https://medium.com/@beccaeharrison/its-a-trap-reylos-racism-and-the-whiteness-of-data-in-the-harassment-of-women-online-be3a7fed040b.
37. Lacina, "Who Hates Star Wars for Its Newfound Diversity?" Emphasizing Lacina's challenges but praising her overall inquiry, James Whitbrook of *Gizmodo* said, "Analysis like Lacina's shows that there is still a long way to go in getting an accurate reading of just how deeply rooted toxic elements in fan communities have become and the affects [sic] they have on individuals." As with the whole essay, this barb reveals the author's resistance to acknowledge racism in fandom. See Whitbrook, "The Washington Post's Analysis of *Star Wars*' Toxic Fandom Doesn't Go Deep Enough," *Gizmodo*, September 6, 2018, https://gizmodo.com/the-washingtonposts-analysis-of-star-wars-toxic-fandom-1828856645.
38. "#SWRepMatters: Celebrating Diversity in a Galaxy Far, Far Away," panel at *Star Wars* Celebration '19 Chicago, April 14, 2019. See also "Our Star Wars Stories" playlist, YouTube, last updated December 22, 2020, https://www.youtube.com/playlist?list=PL148kCvXk8pDC7imn-Xfgpa-XSX6aiZ3H.
39. "Both sides of the ensuing commentary became a long entry on Fanlore. When the AO3 [Archive of Our Own] ship stats came out, inevitably with only one or two Black characters out of 200 in the top 100, people discussed it and started asking why." diversehighfantasy, "Racism in the Star Wars Fandom: The Tumblr Years," *Full-Color Fantasy*, January 15, 2020, https://diversehighfantasy.tumblr.com/post/190278683781/racism-in-the-star-wars-fandom-the-tumblr-years.
40. diversehighfantasy.
41. diversehighfantasy.
42. Stitch, "What Fandom Racism Looks Like: The Star Wars Fandom (Part One, Probably)," *Stitch's Media Mix*, December 14, 2019, https://stitchmediamix.com/2019/12/14/what-fandom-racism-looks-like-the-star-wars-fandom-part-one-probably.
43. Kayleigh Donaldson, "Let's be honest here, Star Wars doesn't have a fandom problem: It has a white male fandom problem . . . ," Twitter, June 5, 2018, https://twitter.com/stichomancery/status/1003979405599870976?s=20; Stitch, "What Fandom Racism Looks Like."
44. Stitch.
45. Stitch, "What Fandom Racism Looks Like—Misogynoir: Black Fans on the Defensive," *Stitch's Media Mix*, May 19, 2019, https://stitchmediamix.com/2019/05/19/what-fandom-racism-looks-like-misogynoir-black-fans-on-the-defensive.

Notes to Pages 182–183   **237**

46. Adam B. Vary, "'Star Wars: The Rise of Skywalker': Finn and Poe Aren't Boyfriends, but J. J. Abrams Hints at LGBTQ Representation," *Variety*, December 3, 2019, https://variety.com/2019/film/news/star-wars-finn-poe-not-boyfriends-lgbtq-representation-1203423286.
47. Between December 18, 2019, and April 1, 2020, I tracked these responses three ways: first, by following the #finnrey and #reylo hashtags on Twitter; second, by using the Brand24 service to analyze mentions of the two hashtags from social media; and third, by advanced searches on Twitter. Brand24 "listens to" keywords of interest across the internet and collects their usage in one interface. It measured engagement between influencers and followers, using artificial intelligence to evaluate whether their messages are positive or negative. The software also exported results into Excel files and PDF reports. I discovered Brand24 while exploring the methodologies of scholars relying on Twitter for data. By bringing the internet's activity to me, I was able to collect, analyze, and interpret more quickly. The AI analysis of sentiment was hit-or-miss, and I did not use this feature. Holes in Brand24's results appeared when accounts were suspended for offensive content, or when users removed posts from their accounts.
48. drhorowitzfine, "Rey or Rose? 'Ah, yes, Rey, man. Rey. It started with her.' John Boyega confirms canon #FinnRey from the beginning," Twitter, March 31, 2020, https://twitter.com/drhorowitzfine/status/1245004257922703362; Brian Davids, "'Star Wars' Co-writer Chris Terrio Sets Record Straight on Perceived 'Last Jedi' Jabs," *Hollywood Reporter*, December 30, 2019, https://www.hollywoodreporter.com/movies/movie-news/star-wars-writer-sets-record-straight-perceived-last-jedi-jabs-1265168.
49. Translated from Portuguese: "#finnrey I'm not a fan of star wars and when I saw the new movies it was obvious that the girl should be with the former soldier of the empire and not with a guy who killed his own father killed innocent people and wanted to kill her, from the moment they changed that, the trilogy became shit." Omauaense, "#finnrey eu não sou fã de star wars e quando eu vi os novos filmes tava na cara que a moça deveria ficar com o ex soldado do império . . . ," Twitter, December 22, 2019, https://twitter.com/omauaense/status/1208861962739867648.
50. WentzWaffles, "#spoiler The Rise of Skywalker was good, not great, just good specifically because of [sic] ReyLo officially happened #RiseofSkywalker #finnrey," Twitter, December 23, 2019, https://twitter.com/WentzWaffles/status/1209330452567330818.
51. MakiiZushii, "Anyways, where is my #finnrey ending, I know a good healthy relationship when I see one," Twitter, December 22, 2019, https://twitter.com/makiizushii/status/1208890504747855873.
52. Anthony M, "loving someone who has repeatedly tried to kill you, stalked you using the force, and thrown temper tantrums when things don't go his way. . . . ," Twitter, December 31, 2019, https://twitter.com/GrayKitsune/status/1212127717333729280#.
53. Klaudia Amenábar, "Also bc if he was white they would've made Finnrey a canon romance and not sidelined Finn and made it the poor baby Kylo

story," Twitter, February 13, 2020, https://twitter.com/kaludiasays/status/1227853520726110208.

54. Steven Goffstein quotes another Twitter user, Dorian Rivas, who said, "I'd like to believe that after the events of TROS [*The Rise of Skywalker*], Rey realizes that she didn't love Ben the way she loved Finn because of how he was there for her ever since they escaped Jakku together. . . ." See Steven Goffstein, "This is my headcanon. #trosspoilers #finnrey," Twitter, January 8, 2020, https://twitter.com/StevenGoffstein/status/1214797188515188737.

55. mar, "#finnrey #art wow!!!," Twitter, December 21, 2019, https://twitter.com/mar67796285/status/1208613888306139136#.

56. awe-and-some, "So I ran. Right into you. And you looked at me like no one ever had. I was ashamed of what I was. But I'm done with the First Order. I'm never going back. . . . ," *Her Satanic Majesty*, accessed September 13, 2022, https://awe-and-some.tumblr.com/post/189963573135/so-i-ran-right-into-you-and-you-looked-at-me; awe-and-some, "they'll tell our story one day // for we have loved in an impossible time, in an impossible way," *Her Satanic Majesty*, accessed September 13, 2022, https://awe-and-some.tumblr.com/post/189964758330/theyll-tell-our-story-one-day; awe-and-some, "You looked at me like no one ever had. We'll see each other again. I believe that," *Her Satanic Majesty*, accessed September 13, 2022, https://awe-and-some.tumblr.com/post/189965177880/you.

57. Winnie The Poe, "I believe a 10 second reylo moment was planned all along as much as I believe bringing back Palpatine was from the start. But this set up of a romantic arc . . . ," Twitter, December 19, 2019, https://twitter.com/WinnieThePoe1/status/1207565274381086720?s=20&t=3xbDRul1NocMAWjlJHewpg.

58. DiviningKnife, "Give us #Finnrey you cowards. Love looks like that, this friendship and affection, goddamn~," Twitter, December 30, 2019, https://twitter.com/diviningknife/status/1211849415146823687?s=20&t=3xbDRul1NocMAWjlJHewpg.

59. JulHS, "My review about #Reylo vs #FinnRey of Star Wars☆," Twitter, January 2, 2020, https://twitter.com/JulHS/status/1212897313179484160?s=20&t=3xbDRul1NocMAWjlJHewpg; Olga Kaf, "SW as shipping wars. #reylo #finnpoe #Finnrey #damerey or something else . . . Ok, it's getting ridiculous . . . I love #starwars like it is . . . ," Twitter, December 27, 2019, https://twitter.com/bloooo_mary/status/1210660385533104129.

60. Justin Chang, "Review: 'Star Wars: The Rise of Skywalker' Is Here to Remind You Just How Good 'The Last Jedi' Was," *Los Angeles Times*, December 18, 2019, https://www.latimes.com/entertainment-arts/movies/story/2019-12-18/star-wars-review-the-rise-of-skywalker-last-jedi.

61. Mike Ryan, "'The Rise of Skywalker' Is a Convoluted and Clumsy End to the Star Wars Saga," *Uproxx*, December 18, 2019, https://uproxx.com/movies/star-wars-rise-of-the-skywalker-review.

62. *The Rise of Skywalker* holds a 53 percent average at Metacritic.com, just two points higher than *The Phantom Menace*, which holds the lowest score for any of the *Star Wars* saga movies. Scores are similar at RottenTomatoes.com, with *The Rise of Skywalker* at the bottom with 51 percent and

The Phantom Menace at 52 percent. The three reviews I excerpt here rate the movie close to that Metacritic average. Mark Birrell, "The 10 Best Star Wars Movies (According to Metacritic)," *Screen Rant*, June 11, 2020, https://screenrant.com/best-star-wars-movies-according-metacritic-critics-scores; Chris Evangelista, "'Star Wars: The Rise of Skywalker' Review: The Saga Ends with a Rushed, Disappointing Finale," *SlashFilm*, December 18, 2019, https://www.slashfilm.com/571184/the-rise-of-skywalker-review.

63. Princess Weekes, "We Need to Talk about Finn (and Rey) in *The Rise of Skywalker*," *The Mary Sue*, December 20, 2019, https://www.themarysue.com/finn-rey-star-wars-the-rise-of-skywalker.

64. Stitch, "Rey/Kylo Shippers: A New Look at an Old Face of Fannish Entitlement," *Stitch's Media Mix*, January 4, 2020, https://stitchmediamix.com/2020/01/04/rey-kylo-shippers-fannish-entitlement.

65. Admittedly, for my own mental health, I gravitated toward videos with lines of inquiry like my own.

66. "Oh No! The Rise of Skywalker Was Real Bad :(," posted December 29, 2019, YouTube, 01:04:46, https://youtu.be/GErIPKjwuDg.

67. "The Rise of Skywalker, Finn, and Character Abandonment."

68. "How 'STAR WARS: The Rise of Skywalker' Should Have Ended," posted February 13, 2020, YouTube, 0:07:58, https://youtu.be/2OnieKUgv3I.

69. "Honest Trailers | Star Wars: The Rise of Skywalker," posted March 24, 2020, YouTube, 00:07:25, https://youtu.be/O7dq_wo5eto.

70. "Finn: The Most WASTED Character in Star Wars History—Rise of Skywalker," posted January 9, 2020, YouTube, 00:10:56, https://youtu.be/n5tKV9ay4as; "The Rise of Skywalker, Finn, and Character Abandonment"; "Oh No! The Rise of Skywalker Was Real Bad :("; "Finn Easily Had the Most Wasted Potential . . . (Let's Talk Some Star Wars)," posted February 9, 2020, YouTube, 00:12:43, https://youtu.be/CL2izCePJIY.

71. "The Rise of Skywalker Finn's BROKEN Character Arc," posted July 19, 2020, YouTube, 00:21:24, https://youtu.be/WLFVKUX4qDs.

72. Phil Szostak, *The Art of "Star Wars: The Rise of Skywalker"* (New York: Harry N. Abrams, 2019), 201.

73. Okiro suggests that the removals from the movie could exist in an "Abrams cut." "The Rise of Skywalker Finn's BROKEN Character Arc."

74. Paisley Gilmour, "Star Wars: The Rise of Skywalker Features the Franchise's First Ever Same-Sex Kiss, but Some Queer Fans Aren't Happy," *Cosmopolitan*, December 19, 2019, https://www.cosmopolitan.com/uk/love-sex/relationships/a30279294/star-wars-first-gay-same-sex-lesbian-kiss-rise-of-skywalker; Shannon O'Connor, "Why That 'Star Wars' Kiss Is a Step Back for LGBTQ Representation," *Hollywood Reporter*, December 20, 2019, https://www.hollywoodreporter.com/movies/movie-news/why-star-wars-kiss-is-a-step-back-lgbtq-representation-rise-skywalker-1264180; Brynne Ramella, "Star Wars: The Rise of Skywalker's Gay Characters Explained," *Screen Rant*, May 19, 2020, https://screenrant.com/star-wars-rise-skywalker-gay-lesbian-kiss-explained.

75. Rebecca Alter, "Wait, What Went Down between John Boyega and *Star Wars* Fans on Twitter Last Night?," *Vulture*, January 1, 2020, https://www

.vulture.com/2020/01/john-boyegas-new-years-eve-star-wars-tweets-explained.html.
76. John Boyega, "Star Wars Romance 😏👀☺️," Twitter, December 31, 2019, https://web.archive.org/web/20211030144329/https:/twitter.com/JohnBoyega/status/1212090062147637251; Charles Pulliam-Moore, "John Boyega's Post–*Star Wars* Honesty Is a Good Thing," *Gizmodo*, January 2, 2020, https://gizmodo.com/john-boyegas-post-star-wars-honesty-is-a-good-thing-1840773091; Stitch, "Quick Coverage: John Boyega Ends 2019 with a Bang (and a Hearty 'Fuck You' to Rey/Kylo Shippers)," *Stitch's Media Mix*, January 1, 2020, https://stitchmediamix.com/2020/01/01/quick-coverage-john-boyega-ends-2019-with-a-bang.
77. Katie McCort, "When Systemic Hatred of Women Online Goes Unnoticed, What Does It Say about Us?," *Medium*, January 15, 2020, https://mythdemeanors.medium.com/when-systemic-hatred-of-women-online-goes-unnoticed-what-does-it-say-about-us-930cccb683e0.
78. hyatt__insomnia, "someone i have followed for a long time (yananiris) was on the thread trying to rebut a few things in the article and discuss it . . . ," Twitter, January 17, 2020, https://web.archive.org/web/20200117171104if_/https:/twitter.com/hyatt__insomnia/status/1218195514228903938; Katie, "The # of times 'reylo' is used is only quantified once & it's only feat. in the methodology. . . . ," Twitter, January 15, 2020, https://web.archive.org/web/20200116205804if_/https://twitter.com/InFormalMajesty/status/1217671878610911232; Yananiris, "This is how they used that 'quantified' data. To say Finnrey fans don't ship Finnrey enough. It is a fancy shipping war mixed in with actual harassment tweets. . . . ," Twitter, January 16, 2020, https://twitter.com/Yananiris/status/1217691110543450115.
79. McCort, "When Systemic Hatred of Women Online Goes Unnoticed."
80. Harrison, "It's a Trap."
81. Chris Agar, "Original Star Wars 9 Script Leaks Confirmed by Colin Trevorrow," *Screen Rant*, January 24, 2020, https://screenrant.com/star-wars-9-colin-trevorrow-script-leaks-confirmed; Jon Arvedon, "Star Wars: Duel of the Fates Concept Art Leaks Online," *CBR*, January 23, 2020, https://www.cbr.com/star-wars-duel-of-the-fates-concept-art-leaks-online; "Pt. 1: A Look at the Star Wars Episode IX: Duel of the Fates Screenplay—Robservations Season Two #317," posted January 13, 2020, 02:16:53, https://youtu.be/5ShS32kJclU; Derek Connolly and Colin Trevorrow, "Episode IX: Duel of the Fates [Original Script]," Internet Archive, December 16, 2016, https://archive.org/details/dotf_20200426/mode/2up.
82. In a move even more willful than George Lucas's refusal to cast Glynn Turman as Han Solo, Trevorrow placed Rey and Poe together romantically, which seemed an even wilder digression from *The Last Jedi* than Johnson's emphasis on Rey and Kylo Ren. See Connolly and Trevorrow, "Episode IX."
83. "Star Wars: The Rise of Skywalker What Did Finn Want to Say T-Shirt," Amazon, January 20, 2020, https://www.amazon.com/Star-Wars-Rise-Skywalker-T-Shirt/dp/B0842TL46N.

84. Anthony Breznican, "J. J. Abrams on *The Rise of Skywalker* Critics and Defenders: 'They're *All* Right,'" *Vanity Fair*, December 21, 2019, https://www.vanityfair.com/hollywood/2019/12/jj-abrams-reacts-last-jedi-rise-of-skywalker.
85. Breznican.
86. Breznican; Davids, "'Star Wars' Co-writer Chris Terrio Sets Record Straight on Perceived 'Last Jedi' Jabs."
87. Hoai-Tran Bui, "J. J. Abrams Explains Unanswered Questions about Rey Reveal, Finn's Message, Rey and Kylo Ren in 'Star Wars: The Rise of Skywalker' [Updated]," *SlashFilm*, December 23, 2019, https://www.slashfilm.com/571298/star-wars-the-rise-of-skywalker-questions-jj-abrams.

Conclusion

1. I excluded characters whose names are known from Lucasfilm licensing alone, including Femi Taylor's Oola. I placed Lupita Nyong'o and Rosario Dawson in two categories, since they are Afro-Latinas. The most recent is Moses Ingram, who appears in the Disney+ series *Obi-Wan Kenobi* (2022).
2. Pete Hull, "Speaking for Darth Vader," *Star Wars Insider*.
3. Dale Pollock, *Skywalking: The Life and Films of George Lucas* (New York: Harmony Books, 1983), 213.
4. Samuel L. Jackson commentary, *Star Wars, Episode III: Revenge of the Sith*, directed by George Lucas (20th Century Fox, 2005), DVD.
5. Brandi Wilkins Catanese, *The Problem of the Color[blind]: Racial Transgression and the Politics of Black Performance* (Ann Arbor: University of Michigan Press, 2011), 74.
6. "Master Class—The Full John Boyega Master Class Session," posted April 17, 2018, YouTube, 00:57:02, https://youtu.be/Xwj8lJhgPt0.
7. "Master Class—The Full John Boyega Master Class Session."
8. Anna Peele, "John Boyega on *Star Wars, Detroit*, and Staying Sane with the Help of Robert Downey Jr.," *GQ*, July 17, 2017, https://www.gq.com/story/john-boyega-star-wars-detroit-and-robert-downey-jr.
9. "Master Class—The Full John Boyega Master Class Session."
10. Geena Hardy, "'The Force Awakens' and the Story of Finn," *Fanfare*, January 29, 2020, https://medium.com/fan-fare/the-force-awakens-and-the-story-of-finn-ee9e325d8c37.
11. Jimi Famurewa, "John Boyega: 'I'm the Only Cast Member Whose Experience of Star Wars Was Based on Their Race,'" *GQ*, September 2, 2020, https://www.gq-magazine.co.uk/culture/article/john-boyega-interview-2020.
12. "MF World Premiere • The Shooting Schedule VII," MillenniumFalcon.com, December 1, 2015, https://web.archive.org/web/20170515233940/http:/millenniumfalcon.com; Robotical712, "Jedi Finn in the Leaked *The Force Awakens* Shot List," *The SWSC*, September 18, 2020, https://swshadowcouncil.wordpress.com/2020/09/18/jedi-finn-in-the-leaked-the-force-awakens-shot-list.

13. Famurewa, "John Boyega."
14. Hardy, "'The Force Awakens' and the Story of Finn."
15. Gretchen Livingston and Anna Brown, "Trends and Patterns in Intermarriage," Pew Research Center, May 18, 2017, https://www.pewresearch.org/social-trends/2017/05/18/1-trends-and-patterns-in-intermarriage; Reginald Oh, "Fear of a Multiracial Planet: *Loving*'s Children and the Genocide of the White Race," *Fordham Law Review* 86, no. 6 (2018): 2761–2772; Allison L. Skinner and Caitlin M. Hudac, "'Yuck, You Disgust Me!': Affective Bias against Interracial Couples," *Journal of Experimental Social Psychology* 68 (2017): 68–77; Vanessa Williams and Scott Clement, "Why Support for Interracial Marriage Is Much More Common Than Interracial Marriage Itself," *Washington Post*, May 25, 2017, https://www.washingtonpost.com/news/post-nation/wp/2017/05/25/why-support-of-interracial-marriage-is-much-more-common-than-interracial-marriage-itself.
16. Brian Jay Jones, *George Lucas: A Life* (New York: Back Bay Books, 2016), 201; Pollock, *Skywalking*, 151.
17. "Alan Dean Foster: Talking STAR WARS, Disney, Star Trek, Humanx Commonwealth and Much More," posted December 22, 2020, YouTube, 02:35:10, https://youtu.be/wntglr8gt3w; Roisin O'Connor, "Star Wars Author Says He Was Told to Remove Finn–Rey Romance from The Force Awakens Story," *Independent*, December 30, 2020, https://www.independent.co.uk/arts-entertainment/films/news/the-force-awakens-finn-rey-alan-dean-foster-b1780261.html.
18. Adam Chitwood, "J. J. Abrams Reflects on 'Star Wars' and When It's Critical to Have a Plan," *Collider*, May 26, 2021, https://collider.com/jj-abrams-star-wars-sequel-trilogy-plan-comments.
19. Similarly, some have concluded that the producers kowtowed to international markets by removing progressive content that would challenge their sensibilities. Echoing the prequel trilogy, international box office revenues made up 52 percent of the totals for the five theatrical releases of the Disney era. Studios must acknowledge international markets, but the franchise's stats across three decades indicate that *Star Wars* is performing as well as it can, especially in China. "Star Wars Franchise Box Office History," *The Numbers*, accessed May 2, 2024, https://www.the-numbers.com/movies/franchise/Star-Wars#tab=summary; Alan Yuhas, "Why 'Star Wars' Keeps Bombing in China," *New York Times*, January 14, 2020, https://www.nytimes.com/2020/01/14/movies/star-wars-china.html.
20. "Franchise: Star Wars," *Box Office Mojo*, accessed August 20, 2022, https://www.boxofficemojo.com/franchise/fr3125251845; "All Star Wars Movies Ranked by Tomatometer," Rotten Tomatoes, accessed June 4, 2022, https://editorial.rottentomatoes.com/guide/all-star-wars-movies-ranked.
21. Charles Pulliam-Moore, "*Star Wars* Fans Are Why I've Never Really Been Able to Love the Franchise," *Gizmodo*, December 14, 2017, https://gizmodo.com/star-wars-fans-are-why-ive-never-really-been-able-to-lo-1821232887.

22. Bethany Lacina, "The Latest Star Wars Film Satisfies the Right Wing. Will the Left Start Trolling?," *Washington Post*, January 18, 2020, https://www.washingtonpost.com/politics/2020/01/18/latest-star-wars-film-satisfies-right-wing-will-left-start-trolling.
23. Amy Harmon, "In TV's Dull Summer Days, Plots Take Wing on the Net," *New York Times*, August 18, 1997, https://www.nytimes.com/1997/08/18/business/in-tv-s-dull-summer-days-plots-take-wing-on-the-net.html.
24. José Esteban Muñoz, *Cruising Utopia: The Then and There of Queer Futurity* (New York: New York University Press, 2009), 10.
25. J. L. Austin, *How to Do Things with Words* (Cambridge, MA: Harvard University Press, 1975), 14–15; Ernst Bloch, *Literary Essays*, trans. Andrew Joron, Jack Zipes, Frank Mecklenburg, and H. Wild (Stanford, CA: Stanford University Press, 1998), 339–344.

Index

Page numbers in italics indicate photographs.

12 Years a Slave (2013), 136
2001: A Space Odyssey (1968), 62

Abrams, J. J.: and Jon Boyega, 196–197; hiring, 148, 171; plans for characters, 153, 172, 182, 191, 199–201, 239n73; reviews of, 184
The Academy, 93
acafan, x–xi, 210n3
African American(s): actors, 42–43, 144, 150, 158, 187, 195–198; anti-Black sentiments, 165, 180; anti-miscegenation laws, 163; artists, 43, 128; Blerd, 145; characters, 236n39; critical thought, 2–4, 63, 76; critics, 202; families, 18; fanship, 2, 7, 81, 89–90, *179*, 180–181, 186; feminism, 154; filmmakers, 43, 136; marketing to, 100; marriages, 144; media criticism, 57–59, 76; and Toni Morrison, 4; musicians, 58, 86–88; nerd figures, 146; and Sidney Poitier, 42, 104, 196; and Richard Pryor, 83; racial consciousness, 65, 67; science fiction, 58; sexualization of, 160; studies, 7, 10; and Darth Vader, 59, 67, 70; and Melvin Van Peebles, 43; women, 3, 30, 70, 105, 166, 169, 181. *See also* Finn; interracial intimacy; Turman, Glynn
Afrofuturism, 58, 80–81, 87
Afrofuturism: The World of Black Sci-Fi and Fantasy Culture (2013), 81
Agents of S.H.I.E.L.D. (2013–2020), 147
Alien (1979), 51–52, 112
aliens: citizenship, 32; computer-generated, 120; and droids, 20; gibberish-speaking, 121; interactions with, 5, 19, 29; interracial intimacy and, 39; rights of, 45; as villains, 26, 40, 131
Allen, Harry, 85
Amidala, Padmé: adoption, 134; character development, 133–135, 185; death in childbirth, 133; pregnancy, 116, 133–134; whiteness, 132, 223n12. *See also* Anakin Skywalker
Anatomy of a Murder (1959), 35

246 Index

Angry Asian Man, 145
anti-intermarriage laws, 6, 9, 42
Appiah, Kwame Anthony, 57
Arabian Nights (1942), 107
Arndt, Michael, 153
Asimov, Isaac, 19
Attack of the Clones (2002): plot of, 132–133, 185, 193; popularity of, 87; premiere of, 131; retcon, 135
Aunt Beru, 122
Avatar (2009), 155–156
Avatar: The Last Airbender (2010), 145
Avci, Neval, 107

Bacon's Rebellion, 8
The Bad Man, 63–65: Jack Johnson, 65, *66*; Stagger Lee, 63–64, 67
Bantha Tracks, 77
Battlestar Galactica (2003), 40, 164, 177
BB-8, 153, 164
Bennet, Chloe, 147, 161
Bernardi, Daniel, 6, 44
Best, Ahmed, 117, 128, *129*, 131, 167, 195, 198. *See also* Jar Jar Binks
Big Daddy Kane, 86: "Just Rhymin' with Biz" (1988)
bikini: as costume, 110; famous actresses wearing, 107; LeiasMetalBikini.com, 109; metal, 104–110; Red Sonja, 107
Binks, Jar Jar: backlash against, *119*, 128, 177; Ahmed Best, 117, 195; racism and, 123, 127–128, 130–131; storyline, 124–125. *See also The Phantom Menace* (1999); toxic fandom
The Birth of a Nation (1915): Mary Alden, 34; blackface, *32*; Blackness, 38, 52, 68; Confederacy, 118; D. W. Griffith, 31; racial mixture, 31, 133; George Siegmann, 34
Biskind, Peter, 42, 118
Black. *See* African American(s)

Black Caesar (1973), 43
The Black Company Man, 66. *See also* Lando Calrissian; Darth Vader
Blackface minstrelsy, 9, 34
Black Girl Nerds, 8
Black Lives Matter, 6
Black Nerd Problems, 146. *See also* The Nerds of Color
Black Panther Party, 63
Black Power movement, 43
Blade (1998), 122
Blade Runner (1982), 51, 194
Blaxploitation: genre, 43–44; movies, 43, 64–65
Blazing Saddles (1974), 43
Blerd, 145–146
Boyd, Todd, 123
Boyega, John: J. J. Abrams and, 148, 196–197; critiques of, 188–189, 195; fan reactions to, 6, 101, 170; Finnrey, 162, 183–184, *188*; *The Force Awakens* (2015), 149, 162, 196; and Oscar Isaac, 158, 176, 197; *The Last Jedi* (2017), 196–197; racism against, *150*, 167, 181, 195, 198; response to racism, 150, 187; Reylo, 144, 162–163, 181; and Daisy Ridley as co-lead, 153, 162–163, 187; social media, *188*. *See also* Finn; Finnrey; interracial relationships
Brackett, Leigh, 97
Branscombe, Nyla R., 206n2
Breitbart, 149
Brian's Song (1971), 96
"bromance" genre, 159
Brooker, Will, 85, 126–127
Brown, Effie, 169
Broyard, Anatole, 60, 70
The Butler (2012), 136

C-3PO: backstory, 13–14; British accent, 37; costume, 36; honorary sidekick, 48; *Star Wars* brand, 77; storyline, 97, 122, 175. *See also* droids; R2-D2
The Cable Act (1922), 32

Calrissian, Lando, 97, *98*; assistant Lobot, 20; Black fans, 86; fan responses to, 101; Donald Glover, 220n23; introduction to, 77; Princess Leia and, 98–99, 112, 193; *Organia* article, 100; race, 86–87, 99–100, 109, 195; rescue of Han Solo, 104–105; sexual attraction, 92, 100, 104
Campbell, Joseph, 213n9
Canby, Vincent, 91
captivity narratives, 106–108
carrington, andré m., 6
casting: J. J. Abrams, 196–197; Black actors, 44–45, 201; *Buffy the Vampire Slayer*, 123; Matt Damon and *Project Greenlight*, 169, 197; fan reactions to, 152, 167; George Lucas and Lucasfilm, 48–49, 51, 110, 179, 195; racially mixed people, 11, 34, 59–60; Gene Roddenberry and *Star Trek*, 48, 51, 200
Catanese, Brandi Wilkins, 104, 195
Cato, Christina, *179*
Chewbacca: with Finn and Rey, 153–154; Kenner toys, 77; Princess Leia and, 27, 105, 112; merchandise, 77; in popular culture, 87; as sidekick, 48; Luke Skywalker and, 173, 175; Han Solo and, 26, 99
Chigurh, Anton, 62
Civil Rights Movement, 18
Civil War, 9, 26, 30–31, 98, 118; Reconstruction, 18, 31
Clinton, Bill, 148
Clinton, George, 58; Dr. Funkenstein, 87
Clinton, Hillary, 167
Cloud City, 68, 97–100, 175
Coffy (1973), 43
Cohen, Ahuva, 115
Collins, Patricia Hill, 174; Black feminist epistemology, 154
colorblindness, 104, 196

color-coding, 35; Blaxploitation films, 65; *Star Wars* films, 35, 37, 45, 59, 92–93; *Twilight* films, 156
cooperation, 5, 193
cosplay, 23, 80, 126, 146, 164, *165*, 178; Leia's metal bikini, 107, 110
Cotton Comes to Harlem (1970), 59
Crain, Jeanne, 34
Critical Mixed Race Studies, 7, 10–11; Association of, xi
cyborgs, 19–20, 39, 194. *See also* Donna Haraway
Cylons, 40

Dameron, Poe: and Finn, 153, 157–160, 180; insubordination of, 172; interracial relationship, 158–159; Oscar Isaac, 153; storyline, 197
Daniel, G. Reginald, 10
Darklighter, Biggs, 93
Darth Sidious. *See* Sidious, Darth
Darth Vader. *See* Vader, Darth
Dawson, Rosario, 148, 241n1
Death Star, 67, 87, 175, 195; destruction of, 5, 24, 26, 42; threat of, 93
debtor and debtee, 5, 124
Delany, Martin, 58
Deneroff, Linda, 102, 152
De Palma, Brian, 49
Dery, Mark, 58
The Desert Song (1929), 107
despotism, 8
Diawara, Manthia, 22
diegetics, 44, 51, 116
DJ Jazzy Jeff & the Fresh Prince, 86–87
Donalson, Melvin Burke, 159
Driver, Adam: Finnrey, 144; Reylo, 165. *See also* Kylo Ren
droids, 5, 14, 20, 105, 122–123, 193; race and, 19, 37, 69. *See also* C-3PO; R2-D2
Duel of the Fates (2020), 190

Ebert, Roger, 91
Ejiofor, Chiwetel, 62
Electric Dreams (1984), 80
Emperor Palpatine. *See* Palpatine, Emperor
The Empire, 86; dislike of, 94; as evil, 93; fighting against, 48, 93; hierarchy within, 62; search for Rey, 154; Darth Vader, 60
The Empire Strikes Back (1980): anticipation for, 77; box office, 121, 222n55; Lando Calrissian, 50–51, 98, 100, 104, 193; Princess Leia, 50–51, 97, 98, 104, 193; racist backlash to, 96, 100; romance narratives, 50–51, 98, 103–104, 193; Luke Skywalker, 69, 128; storyline, 22, 26, 97, 205n1; Han Solo, 50; Darth Vader, 68–69, 181; watch parties, 85; Yoda, 128
enslavement, 9, 106
Esteban Muñoz, José, 2, 103, 202
ethnoracial preferences, 137
E.T. the Extra-Terrestrial (1982), 80
eugenics, 9, 30, 120, 130, 151, 156
experimentation, 35, 38, 52–53, 155
Ewoks, 93, 108
Expanded Universe texts, 110

family: adoption, 134–135; conceptions of, 18, 124, 162–163, 167; interracial, 40; making, 35, 40, 47–48, 116–117, 203; unknown, 70; values, 164, 202
Family Matters (1989–1998), 146
fandom, 84, 206n2; conformity, 6; racism, 180, 236n37; revenue, 191; whiteness, 1, 181. *See also* The Nerds of Color
Fandom, 141, 177
fan fiction: awards, 77; creating characters, 74; editors of, 152; feedback loop, 110–112; racism, 180; sexual relationships, 92, 101, 103, 180; shipping, 75, 112, 143–144, 160, 166, 202
fanship: authenticity, 112; Black, 81, 88–90, 179, 217n23; conventions, 77; early, 59, 73, 76; and fandom, 206n2; "Han shot first," 121; in musical lyrics, 88; people of color, 6, 80–81, 183–184; racism, 189; shared community, 84; toxic expressions of, 117, 204; and whiteness, 2, 22, 76, 110, 198. *See also* toxic fandom
fanzines, 7, 74–77, 101–103; x-rated content, 102
Feagin, Joe, 14–16
feminism: audience response to, 174; in film, 113; in literature, 95; parochial white, 113, 155, 190, 222n56; and shipping, 143
Fett, Boba, 77, 88, 116, 171
Finn: J. J. Abrams and, 148, 197; backstory, 158, 186; Chewbacca, 153–154; critiques of sidelining character, 183–187, 195, 197, 200, 202, 237n53; Poe Dameron, 153, 157–160, 180; fan reactions to, 101, 165–166, 195; Force sensitive, 172, 191; interracial intimacy, 142, 152, 193, 196; interracial relationship, 22, 158–160, 164, 196; Jakku escape, 153, 238n54; *The Last Jedi* (2017), 175–176, 193, 197; racism against, 231n68; reduced marketing, 175, 181; Rey, 153–154, 162–165, 187, 190, 193; *Rise of Skywalker* (2019), 186; sequel trilogy (2015–2020), 101, 195–196; Stormpilot, 157; as stormtrooper, 149, 157–158, 162, 165, 182; storyline, 48; Rose Tico, 174–176, 182, 193. *See also* Boyega, John; Finnrey; Finnrose; Finnpoe; shipping

Finnpoe or Finn-Poe, 158–159, 180, 182; Stormpilot, 157, 160. *See also* shipping

Finnrey: anti-Blackness, 190; backlash against, 165, 188–190; John Boyega, 183–184, *188*; in comparison with Reylo, 144, 164–165, 183, 187–190, 196; critiques of Lucasfilm, 183–184; Adam Driver, 144, 165; fan art, 162; fan support, 164, 180, 183–184, 189; interracial relationships, 142, 199; Kylo Ren, 187; Katie McCourt, 188–189; media coverage, 164; racism, 190; Daisy Ridley, 162–163, 184, 187, 190, 200; social media, 237n47, 237n49, 240n78. *See also* Finn; Quinn, Holly; Rey; shipping

Finnrose, 176, 182

Firefly (2002–2003), 39, 112, 139, 145, 149

Firmstone, Jane, 101

First Order, 153, 157–158, 172, 176, 182, 190

Fisher, Carrie: career, 194; Princess Leia, 48, 92–93, *98*, 99, 108–109, 179; shipping, 200; *Wishful Drinking* (2006), 109

Fiske, John, 2, 206n2

Flash Gordon (1936), 217n23, 41–42, 51, 97

Florini, Susan, 217n23

The Force Awakens (2015): Bechdel Test, 233n15; box office, 170, 173, 201; reactions to John Boyega, 149, 151, 196–197; cast, 182, 196; Finnpoe, 158–159, 180, 182; Finn sidelined, 186; interracial relationship, 153, 155, 194, 201; Kylux, 157–158; merchandising, 175; responses to, 70, 141, 198; Stormpilot, 157, 160; storyline, 153, 172, 193, 200; villainy, 175; whiteness, 154.

See also Finnrey; prequel trilogy (1999–2005)

Ford, Harrison, 49–50, 99, 137, 194. *See also* Han Solo

freedom: agency, 22, 93–94; of choice, 95; personal, 91, 94; political; and race, 8, 147, 160; reproductive, 151; sexual, 33, 112

Fruitvale Station (2013), 136

Fugees, 87

Gamergate, 148–150, 166–167, 186

Gardner, Ava, 34

General Grievous, 21, 194

genocide, 103, 185; white, 151–152

Gliddon, George, 9, 19, 46

Glover, Donald, 140, 220n23. *See also* Calrissian, Lando

Gone with the Wind (1939), 50

The Good Earth (1937), 34

The Great White Hope (1970), 43, 65, 66; Jane Alexander, 65; Jack Johnson, 65–66

The Guardian, 102, 106, 173

Guardians of the Galaxy (2014), 155

Guess Who's Coming to Dinner (1968), 42, 49, 104, 200–201

"half-breed," 46, 48

Hall, Stuart, 3, 37, 64

Hamill, Mark, 194

Han Solo. *See* Solo, Han

Haraway, Donna, 20

Harris, Trudier, 213n11

Harrison, Becca, 178, 189–190

Harris-Perry, Melissa, 70

Harry Potter films, 19, 39, 156

Have Gun, Will Travel (1957–1963), 44

Hays Code prohibitions, 23, 34–35, 42

hegemony, 15, 108

Hellekson, Karen, 84

The Henchman, 62
hip-hop, 58, 87, 100; lyrics, 7, 81, 85
Hoberman, J., 130
Hobson, Mellody, 135–139, *138*
Hollywood Diversity Report, 170
Holmes, Sherlock, 56
hooks, bell, 3, 22, 142
"Hoth Admiral," 103
"Hoth Captain" (1981), 104
How It Should Have Ended, 141–142, 186
hybridity, 19, 51, 108, 201

I Dream of Jeannie (1965–1970), 107
Imitation of Life (1934), 9
Imperial Entanglements, 103; Karen Osman, 152
Instant Funk, 86
interracial intimacy: *Avatar* (2009), 155–156; Lando Calrissian, 193; and civil rights, 33, 91; definition and overview, 17, 39; depicted in films, 31, 122; fan responses to, 144; Finn, 142, 193; Finn-Poe, 158; *Harry Potter* series, 156; interracial and transnational adoption, 18; Kylux, 157–158; Princess Leia, 95, 193; mongrelization, 18; popular culture shifts, 1, 6, 10, 30, 122, 155–156; racism and white supremacy, 30, 34, 150–152; research about, 10–11, 209n3; Rey, 142, 193; *Star Wars* films, 12; *Star Wars* producers, 8, 200–201; Stormpilot, 157; symbolic, 6, 32, 35, 38–39, 51–52, 155, 193; Darth Vader, 193; white racial frame, 16. *See also* Finnrey; Reylo
interracialism: concealment of, 30–31, 34, 42; in film and television, 40, 52, 155; and kinship, 115; limited presence in *Star Wars*, 7, 11, 95, 193, 201, 203; minority sidekicks, 157; Gene Roddenberry and, 44, 51; shipping, 143
interracial marriage: *Guess Who's Coming to Dinner* (1968), 42; interracial intimacy, 17; laws against, 6, 30, 32, 163; notions of racial progress, 165; research about, 120; white supremacy and, 151, 163
intimacy: characters deemed unworthy, 26; interspecies, 1, 133; and kinship, 12, 117, 185; kisses, 115; and romance, 12, 48, 117, 185; sex, 48, 115, 187; with unnatural offspring, 122. *See also* interracial intimacy
intraracialism: intimacy between Rey and Kylo Ren, 22, 142, 144; kinship, 115; Luke's adoption, 135
Isaac, Oscar: and John Boyega, 158, 176, 197; Poe Dameron, 153, 157; interracial romance, 202; racial identity, 158, 176

Jabba the Hutt, 105, 121
Jackson, Samuel L., 194–195, 197–198
Jackson Mendoza, Rebecca, 135. *See also* retcon
Jar Jar Binks. *See* Binks, Jar Jar
Jawas, 48, 89, 122
Jay Electronica, 88
Jedi: ancient texts, 174; care for Jar Jar Binks, 117, 124–125; Code, 133; Council, 132, 231n68; fan opinions of, 149; Qui-Gon Jinn, 124; Obi-Wan Kenobi, 62, 124; Knights, 124, 162, 186; in musical lyrics, 88; and Sith, 37; Anakin Skywalker, 133, 146; Luke Skywalker, 62, 97, 105, 128, 174; Darth Vader, 59, 62;

Mace Windu, 195; Yoda, 97, 128, 146
Jenkins, Henry, 104
Jim Crow, 17–18, 34, 52, 99
Jinn, Qui-Gon, 124
Johnson, Rian, 109, 172, 175–177, 191, 201. See also *The Last Jedi* (2017)
Jones, James Earl, 43, 66, 95; fan responses to Darth Vader, 65, 214n18, 215n23; in musical lyrics, 86; race and casting, 68, 70, 195; voice of, 38, 55–57, 67, 69, 194. See also Darth Vader
Jones, Jennifer, 34
Joseph Burstyn, Inc. v. Wilson (1952), 35

Kael, Pauline, 91
Kaplan, Andreas, 143
Kasdan, Jonathan, 220n23
Kasdan, Lawrence, 106, 153
Kennedy, Kathleen, 6, 147–148, 171
Kenobi, Obi-Wan: casting, 48; in musical lyrics, 87; *The Phantom Menace* (1999), 124; search for, 13; Anakin Skywalker, 56, 74; storyline, 153, 195
King, Martin Luther, Jr., 16–17, 126–127
Kool Moe Dee, 86
Ku Klux Klan, 31
Kurosawa, Akira, 48
Kweli, Talib, 87
Kylo Ren: character development, 166, 173, 175, 181, 185; death, 183; Adam Driver, 144, 165; *Duel of the Fates*, 190; fanship, 165, 223n12; *The Force Awakens*, 153; and Rey, 142, 144, 154, 160–162, 165, 183–187; Reylo, 166; shipping, 22, 142, 157, 160–162, 180; toxic masculinity, 172–173. See also Reylo

Lady Sings the Blues (1972), 96
The Last Jedi (2017): box office, 172; John Boyega interview, 196–197; "Chauvinist Cut," 174, 234n23; critical reputations, 141; critique of white chauvinism, 173; director Rian Johnson, 109, 191, 201; fan responses, 186; Finn, 175–176, 193, 197; Kylo Ren, 181; Annalise Ophelian of *The Guardian*, 173, 233n15; Rey, 154; Rose, 176, 193; storyline, 174, 190; toxic fandom, 178, 199
LaVerne, Julie, 34
Leia, Princess: adoption by Bail Organa, 134–135; Lando Calrissian and, 98–99, 112, 193; Chewbacca and, 27, 105, 112; *The Empire Strikes Back* (1980), 50–51, 97, 98, 104, 193; interracial intimacy, 95, 193; Kenner toys, 77; kisses with Luke Skywalker, 24, 50, 74, 97, 112, 115; metal bikini, 108, 110; *The Phantom Menace* (1999), 135; *Return of the Jedi* (1983), 51, 56, 104, 106, 115, 193; sex, 109; Luke Skywalker as sibling, 56; "Slave Leia," 109–111, *112*. See also Fisher, Carrie
Levine, Cynthia, 102, 152
LGBTQ+: fans, 160, 182; representation, 152, 220n23; visibility, 104
lightsabers, 12, 24, 87, 89, 186
Liss, Steven, 120. See also intermarriage
Liston Smith, Lonnie, 86
Live and Let Die (1973), 43
Logan's Run (1976), 82, 113
Lost (2004–2010), 182
Lothian, Alexis, 2
Loving v. Virginia (1967), 35
Love Is a Many-Splendored Thing (1955), 34

Lucas, George: absence of Black characters in work of, 83; Lando Calrissian, 101, 104; casting, 48–49, 51, 110, 179, 195; colorblind thinking, 95–96; and colors, use of, 64; compared with Disney years, 200; critiques of, 129–131; family-making themes, 124, 203; fan types, 127; Mellody Hobson and, 135–139; influenced by, 14, 16, 36, 41, 91–94, 113; interracial relationships, depicting, 50, 112, 137; Obi-Wan Kenobi, 74; Princess Leia, 69, 92, 104, 109; race topics, 8, 19, 42, 83, 115, 117, 125–126; *Red Tails* (2012), 136; retcon, 56, 69; and Gene Roddenberry, 7, 30, 48, 51; Anakin Skywalker, 74; Luke Skywalker, 51, 69; Han Solo, 49; Special Editions, 121, 123; Glynn Turman, 49–50, 200; Darth Vader, 67–68, 74, 214n18; women characters, 134–135

Lucasfilm: acquisition by Walt Disney Company, 147; casting, 48–49, 51, 110, 179, 195; fan critiques of sidelining Finn, 183–184; leadership changes, 163; *The Phantom Menace* (1999), 125; Howard Roffman, 102; Colin Trevorrow, 171, 190; whiteness, 200; YouTube channel, 178, 180. See also J. J. Abrams; fanzines

The Machine, 62
The Mack (1973), 43
Mad Magazine, 70, 71
Mahtani, Minelle, 11
The Man (1972), 66
The Man with the Golden Arm (1955), 35
Martin, Amiyrah, 89, 90, 179
Martin, Trayvon, 60

masculinity: Blerds, 146; heterosexual, 131; nerds, 78; toxic, 172–173; in *Twilight*, 156; white fans, 14, 23, 152
Matrix trilogy (1999–2003), 41
McCarthy, Todd, 130
McIntosh, Peggy, 22, 76
MCU Fandom Hates People of Color, 8, 147
Meco, 86
Media Action Network for Asian Americans, 145
microaggressions, 67, 89, 147, 199
midi-chlorians: explanation of, 116; fan response to, 128, 224n35; storyline, 134–135, 193–194, 223n12
Mifune, Toshiro, 48
militarism: against, 8, 45, 173, 196; Rose Tico, 176; Darth Vader and, 22, 92
Millennium Falcon, 97–99, 121
mirroring, 4–5, 203
Mitchell, Elvis, 96
mixed race: acafans, 209n3; analysis, 10–11, 63, 203; critical studies, 7, 11; Lena Horne, 34; identity, 4; interracialism, 203; onscreen intimacy, 40–41, 52
morphing, 5
Morrison, Toni, 4
Motion Picture Association, 12, 33
Motion Picture Producers and Distributors of America (MPPDA), 33
Myrdal, Gunnar, 99

Nama, Adilifu, 6, 37, 99
Nas, 87
National Lampoon, 78, 79, 146
Naturalization Act (1790), 32
Nelson, Alondra, 80
nerds, 78–80, 79, 146; film characters, 78
The Nerds of Color, 8, 145. See also Black Nerd Problems
New Criticism, 61, 130, 213n9

Nichols, Nichelle, 45–46
Nimoy, Leonard, 46, 47. *See also* Spock
Nineteenth Amendment (1920), 32
Nishime, LeiLani, 38–39, 52
No Country for Old Men (2007), 62
nonwhite: actors, 156–157; ancestry, 13; anti-miscegenation laws, 163; chattel, 105; intimacy, 176; Jabba the Hutt, 105–106; Toni Morrison, 4; sexual predator, 105. *See also* whiteness
nostalgia, 38, 91, 116, 118
Nott, Josiah, 9, 19
Nowakowska, Maggie M., 74
Nyong'o, Lupita, 170, 241n1; Maz, 154

Obama, Barack, 6, 46, 145, 155
Octoroon (1859), 16, 68
Official Star Wars Fan Club: Maureen Garret, 103; Craig Miller, 74–75, 103
One Million Years B.C. (1966), 107
oppositional Black gaze, 3
oppositional reading, 22, 57, 84
Organa, Bail, 134–135. *See also* retcon
Osuji, Chinyere K., 137

Pace v. Alabama (1882), 30
Palpatine, Emperor, 56, 182, 191
Park, Grace, 40, 177
Patterson, Orlando, 13
Paul, Jim, 35
The Pawnbroker (1964), 35
Payne, Julianne, 164, *165*
The Personification of Evil, 62
The Phantom Menace (1999): Padmé Amidala, 133; backlash against, 128, 131, 166, 178; Jar Jar Binks, 124; casting, 194; expectations of, 17, 121, 131; fan expressions, 118; Nute Gunray and the Neimoidians, 123; Qui-Gon Jinn, 124; Obi-Wan Kenobi, 124; Princess Leia, 135; Lucasfilm, 125; midi-chlorians, 128, 193; positive minority representations, 123; racial stereotypes, 117, 123; reviews of, 130, 238n62; scholarship about, 126–127; storyline, 124, 132; Watto, 123; whiteness, 113; Yoda, 146. *See also* prequel trilogy (1999–2005); toxic fandom
Phi, Bao, 145
Pinky (1949), 34
PopSugar.com, 213
Pratt Guterl, Matthew, 5
prequel trilogy (1999–2005): backlash against, 22, 117, 167, 195; box office, 223n14, 242n19; family/kinship, 116; fan responses to, 7; gender and race, 115–116, 123, 167, 173, 200; interracial relations, 193; Ben Kenobi, 73; in musical lyrics, 88; release dates, 17; retcons, 134; storyline, 48, 185; Darth Vader, 73; whiteness, 223n12
Princess Leia. *See* Leia, Princess
Production Code Administration (PCA), 33, 52
Project Greenlight (2001–2015), 169–170, 197
proslavery scientists, 9, 38
Pryor, Richard, 44, 82, *83*

Quinn, Holly, 155, 180, 202, 231, 165–166n68. *See also* Finnrey; Reylo; shipping
Quinn, Zoe, 148–149. *See also* Gamergate

R2-D2: backstory, 13–14; C-3PO, 13; honorary sidekick, 48; Kenner toys, 77; Obi-Wan Kenobi, 56; in musical lyrics, 86; *Star Wars* brand, 77; storyline, 20, 56, 97, 122, 173; Uncle Owen, 13. *See also* droids
racial frame, 4, 14–15, 136
racial passing, 9

racial rules, 99. *See also* Lando Calrissian
Raiders of the Lost Ark (1981), 194
rap lyrics, 87. *See also Wired* magazine
Real Thing, 86
Rebel Alliance, 5, 37, 60, 69, 86, 93, 175
Redman, 88
Red Tails (2012), 136
retcon (retroactive continuity), 56, 69, 121, 134–135, 191. *See also* prequel trilogy (1999–2005)
Return of the Jedi (1983): Padmé Amidala, 134; Black fans, 76; box office, 121, 222n55; Ewoks, 93; fanship, 22, 76, 110; Princess Leia, 51, 56, 104, 106, 115, 193; metal bikini, 104, 108, 110; in musical lyrics, 86; Orientalism, 106–107; Emperor Palpatine, 182; retcon, 56; Luke Skywalker, 51, 56, 69, 153; storyline, 51, 134, 153; Darth Vader, 64, 70, 72
Revenge of the Nerds (1984), 78, 146
Revenge of the Sith (2005): Padmé Amidala, 133; continuity with prequels and original trilogy, 73, 134–135, 185
Rey: BB-8, 164; fan reactions to, 165–166; Finn, 153–154, 162–165, 187, 190; interracial intimacy, 142, 193; interracial relationship, 22, 164; Jakku escape, 153, 238n54; and Kylo Ren, 22, 142, 144, 153–154, 160–162, 165, 183–187; *The Last Jedi* (2017), 154; *Rise of Skywalker* (2019), 154, 186–187; search for, 154; sequel trilogy (2015–2020), 56, 109; storyline, 48, 153. *See also* Finnrey; Reylo; Ridley, Daisy; shipping
Reylo: John Boyega, 144, 162; Adam Driver, 165; fan art, 231n68; fan support, 162, 183–184; and Finnrey, 144, 164–165, 187–190, 196; and Finnrose, 176; Kylo Ren character arc, 181–185; Katie McCourt, 188–189; onscreen kiss, 183; and Holly Quinn, 180; racism, 161, 178; Daisy Ridley, 144, 162, 165; social media, 237n47, 237n50, 238n57, 238n59, 240n78; whiteness, 144, 162; white racial purity, 181. *See also* Kylo Ren; Rey; shipping
Reysen, Stephen, 206n2
Rhymes, Busta, 87
Ricca, Brad, 105
Rich, Adrienne, 15
Ridley, Daisy, 109, 144, *150*, 153; attacks against, 167; Finnrey, 162–163, 184, 187, 190, 200; and Kylo Ren, 165; social media, 166, 202. *See also* Finnrey; interracial relationships; Rey; Reylo
Rinzler, J. W., 36
Ripley, Ellen, 51–52, 112
Rise of Skywalker (2019): edits during filmmaking process, 201; fan responses to, 141, 183–185, 190; Finn, 186; Rey, 154, 186–187; ships, 182
Rocky III (1982), 71, 158
Roddenberry, Gene: background, 44; casting, 48; centering of diversity, 45–46, 51, 200, 203; and George Lucas, 7, 30; philosophy of amalgamation, 52
Roffman, Howard, 102, 220n25
Roosevelt, Franklin Delano, 94
Root, Maria P. P., 10
Roots (1977), 23, 26, 96
Rosemary's Baby (1968), 40
Ross, Charles, 215n23
Rowling, J. K., 19, 156

Sabrina (1954), 23, 194
Said, Edward, 106–108
"Save *Star Trek*" Movement, 78
Schiappa, Justice, 179

Schultz, Michael, 50, 160
science fiction fanship, 2
ScreenCraft.org, 213n9
Screen Junkies (2011–present), 141–142
Selma (2013), 136
sequel trilogy (2015–2020): depictions of romance, 48, 185, *188*; director, 171–172; fan responses, 101, 150, 180; Finn, 101, 195–196; interracial intimacy, 92, 152, 194; minority voices, 142; Rey, 56, 109; Kylo Ren as hero, 181; Reylo ship, 144, 162
Serenity (2005), 39, 62
servitude, 5; cyborgs, 19–20; of nonhumans, 12, 193; and whiteness, 107, 124
sex: Lando Calrissian, 92, 96, 100, 220n23; casual, 35; comparison between *Star Trek* and *Star Wars*, 45, 47; family making, 35, 48, 51; Finn and Rey, 187; Carol Hanisch, 94–95; hidden in *Star Wars*, 12, 91, 104, 134; industry, 33, *111*; Princess Leia, 109; nonconsensual, 132; object, 105–106; and race, 11; same-sex kiss, 187; same-sex relationships, 160; symbol, 92, 100, 109. *See also* interracial intimacy
Shaft (1971), 43, 65
shipping, 75, 112, 143–144, 160, 182; antagonism among fans, 183–184, 188–189; racism and, 165–166, 176, 178, 180, 202. *See also* Finn-Poe; Finnrey; Finnrose; Reylo
Shmi, 132–133, 193. *See also* Anakin Skywalker
Short Circuit (1986), 78
Show Boat (1951), 34
Sidious, Darth, 134, 191
Silver Streak (1976), 44
Sine, Victor, 164, *165*

Sith: Death Star, 195; Darth Sidious, 134; Anakin Skywalker, 134; storyline, 37; Darth Vader, 69, 73
Sixteen Candles (1984), 78
Skywalker, Anakin: and Padmé Amidala, 133–134, 185, 195–196, 223n12; *Attack of the Clones*, 132, 185; Kenner toys, 130; lightsaber, 149, 197; Jake Lloyd, 130; in musical lyrics, 88; storyline, 132, 185; Darth Vader, 48, 56, 132; Watto, 123; whiteness, 72
Skywalker, Luke: adoption, 134–135; birth by Padmé Amidala, 116, 133; casting, 49; death, 174; droids, 13; fan fiction, 74, 101; fan responses to, 120; in hiding, 153, 162, 173; as Jedi Knight, 105; joining the Rebel Alliance, 93–94; kisses with Princess Leia, 24, 50, 74, 97, 112, 115; learning about father, 133; Princess Leia as sibling, 56; lightsaber, 149, 154, 197; in musical lyrics, 87–88; rescue of Han Solo, 105; self-sacrifice, 173; Han Solo and, 42; storyline, 36, 191, 196; training with Yoda, 97, 128; Darth Vader, 48, 62, 68–70, 175, 181, 215n23; whiteness, 37, 68, 106
Skywalker, Shmi, 132–133, 193
slash fiction, 75, 104
Slave Girl (1947), 107
Smith, L. Neil, 100–101
Smits, Jimmy, 135. *See also* Bail Organa
social Darwinism, 9, 30
social media: appeasement of fans, 184; Black users, 181; efforts toward social equality, 17; empathy and, 143; hashtags, 237n47; interactions among users, 90, 141–142, 163, 166; Tumblr, 7, 147; Twitter, 7

Solo, Han: Lando Calrissian and, 195; casting, 45, 240n82; Chewbacca, 26, 99, 153; costume color, 37; *The Empire Strikes Back* (1980), 26, 100; fanzines, 74; *The Force Awakens* (2015), 153; Harrison Ford, 49–50, 99, 137, 194; "Han shot first," 121; Princess Leia, 26, 97, 108, 112; *Return of the Jedi* (1983), 104; storyline, 100, 220n23; Glynn Turman, 43, 49, 50, 200, 240n82; Billy Dee Williams, 100
Some Like It Hot (1959), 23, 35, 161
Sounder (1972), 43
Species (1995), 122
Splice (2009), 122
Spock, 46, 75, 100, 164. *See also* Leonard Nimoy
The Spook Who Sat by the Door (1973), 43
Staiger, Janet, 85
Stanfill, Mel, 1, 152
Stargate (1994), 41
Star Trek (2009), 148, 155
Star Trek: The Next Generation, 52
Star Trek: The Original Series, 30, 44–45, 155; Daniel Benardi, 6; cultural relativism, 48, 51; diversity of cast, 200; fanzines, 74–75, 77–78, 80; mixed-race experiences, 46; sex and, 47; shipping, 75; Spock's origin, 46, 164. *See also* Roddenberry, Gene
Star Wars (1977), in musical lyrics, 88
Star Wars Official Poster Monthly, 73
stormtroopers: Finn, 149, 157–158, 162, 165, 182; First Order, 153, 190; *menpō*, 36; race and, 36, 198; *Troops* (1997), 122; Darth Vader, 55. *See also* Kylo Ren
Super Fly (1972), 43, 65
Sweet Sweetback's Baadasssss Song (1971), 43

Takei, George, 46
Tano, Ahsoka, 148
Tatooine, 14, 36, 93, 121–122, 132
Taylor, Femi, 105, 241n1
Taylor, Shawn, 81–82: "The Dark Side of Star Wars" (2013), 81, 216n16
technophilia, 8
The Terminator (1984), 51–52, 62
Terminator 2: Judgment Day (1992), 5
Thompson, Clive, 143
Thor (2011), 113
Threepio. *See* C-3PO
Tico, Rose, 174–177, 179, 195, 202
Time magazine, 12
Toomer, Jean, 60
toxic fandom, 120, 167: authority, 117; entitlement, 118; possessiveness, 117–119; racism, 177. *See also* Best, Ahmed; Binks, Jar Jar
tragic mulatto stereotype, 9, 16, 69
Tran, Kelly Marie, 6, 179, 197, 202. *See also* Tico, Rose
Travers, Peter, 129–131. *See also* *The Phantom Menace*
A Tribe Called Quest, 88
The Trickster, 63
A Trip to the Moon (1902), 29–31
The Triumph of the Will (1935), 93
Troops (1997), 122
Trump, Donald, 6, 149, 167, 190
Tumblr, 159, 162; blogs, 7–8; fans of color, 147, 231n68; shipping, 165; withdrawal from, 166
Turman, Glynn, 43, 49, 50, 200, 240n82
Twilight: films, 156; novels by Stephenie Meyer, 95

Uncle Owen, 13, 115, 122
Uproxx, 184

V (1983), 40
V: The Final Battle (1984), 40, 51
Vader, Darth: African Americans and, 59, 67, 70; blueprint, 21; the

Empire, 60; *The Empire Strikes Back* (1980), 68–69, 181; The Henchman, 62; interracial intimacy, 193; Jedi, 59, 62; The Machine, 62; mechanical breathing, 21, 62; militarism and, 22, 92; Lydia Millet, 64; The Personification of Evil, 62; prequel trilogy (1999–2005), 73; *Return of the Jedi* (1983), 64, 70, 72; Sith, 69, 73; Anakin Skywalker, 48, 56, 132; Luke Skywalker, 48, 62, 68–70, 175, 181, 215n23; Matt Sloan, 214n18; *Star Wars* brand, 77; voice of, 38, 55–57, 67, 69, 194; the "What are you?" question, 61. *See also* James Earl Jones
Vietnam War, 91, 93
vortextuality, 143

Wanzo, Rebecca, 76, 206n2
Wargames (1983), 80
Weaver, Sigourney, 112
Weird Science (1985), 80
western movies, 14, 44, 106, 121
Whannel, Garry, 143
What Happened in the Tunnel, 30–31
white: actors, 104; chauvinism, 173; fans and masculinity, 14, 23, 152; fanship, 2, 22, 76, 110, 198; feminism, 113, 155, 190, 222n56; filmmakers, 43; genocide, 151–152; racial frame, 16; racial purity, 181; racism and interracial intimacy, 30, 34, 150–152, 163, 202; supremacy, 176. *See also* nonwhite
whiteness: Padmé Amidala, 132, 223n12; anti-Black racism, 4, 37; critiques of *Star Wars*, 1, 181, 183; fan investment, 2, 76, 93, 131, 199; Princess Leia, 93, 105, 110, 154; Lucasfilm, 200; Trayvon Martin, 60; *The Phantom Menace* (1999), 113; prequel trilogy (1999–2005), 223n12; Reylo, 144, 162; Edward Said, 106; servitude, 107, 124; Shmi Skywalker, 132; Luke Skywalker, 37, 68, 106; Darth Vader, 68–69; "white stories," 64–65; white supremacy, 9, 11, 15. *See also* nonwhite
Williams, Billy Dee: Avon, 101; career, 95–97; casting with white actors, 104; Colt 45, 100; Donald Glover, 220n23; public treatment, 100; racial identity, 100, 195; as sex symbol, 92, 96, 100; spillover effect, 43. *See also* Calrissian, Lando
Wilson, Angel, 159
Wired magazine, 87, 173
Womack, Ytasha L., 81, 87
Wong, Anna May, 34
Wookiee, 26, 30, 105, 112, 154; Wookieepedia.com, 177. *See also* Chewbacca
Wu-Tang Clan, 87

YouTube: fan accounts, 88–90, 202; Lucasfilm channel, 178, 180; Midnight's Edge channel, 200; reviews of *The Rise of Skywalker*, 184–186; Screen Junkies channel, 141; and social media, 7, 141
Yu, Philip, 145

Zimmerman, George, 60